VISUAL

VISUAL HISTORY

Images of Education

Ulrike Mietzner, Kevin Myers
& Nick Peim (eds)

PETER LANG
Oxford · Bern · Berlin · Bruxelles · Frankfurt am Main · New York · Wien

Bibliographic information published by Die Deutsche Bibliothek
Die Deutsche Bibliothek lists this publication in the Deutsche National-
bibliografie; detailed bibliographic data is available on the Internet at
‹http://dnb.ddb.de›.

British Library and Library of Congress Cataloguing-in-Publication Data:
A catalogue record for this book is available from The British Library,
Great Britain, and from The Library of Congress, USA

Cover design: Thomas Jaberg, Peter Lang AG

ISBN 3-03910-151-X
US-ISBN 0-8204-6961-0

© Peter Lang AG, European Academic Publishers, Bern 2005
Hochfeldstrasse 32, Postfach 746, CH-3000 Bern 9, Switzerland
info@peterlang.com, www.peterlang.com, www.peterlang.net

Printed in Germany

Contents

NICK PEIM

Introduction: The Life of Signs in Visual History

The concept of representation has come to occupy a new and important place in the study of culture.[1]

by definition, all that is past does not exist. To be accurate the object of history is whatever is *represented* as having hitherto existed.[2]

Historians in pursuit of signs

The work of history is always a work of interpretation. History does not speak for itself. It is always something that has to be, in one way or another, told – or, at least, represented. The painstaking work of archaeology is a matter of piecing together data, a work of re-constituting and reconstruction. The reassembled bits and pieces of an archaeological enterprise have to be sifted, gathered together and put into order. Those bits and pieces might be taken for signs, signs of the past that are organized according to a twofold logic of form: the form of the thing and the form of its reconstruction. Between these two forms is an inevitable gap. The reduction of the gap between object or event and representation is the work of the historian. In this meaning-making process atomistic signs and sign configurations are being constructed into more or less coherent texts. These texts inevitably are organized in discourses. Discourses in turn classify knowledge into fields, orders, practices. Discourses shape the production of know-

1   S. Hall, *Representation: Cultural Representations and Signifying Practices* (London: Sage, 1997), p. 15.

2   B. Hindess and P. Hirst, *Pre-Capitalist Modes of Production* (London: Routledge and Kegan Paul, 1975), p. 309.

ledge, the types of texts it produces, how they get read and what kinds of subjects they engage with. This process of the archaeology of signs might stand as a kind of metaphor for the production of knowledge in history.[3]

The following essays all engage with issues of representation in the field of the history of education. They come together by dint of a common interest in the visual in the history of education. In this collection, some address photography, finding fascinating, even haunting but sometimes elusive data; some provide an account of the theoretical topography of photographic data; some seek to engage with the rhetoric of film in and about education. Others engage with visual components of children's literature to explore a history of visual representation, or focus on visual materials from past class-rooms. Other pieces have a more pedagogical orientation, exploring visual material in the teaching process or deploying visual material to explore the subjectivities of students. This collection then has come of out of different modes of engagement with the visual in the history of education. The contributions are not all theoretically oriented to a singular model. They represent an instance of what Bernstein refers to as the 'collection code': the accumulation of perspectives and paradigms of knowledge that sit more or less comfortably alongside one another, rather than a hierarchically ordered schema.[4] They are all theoretically informed, however. It is just that there is not a general position being advocated. The historical perspectives gathered here are the outcome of a process of exchange, including the exchange of differences of perspective, focus and orientation. None of the essays here claim to have displaced other forms of historical knowledge. They all seek with some serious intent to recover something of the socio-historical realities that give meaning to the objects they en-counter. Nevertheless, the collection is the product of a general movement, a shift in the very idea of the archive, a shift in the orien-

---

3   See M. Foucault, *The Archaeology of Knowledge* (London: Tavistock, 1977).
4   B. Bernstein, *Pedagogy, Symbolic Control and Identity* (Oxford: Rowman and Littlefield, 2000), pp. 10–11.

tation towards data, a reconceptualization, in effect, of both subject and object in history and of history as a discourse of knowledge.[5]

At the same time, there is an implicit consensus here that history cannot be seen as the accumulation of a steadily growing stock of knowledge. These essays agree implicitly that history is fundamentally *hermeneutic* in character. The classical (Greek) distinction that marks the emergence of history as radically different from myth has come full circle.[6] One of the effects of semiotics has been to restore the idea of myth into history. The destabilizing of the field of knowledge is at least partly a product of the logic of the sign with its disjuncture between signifier and signified. Fundamental to Saussure's nascent semiotics is the description of the logic of the sign as arbitrary. There is no necessary connection between signifier and signified.[7] The signifier relates to the signified (language to the 'real') only through the binding force of convention. Convention is not a static force, but is at the centre of Volosinov's 'struggle over meaning'.[8] Social life itself, in Saussure's formulation, is seen as being organized through and around signs. Signs belong to orderings that constitute systems of knowledge and meaning and that organize the otherwise amorphous stuff of the world. For the historian, then, semiotics would seem to be central to the business of reconstructing past social realities. As Jones, Limond and Peim (chapters 7, 6 and 8) in the present collection indicate, these realities are constituted out of material that includes the 'mythic' whether in the form of 'documentary' or fiction.

The book arises from a gathering of historians of education at the EERA conference in Edinburgh in September 2000. It had become a habit for this group to address things visual as a way of rethinking history beyond conventional strictures of narrative and beyond con-

---

5   See I. Grosvenor, M. Lawn, K. Rousmaniere (eds.), *Silences and Images: The Social History of the Classroom* (New York: Peter Lang, 2000); also *Paedagogica Historica*, 36 (2000), 1.

6   See P. Cartledge, *The Greeks* (Oxford: Oxford University Press, 1993), pp. 18–35.

7   F. de Saussure, *Cours de linguistique generale* (Paris: Payot, 1922).

8   V. N. Volosinov, *Marxism and the Philosophy of Language* (Cambridge, MA: Harvard University Press, 1986), pp. 99–106.

ventional paradigms of progress or good practice. The group met in Edinburgh with a collection of papers that were to deal with questions of the visual, including moving images, in relation to the history of education. The group enjoyed a convivial and productive series of meetings through the conference, providing some anchoring for the experience.

The visual turn

In the human sciences a great deal has been written over the past thirty years or so about *the linguistic turn*, the preoccupation with the role of language and signs in the field of knowledge.[9] The concern with the *question* of representation problematizes the classical unconcern with representation. The key issue at stake in the classical Western idea of representation is the question of 'truth', 'correspondence' or 'authenticity'. Language is assumed to be the vehicle for a thought that it resonates with in a more or less direct relation with what it represents.[10] Cultural studies and related domains of contemporary knowledge have moved the emphasis on signifying practices from reflective and intentional modes of working with meanings to a more constructivist approach. On this view truth is not so much something out there to be uncovered and revealed, it is to be pieced together, constructed according to practices that are both established and contested. To engage with this hermeneutic approach is to engage with fundamental questions about the meaning of signs. Do images simply reflect something that is there? Or do images reflect the intention of a conscious act of representation, undertaken by a subject in specific conditions and in a specific historical moment? Or do

9   See R. Rorty (ed.), *The Linguistic Turn* (Chicago: The Chicago University Press, 1967) and C. Norris, *The Contest of Faculties* (London: Methuen, 1985), p. 201.
10   M. Foucault, *The Order of Things* (London: Tavistock, 1970), pp. 78–120.

images have a logic of their own that operates relatively autonomously from their context of production and the intentions of a producer?

It is with the 'visual turn' that this book occupies itself. While semiotics belongs to no particular domain of knowledge, it has become associated with cultural studies and other hybrid practices. Semiotics has had a significant influence on philosophy, on the understanding of systems of ideas and knowledge.[11] Semiotics was originally conceived of by de Saussure as the 'science of signs in society'.[12] The linguistic turn is a kind of shorthand in effect for a general concern with matters of representation.

It would be misleading, though, to represent the group of writings here as consisting of, or even working towards, a general consensus of the significance and value of the visual in respect to the history of education. The present volume does not claim to represent an agreed and fully worked out 'paradigm shift'. The turn towards the visual here is not a turn away from other modes, other senses of doing history.[13] The visual here is seen as offering a specific (but certainly not separate) form of knowledge that requires its own modes of apprehension. It offers a *complementary* form of historical knowledge (see Grosvenor and Lawn, chapter 3). The concern here expressed with the visual arises from particular ongoing engagements with aspects of the history of education. This engagement with the visual will no doubt have some significant impact on our idea of 'the archive' and of the proper practices of historiography, but makes no claim to privilege the domain of the visual as offering a special kind of access to the past in education. The whole problematic, in fact, of the relations between the visual and other forms of knowledge is variously grappled with here. We include, for example, an essay that explicitly challenges a perceived privileging of the visual in the history of education (see chapter 10). These issues no doubt have resonances for the practice and theory of history of education in general.

11   Ibid.
12   F. de Saussure, *Cours de linguistique generale* (Paris: Payot, 1922) p. 33: 'une science qui étudie la vie des signes au sein de la vie sociale'.
13   See *Paedagogica Historica*, 36 (2000), 1.

A science of signs?

Is it possible to speak of a *science* of signs? The idea of a general 'science of signs' is frequently credited to Ferdinand de Saussure (1857–1913). Language was Saussure's ostensible concern; but language, as Saussure implicitly recognized, is one of a number of signifying practices in social life. The introduction of this idea of *general* semiology is frequently cited as the source of the twentieth century's obsession with issues of representation. Some would say signs are what we 'are', in a quite literal as well as a symbolic sense. The contemporary concern with signs gives rise to a sense of the symbolic field as being what constitutes identity. Although ostensibly a linguist, Saussure was quite well aware of this expanded application of the primary definition of the sign: hence his own imagining of a science of signs in society.

Saussure's famous description of the sign as divided into signifier and signified has given rise to a whole philosophy of meaning and series of disputes and debates about the very nature of the sign and its complex logic. This primary division (S/s) has produced a cluster of issues and debates in the field of meaning.[14] From the Saussurian 'moment' a number of significant areas of study have evolved, including modern linguistics, discourse analysis with its various subdivisions and more generally cultural studies, the whole field of semiotic concern with representation defined by Greimas as a domain 'in search of a name'.[15] The question of the relations between the material component of the sign and its meaning has both problematized and enriched the relations between language and the social. This many-sided 'semiotic' movement has made possible the reformation of the very idea of the political, for example, opening up the various possibilities envisaged and realized by a 'politics of everyday

14   Saussure, op. cit., p. 158.
15   See A. J. Greimas, *On Meaning* (London: Frances Pinter, 1987), p. 180.

life', and the extension of the political into various domains and practices of signification.[16]

Saussure's account of the sign as divided (what Lacan refers to as 'the cut') opens onto the series of concepts – difference, trace, slippage – that get woven into contemporary theories of the symbolic.[17] Saussure's key division between the signifier, understood as the material component of the sign, and the signified, understood as what is referred or 'pointed' to, enables the association between material practices of meaning to be related to the psychological dimension of meaning and ideas. In this movement, however, the sign is rendered problematic. What does the signifier point to, or signify? Is it the concept or the thing? Is this concept or thing ever a stable unity, a 'fact constituting the world', as the early Wittgenstein would have it?[18] It seems that Saussure's description inevitably gives rise to the idea that signs are more to do with social *realities* than with plain and simple reality. This is the implication of the revisiting of Saussure's divided sign that constitutes Derrida's general theory of language and representation.[19]

The second major division Saussure announces is the difference between system and statement – or *langue* and *parole* – where *langue* refers to language as a whole, language as system, and *parole* refers to any specific instance of language in a real utterance, text or exchange. Saussure declares, rather like Chomsky, that it is *langue* that is the 'true' object of linguistics.[20] The empirical, in terms of actual manifestations of language in specific social contexts, is regarded by Saussure as a kind of dust cloud that obscures the truth of language. This position is roundly contested, for instance, by Bourdieu's insistence that language only exists as social practice. In a Lacanian

---

16   See M. Blonsky (ed.), *On Signs* (Baltimore: Johns Hopkins University Press, 1985).

17   J. Lacan, 'Sign, Symbol, Imaginary', in Blonsky (ed.), op. cit., pp. 203–9.

18   L. Wittgenstein, *The Tractatus Logico-Philosophicus* (London: Routledge and Kegan Paul, 1961), p. 5: 'The world is the totality of facts, not of things.'

19   J. Derrida, *Of Grammatology* (Baltimore: Johns Hopkins University Press, 1976) and *Positions* (London: Athlone Press, 1987).

20   See R. Harris, *Saussure and his Interpreters* (Edinburgh: Edinburgh University Press, 2001), pp. 8–9.

sense, however, *langue*, the system, the order of language, is itself the very product and ground of social being. It is precisely what enfolds the subject, irrevocably, in the symbolic order of meaning in the social. Through signs, features of identity are constituted: name, self-image, social relations, orientations to meaning.[21]

Saussure's third main division is the difference between the paradigmatic and the syntagmatic. This difference arises from two relations of difference that can be seen to operate in signs. The paradigmatic refers to the difference in meaning that words have in relation to non-present elements. So the word 'dog' means what it does (negatively) by virtue of its difference from the word 'cat', etc. The syntagmatic recognizes that signs do not appear by themselves but always appear, if at times by implication, in relation to other signs and elements in the system. In other words, there is an external relation to non-present elements; and there is also an internal location for meaning in relation to local elements. What this tells us is that meanings are determined by their relations to other meanings but they are also determined by their relations to the system's rules governing possibilities of combination. Their appearance is thus logically determined as well as determined by the demands of meaning. Furthermore, both meaning and logic of combination are always realized in specific social contexts. All this seems to imply strongly that it is more appropriate to speak of a *social science* of signs than of a science in the sense of a fully integrated, hierarchically systematic encoding of knowledge.

21   This general position is associated with Lacan, particularly, in the field of psychoanalysis; and can be found in sociolinguistic versions in B. Bernstein, *Class, Codes and Control*, vols 1–4 (London: Routledge, 1971–90) and M. A. K. Halliday, *Language as Social Semiotic* (London: Edward Arnold, 1978).

Signs, referents and realities

Saussure's nascent semiotics is often distinguished from other attempts to define relations and processes of signification and meaning. Other theorists have proposed different models of semiotic description. C. S. Peirce's semiotics seems to be founded on what has become a more traditional, conventional and common-sense notion of communication. Peirce, like Jakobsen after him, sees semiotics as concerned essentially with representation where something stands to somebody for something else in a linear relation. Peirce's description of the sign (representamen: interpretant: object) includes the idea of the 'referent', the real something that the sign indicates. Furthermore, Peirce's description tends to make less of the arbitrary relation between the material component of the sign and its referent, seeing signs as always motivated and inflected with interest.[22] This in turn is made problematic by the fact that the referent is indicated by the interpretant, taking the sign back into the realms of ambiguity, uncertainty and polysemy. Peirce's taxonomy of signs, consisting of index, icon and symbol, provides a guide to levels of abstraction, but always indicates that signs are not and cannot be directly related to what it is that they signify. As Chomsky puts it, according to Peirce reference is a triadic relation: 'person X refers to object Y by sign S where Y's [sic] are real objects in the world.' Then Chomsky reminds us: 'Rather, person X refers to Y by expression E under circumstances C, so that the relation is at least tetradic; and Y need not be a real object in the world or regarded that way by X.'[23] There is always a relation between (signifier and signified, again) and it is the *between* that provides the element of ambiguity. While elaborating a typology of modes of production of sign functions, Umberto Eco has questioned the desire to provide an exhaustive list of 'modi significandi'. Eco's notion of semiotics always reminds us that signs operate within specific and highly rule-bound social practices, that these practices are

---

22   See G. Kress, *Before Writing* (London: Routledge, 1997).
23   N. Chomsky, *New Horizons in the Study of Language and Mind* (Cambridge: Cambridge University Press, 2000), pp. 149–50.

both culturally specific and infinitely variable while also bound by the mostly unwritten laws of genre. It is in their social being that signs get ascribed particular and more or less determinate meanings.[24]

A turn towards specifically visual objects or signs of culture had already appeared at the beginning of the twentieth century. Aby Warburg in Hamburg was one of the first art historians to express an interest in objects of popular culture such as stamps, newspaper photographs or advertisements.[25] This tradition of picture or image theory deals with the specifically iconic quality of pictures but with a concern to specify the social meanings they represent. The surface of the picture or image provokes a simultaneous perception of space, colour, symbols, objects, forms, in contrast to the linear modality of verbal texts. These elements of the visual field, consciously and unconsciously, constitute the specifically *iconic* meaning of pictures. The methodological implications of iconology were developed by Erwin Panofsky, who especially looked at iconic meanings in pictures.[26] These interpretations seek to give insight in meanings that concern not only the visual object itself but also the time and place in which and where the object was made. Image analysis can thus produce an index of the *Weltanschauung* of time and place providing data relating to the social milieux of visual objects.[27] Debates on image, picture and media sciences continue, and reach into diverse fields of knowledge including neuro-sciences, anthropology and cultural studies.[28]

---

24   U. Eco, *Semiotics and the Philosophy of Language* (Bloomington, USA: Indiana University Press, 1984).

25   See E. H. Gombrich, *Aby Warburg: An Intellectual Biography* (London: The Warburg Institute, University of London, 1970).

26   E. Panofsky, *Meaning in the Visual Arts* (New York: Doubleday&Company, 1957). A critical discussion of Panofsky's iconology in the light of semiology is found in W. J. T. Mitchell, *Picture Theory* (Chicago: The University of Chicago Press, 1994).

27   The history of iconology and art history is also a history of emigration and expulsion from Germany of Jewish thinkers, especially to Great Britain and the United States. See K. Michels, *Transplantierte Kunstwissenschaft. Deutschsprachige Kunstgeschichte im Amerikanischen Exil* (Berlin: Akademie, 1999).

28   *Frames of Viewing*, a conference in Berlin in May 2002, sponsored by the Getty Research Institute and the Haus der Kulturen der Welt, illustrates this extension

Relations between signs and reality have been contentious in many ways. The correlation of meaning with intention (or consciousness) and the notion of language and text as communication as the passing of 'c from a to b' is the very stuff of 'logocentrism' and belongs to the metaphysics of direct communication, in Derrida's terms.[29] The difference between a notion of meaning as describing (straightforwardly and logically) states of affairs in the world is contrasted with a position that sees meaning as rooted in a 'form of life'. That is the movement made by Wittgenstein from the early positivistic philosophy of meaning in the *Tractatus Logico-Philosophicus* to the more constructivist conception of meaning evident in *Philosophical Investigation*s and other later texts. Hjelmslev's distinction between 'expression' and 'content' conforms to the difference between signifier and signified but does not serve to clarify the problem of reference. What is the ontological status of the content of any sign or signifying event? Fredric Jameson argues that it is the whole semiotic 'system' that runs parallel to reality; but again that doesn't guarantee *correspondence*, just as Chomsky's powerful case for innate hard-wired structures for language ('universal grammar') indicates a commonly shared genetic inheritance but only at the level of 'deep' grammar and does not claim to guarantee a fixing of signs to reality.[30] Semiotics has to deal with the internal relations of the system of signs and with the external relations of that system and its elements with 'the world'. This internal – external doubleness in turn requires a language to describe relations *within* texts: semantics, syntax, forms; and relations *between* texts: genre, discourse, intertextuality.

---

of scope. Numerous discourses of knowledge were brought to bear on the visual arts, including cognitive sciences, history, anthropology, philosophy, film and media studies. See also M. Banks and H. Morphy (eds.), *Rethinking Visual Anthropology* (New Haven and London: Yale University Press, 1997); N. Mirzoeff, *An Introduction to Visual Culture* (London: Routledge, 1999).

29   J. Derrida, *Positions* (London: Athlone Press, 1987).

30   F. Jameson, *The Prison-House of Language: A Critical Account of Structuralism and Russian Formalism* (Princeton: Princeton University Press, 1972), pp. 32–3; N. Chomsky, *Aspects of the Theory of Syntax* (Cambridge, MA: MIT Press, 1965), p. 6.

Halliday's systemic functional linguistics provides an account of signs and texts as always embedded in social realities: language is defined as '*social* semiotic'. In analysing signs and texts we must always take the social dimension into account: there can be no adequate description of how signs work purely, for example, at the level of either meaning or internal logic. Signs appear and work entirely within specific situations of context. Situations of context are always institutional in character. Within them the discourses of social practice occur. Semantic elements and syntactic configurations are motivated within situations of contexts. Signs exist within forms of social semiotic. Halliday's account of signification in social context has strong (potential, at least) reference to the domain of the visual, providing a working language of description, offering a model for a general account of a semiology.

Looking for a landmark in the development of applied semiotics one might cite the publication in 1957 of Roland Barthes's *Mythologies* and the emergence of the journal *Communications*, dedicated to the analysis of social symbols and collective representations. Using semiological techniques derived from Saussure and a theory of social relations derived from Marxism, such early semiology was based on the project of unmasking the ideological, revealing the operations of ideology in the everyday world of signs. As semiotics came to refine and establish its 'scientific' credentials, the general movement of cultural studies explored the sign at work in *all* aspects of social life: in architecture, in the urban landscape, in cinema, in television, in the very sign-saturated business of the self and in all forms of social rituals. This new extensive semiotic anthropology has concerned itself with the mythic generation and circulation of signs, sign-systems and meanings. This expansion of the Saussurian idea suggests that any account of signs at work must involve more than an algorithm of signs, reference and reality. The complexities of photographic representation, for instance, are dealt with in the chapter dedicated to methods of image analysis in social science research (see Mietzner and Pilarczyk, chapter 4).

Contested objects, contested meanings

In the different positions that can be identified in relation to questions of meaning in and through signs, there is a consistent problematic. None of the elements in the signifying process – signs, meanings or subjects – exists in the unambiguous world of direct communications. One of the consequences of the declaration of a 'science of signs in society' involves bringing together the social with the world of signs. Social life is conducted in and through signs. Among the various ways of configuring the complex set of relations involved in the semiotic, it is consistently the case that the productivity of signs, meanings and subject (none of them being fixed, determinate elements in a closed structure) works against a monologic model of communication or theory of meaning. With the advent of postmodern perspectives, the sign occupies a critical role in systems of thought, knowledge and belief. The sign is at the decentred centre of the postmodern perspective. Philosophy and semiotics come together. Thought is equated with signs, texts, discourses (Husserl, Heidegger, Derrida). Identity is forged in and through signs (Freud, Lacan). History is discourse (Foucault). Knowledge is constituted of organized sign systems (Lyotard, Bernstein). The so-called end of grand narratives, as the postmodern account of the contemporary has it, means that everything, in terms of truth claims, science and objectivity, is up for grabs.[31] In the domain of knowledge, it is no longer possible, since the incursion of various discourses on language in anthropology, cultural studies, sociology and philosophy, to avoid the sign and the question of meaning. It is not just that the slipperiness of meaning has been recognized, but more a case of a radical departure from the common-sense notions of reference and truth. The 'semiotic turn' problematizes our very relationship with knowledge. The focus given to the sign, to (an expanded conception of) text, to discourse and to the problem of representation means that the historical archive can no longer pretend (if ever it could) to be a safely stable, cohesive and singular entity.

31   J.-F. Lyotard, *The Postmodern Condition* (Manchester: Manchester University Press, 1986).

Similarly, historiography must be subject to the same decentring and polysemic logic. As we engage with historical issues the question of representation and all its attendant questions – of meaning, interpretation, reference, denotation, connotation and so on – impinges on the very object we seek to engage with and define. On this view, history becomes a matter of the construction and interpretation and arrangement of signs.

Whichever model of communication we may look at, the issue of representation is always structured by the difference between the act and mode of representation and what is represented. Further complications arise on consideration of the recontextualizing of representations that occur in the work of historians.[32] What this means in effect is manifold. In and among the various modalities of the semiotic enterprise is a concern to account for relations of mobility. The upshot is that the *objects* of history, the material resources of the practice of historical research and of the creation of historical knowledge, are subject, always, inevitably, to interpretation. Secondly it also means that the very objects of history 'themselves' are not of certain and self-announcing definition. The objects of history are generated from signs and from the complex and fundamentally split process of signification. This indeterminacy of the historical object is dramatically represented by contests over what constitutes history and with relatively recent developments in the construction of significant 'new' and alternative histories.

The 'uncertainty principle', then, gives rise to a dynamic field of discourse where objects get produced and their very identity is contested. It is into this domain that the following contributions enter, to establish a range of different types of history, in many cases arguing for the consideration of new types of historical object, new types of historical archive, as well as offering a rearticulation of the multiple ways of interpreting and making sense of the history of education. As variously practised in these essays, a clear sense emerges that to engage with the visual in the field of the history of education is,

---

32   B. Bernstein, *Pedagogy, Symbolic Control and Identity* (Oxford: Rowman and Littlefield, 2000), pp. 31–5. Bernstein's idea of recontextualization is relevant to the adoption of semiotics by history.

among other things, to question the kinds of history that we produce and to bring into explicit focus the question of representation as a factor that determines the historical field.

Signs and subjects

It is perhaps in poststructuralist theories the that the most radical version of a semiotic theory is expressed. The poststructuralist intervention, on the whole, disturbs the very stabilities that construct formalist and structuralist thinking on signs and meanings. Foucault's description of Velazquez's *Las Meninas* problematizes the subject-object relation in the field of the visual.[33] In the work of Lacan, the sign is the fundamental principle at the decentred centre of the human subject. Signs are more than the medium through which we think and act and exist in the world. Signs are constitutive of our being in the world. In Lacan's psychoanalytic account of identity the subject is caught up in a symbolic order. This is necessarily external to the subject but becomes internalized through the process of the acquisition of language and entry into the symbolic order. But this acquisition is not simply an added capacity or ability to use. Signs organize the subject, splitting the subject into conscious and unconscious as the subject becomes subject to the law of the signifier. The symbolic order is not something external to the subject. It structures the subject's experience and knowledge (of both self and world). The subject is always already a subject of the sign. There is a correspondence here with Foucault's notion of the subject of discourse.

In the engagements with the visual in this volume there is a frequent if not insistent recognition and exploration of the relations between the social subject (the subject of education, for instance) and the visual objects that occupy the field of experience and knowledge. The subject, in this sense, is the subject recreated, resituated through

33 M. Foucault, *The Order of Things* (London: Tavistock Press, 1970), pp. 3–16.

the discourse of history. But the subject in question here is also the subject of knowledge (the present writer, colleagues in the ECER history group, historians of education) who attempts to define an idea, a practice, a specific text or series of texts in the process of redefining an object, a series of objects, an event, an experience. In the process, it might be said that there is a redefining of the subject's relation to a field of knowledge. This subject of history cannot be erased from the discourse of representation enacted here. Just as the subject is caught in the field of the visual by the impersonal gaze of 'the Other', the subject is the active agent in the world of images demanding to be recognized as real.[34] The 'issue' of the subject is addressed in the present collection in chapters dealing with the use of images in nineteenth-century elementary-school classrooms (see Myers, chapter 1) as well as in relation to the contemporary pedagogic context where images are utilized as a distancing means of exploring the mythology of self (see Bunyard, chapter 11).

The subject is always somehow both present and absent in the visual in pictures, in photographs and in film.[35] The problematic of representation is perhaps most dramatically realized through the 'caught' subject of visual technologies (more so than with the 'fabricated' subject of less 'mechanical' technologies of representation). For the photographic image induces us think, in the first place, at least, of a person more than a subject, of an individual perhaps more than a figure or metonym encased in a social space. And yet the logic of the representation, the logic of the sign, does not cease at the point when we recognize (or 'misrecognize') the figure as a point in the trajectory of a life. We learn to read photographs as much as we learn to read other textual forms. It is appropriate, then, that the photograph occupies some of the more theoretical explorations here, in terms of beginning to formulate a sense of the photograph as a specific textual

---

34   J. Rose, *Sexuality in the Field of Vision* (London: Verso, 1986), p. 194: 'the subject is caught by a look which it cannot see but which it imagines in the field of the Other.' Rose also refers to Metz's theorizing the relation of the subject to 'mere' images demanding to be recognized as real (p. 195).

35   For a remarkable account of the 'ghostly' nature of representation see J. Derrida and B. Stiegler, *Echographies of Television* (Cambridge: Polity Press, 2002).

form within the general archive of the history of education (see Mietzner and Pilarczyk, chapter 4).

The contributions offered in this volume never make the claim that the subject can be erased in this quest for the reconstitution of the object. Here the visual provides a series of occasions for re-engaging with education in a number of different contexts and modes. Some of these engage with issues of subjectivity directly as in the case of the exploration of the subjectivity of the would-be historian. Sirke Happonen has provided here a sustained account of the subject's experience of visual texts in children's fiction, for example (see chapter 2). The coded representation of subject identity and activity is explored as well as, in other sections, the formation of the subject in policy and governance through the visual rhetoric of film (see Jones and Vuorio-Lehti, chapters 7 and 5). Pedagogy is explored bringing together the more conventional material of academic history with an awareness of the production of the learning subject in the pedagogic relation (see Myers, chapter 1). Various myths of subjectivity are explored through film. The governmental role of pictures in early elementary urban classrooms is explored as a technology of person-formation (see Peim, chapter 8). Nowhere is the logic of subject representation more dramatically realized in this collection than in Moholy-Nagy's strange realism reflecting the alien social world of Eton (see Grosvenor and Lawn, chapter 3). In all this, an account is given of how the social subject is portrayed and relayed back to the viewer. It is clear that accounting for the meaning of images also means accounting for ourselves, our own subjectivities. Often the engagement with the visual involves a visceral element (as Roland Barthes's account of the 'punctum' suggests) forcing our engagement to be dislocated from the strictly conventional.[36]

36   R. Barthes, *Camera Lucida* (London: Vintage Press, 1993), pp. 27–8.

Contexts, discourses

Of course, visual signs and visual texts do not exist as independent entities in our world. We are, it is frequently noted, more or less constantly exposed to images of various kinds. How we experience them, however, is a complex matter that relates to the very problematic issue of how signs work in society. This is no securely hierarchical and objective science. There are innumerable theories and positions that present different ways of understanding the visual field. These range from the psychoanalytic, with its often intense engagement with the structure of the subject both within and in relation to the field of vision, to the ethnographic, which is more concerned with trying to account for how visual meanings are actually engaged with in the lived experiences of actual social subjects. We can begin to account for the complexity of the fundamental account of the engagement with the visual in terms of an account of the visual sign, an account of visual texts, their taxonomy and generic features. But on the other, non-formalist, side we must also account for the contexts of visual texts, their relations with other texts, visual and otherwise, the specific codes of the specific languages they deploy, their relations with the meanings that circulate through texts, contexts, subjects and discourses.

Systemic functional linguistics offers a useful comparative frame of reference. Halliday defines language as 'social semiotic'.[37] Language is embedded in social contexts that are themselves semiotically-saturated environments. In exploring what are interestingly referred to as 'lexico-grammatical structures' Halliday determines that meanings cannot be understood outside of the *functions* that can apply to certain situations of context. Language in use, Saussure's *parole* or Chomsky's performance, is dependent for its meaning and effect on the complex ordering of context. According to Halliday, the various contexts of usage can be defined and must be written into any attempt to write a grammar of signs that is capable of grappling with meaning. In effect,

---

37   M. A. K. Halliday, *Language as Social Semiotic* (London: Edward Arnold, 1979), pp. 108–26.

this also means that language is not a closed system, that it is always reaching beyond itself but also that it is caught up in practices of meaning and practices of sense-making. Context is composed in this sense of many different elements, including the social order at work in the business of meaning-generation. We may equally apply this logic to 'visual language'.

A structuralist analysis may be able to reveal internal relations within texts.[38] But even structural analyses must begin to address the generic frameworks of textual identity. Meaning-making processes are always moving beyond the confines of the text 'itself'. Boundaries are uncertain and impossible to define. The photograph cannot be understood as bearing meaning in its own right. Mr Shoveller does not announce himself through the medium of the photograph, fully formed and determinate (see Peim, chapter 8). Nor can we trace the meaning of Mr Shoveller to an archive, or another point of origin or originary context, that will exhaustively explain his meaning and confirm its limits. Maholy-Nagy's photographs of Eton reverberate with enigmatic meanings that are the product of a strange and alien social environment as well as often startling perspectives and composition. In these cases neither 'lexicon' nor 'grammar' can exhaust the signifying productivity of the images in question (see Grosvenor and Lawn, chapter 3). And in a historical sense, the 'context' can only be effectively reproduced through recourse to other such textual evidence. There is also the 'juridical' component: what kind of evidence counts, rules for its organization, presentation, who is authorized to make interpretations, to define objects. Images are caught up in discourses embedded in material practices. History cannot be innocent of the sociology of knowledge.

It would be misleading then to claim that semiotics or the science of signs in society represented the name of a unified field of thought or a cohesive method for engaging with historical (or other) evidence. The essays in this collection reflect the diversity of the field and some hopefully useful and illustrative modes and occasions of engagement

---

38   See T. Hawkes, *Structuralism and Semiotics* (London: Methuen, 1977), on
      Roland Barthes's codes. Even these codes must include the cultural reference
      code and the hermeneutic.

with signifying material. What this collection doesn't do is to lay claim to a new mode or model of history. While there may be the rumblings of a paradigm shift in some of the essays enclosed here, there is frequently an attempt to use visual images to positively supplement other kinds of historical evidence.

Sign languages: meanings and theories

With the poststructuralists the positivistic tendencies of the science of signs have had to confront the 'law of contamination', the sliding of the signifier under the signified, the decentring of the subject, the association of the sign with the unintended workings of the unconscious and with the historically contingent nature of discourses. From this position, the science of signs recognized itself more as a social science (belonging to the collection code rather than to the integrated code), concerned with the dialogic, agonistic, decentring effects of signs in the dynamic sphere of social life and its meaning-making processes.

Visual signs, even when they may appear to bear a close resemblance to the things they refer to, are still signs. They carry meaning and require interpretation, even if that interpretative process remains unconscious. For visual signs to convey meaning at all, a visual 'language' must exist. Visual signs belong to an order or a system of organization that determines, to some significant degree, how we look at them, the range of sense-making options available, the kinds of meaning we ascribe to them and where we might place them in our general sense of the larger order of things. For signs to make sense there must be a *more or less* shared set of meanings that attach to specific signifiers. That is not to say that the signs can determine their own meanings, or that meanings are somehow fixed in shared assumptions. On the contrary, meanings are always contested and variable. This again relates to the difference between the sign and what it represents, even, as indicated above, where the two may seem to be very close, as for example with common-sense assumptions about photography as revealing a kind of iconic truth about the world through the effects of a disinterested chemical process. In the Peircian account of sign systems a radical difference is made between a sign which is indexical and a sign which is iconic. In fact, it is when signs are most automatically taken for what they represent that we may be most alert to the presence of ideology or the embedding of meaning within systems of ideas that are taken for natural and naked truth. This is the very condition of representation. Iconic signs are also always symbolic and indexical.

Towards a semiotic theory

If a systematic theory were to be offered here it would need to address the following specific semiotic issues:

- *the structure and logic of the sign*: fundamental matters of how signs work;
- *modality and representation*: or the exploration of the reality-status of signs and the discourses they inhabit. Modality refers to ways in which we may make distinctions, for example, between textual forms that refer more closely to conceptions of reality than others through different modes, but which may at the same time make different claims to their truth-status;
- *paradigms and syntagms*: where the distinction is made between vertical and horizontal axes of meaning. The paradigmatic corresponds to the meaning potential of signs beyond themselves; the syntagmatic relates to the organization and ordering of signs within specific rules of combination, textual forms and discourses. All theories of meaning must deal with this duality;
- *denotation, connotation and myth* refer to different aspects of signs and their relations with meaning. Denotation refers to the

more direct relation between a signifier and a signified, whereas connotation refers to the more nebulous suggestions that may accrue to the signifier, its 'poetic' or symbolic potential above and beyond its more literal reference. This distinction is important in grasping the mythic content of language where meaning exceeds a simple direct reference and takes on a more socio-symbolic resonance;

- *rhetorical tropes* refer to the specific resources, tactics and strategies that signs, texts and discourses deploy as resources of signification to produce representations, and to give them specific form;
- *codes* are the inexplicit rules for putting together combinations of signs in meaningful arrangements. Codes operate at the level of encoding and decoding, but there can be no clear separation between them, every decoding famously being another encoding. There can be no meaning for signs without codes. Signs do not, therefore, 'speak' for themselves;
- *articulation* refers to the relations in a code between the fundamental units of meaning. Articulation is the condition that enables combinations of units to form more or less complex meanings;
- *intertextuality* refers to the web of meanings that is at work between any one text and others. Texts refer to one another and echo one another both consciously and unconsciously. Meanings always reverberate with their realizations in other texts, in other contexts. Hence, meanings cannot be fully present and self-sufficient in any given single text.

This rough outline can only provide the starting point perhaps for a theory of the semiotic. In addition, specific discourses of knowledge will relate to the different themes appropriate to photography, say, or film. Equally important is the need for a discourse addressing the generation of meanings and their exchange in specific social contexts, a dialogic theory of 'audiences' and institutions that brings reception into the loop of the production of meanings. In the domain of education, this further depth seems especially significant in any attempt to capture lived realities.

Signs of history

Knowledge in history, then, does not subscribe to a single overarching paradigm. There is no correspondence between the account of science offered by Kuhn's analysis and description. There is no sovereign 'master' theory or presiding position. It seems that the human 'sciences' are subject to the decentring logic of the poststructuralist and postmodern nexus or to the hermeneutic emphasis of Gadamer. This means that the field of representation cannot be exhaustively accounted for 'scientifically' by predetermined and foolproof method. The position of the subject, indeed the very complex fact of subjectivity, has to be taken into account. This means rethinking some familiar ideas like ideology, intention and reception in the field of representation including the visual. The social and interested dimension of meaning cannot be written out of the account.

This collection is not concerned only with the documentary potential of visual material in history. It does seek to explore a range of visual materials as specific forms of historical 'data'. These data do not and cannot speak for themselves directly through 'the dark backward and abysm of time'. The painstaking work of framing, placing, locating visual images and texts in relation to a field both past and present engenders complexities, issues of interpretation and sense-making and status.

The problem of status and approach (how do we read different types of historical data?) seems particularly emphatic in relation to visual material that comes within the ambit of fiction. But a similar uncertainty may arise with other categories. What approach is appropriate to government documentaries, promising a bright new age? What approach is appropriate for Moholy-Nagy's peculiarly arresting photographs of Eton College? Is there a method that can encompass these different instances of visual data in the field of the history of education? On a number of occasions this collection also addresses fictions of various kinds within or relating to the field of education. What is the motivation and the direction of this kind of exploration? In what sense does material from popular culture enter into the domain of history? What are the relations between fictions and non-fictions, in terms of textual orders, text types, modes of reception, sense-making and meaning within a field?

To some extent these questions are explored explicitly. The relations between the fictional and the documentary are closely bound up with questions about the status of text, document, archive and the nature of the relations between data and interpretation. These questions touch on vital matters that promise to transform and re-energize historical studies, both opening the field to include reference to a vastly expanded range of data and prompting a rethinking of the relations between knowledge, ideas and perspectives. In this context, the historical meets with other domains: the approach must become multidisciplinary. Fictions of various kinds provide further examples, further semiotic data and at the same time further issues and problems for interpretation and determination. The explorations here engage with fictions in attempts to explore the historical forms of representation relating to education within a culture (see Catteeuw *et al.*, Happonen and Vuorio-Lehti, chapters 9, 2 and 5). Again, the process of recreation and reproduction is an inescapable component of this kind of work.

There is the question of whether the incursion of the visual into the history of education constitutes a radical shift in the order of things, particularly in the nature of the archive. Does the visual require a different mode of engagement, different forms of interpretation? Does the visual require different kinds of tactical deployment in arguments? Does the visual open new and different spaces for exploration, for active engagement and re-engagement with the classical issues of the history of education? And does the visual open the possibility of an approach to hitherto unexplored spaces and dimensions? Does this engagement effect a different conception of the field, of its objects, modes of engagement, subject positions, of its method and of its archive? The determination of these questions rests with the movement of the discourse. In one sense it is already very obviously and clearly evident that the archive is not a stable and fixed something, as new discourses enter into the field and open new objects and new ways of engaging with history. Women's histories provide a vivid and perhaps drastic example of the reconstitution of the field of history through the opening up of a new and different space of knowledge. The field is not simply expanded by the intrusion of hitherto excluded knowledge. Its borders are interfered with; its ontological status is problematized, reorganized and redefined.

History as signs of difference

What we are examining, then, are signs, texts and the traces they bear of past meanings, past intentions, past institutions, past relations. Of course, we can only view these from present perspectives. This is a necessarily hermeneutic process and cannot come to rest either in the capture of the essence of what it is that we seek nor in a total explanation. Derrida's concept of 'writing' reminds us of forgotten but essential elements in the signifying process, such as the temporal dislocation of the sign.[39] In the description of the sign as *trace* we are confronted with our own meaning-making intentions, both as subjects of history and as would-be historians. Between the signifier and the signified there must be recognized something corresponding to 'the will to knowledge'. The point about Derrida's idea of the trace is that it refers to an absent presence. The trace signifies the absence of what *was* present. And it is in the interplay between this presence and this absence that discourse intervenes. Thus the logic of the trace demands that the material social world of discourse be taken into account as a fundamental condition of the sign.

The signifier indicates no immediate presence of the signified: on the contrary. Discourse gives shape, provides context, activates a range of possible meanings and even enables the possibility of exchange. The photographic image, the image of Eton College in the 1930s, for example, may seem to 'capture' real objects in real social space (see Grosvenor and Lawn, chapter 3). There is something in this. The vivid contrasts and subtle shades of the photographs may

39   J. Derrida, *Of Grammatology* (London: The Johns Hopkins University Press, 1976); and *Positions* (London: Athlone Press, 1987).

entice us into the sensation of a living moment. But the process of transformation that the technology of reproduction enacts is vital to realizing the curious and enigmatic logic of the photographic image. Even in its most apparently naturalistic mode, the photographic image drastically transforms the objects and space it appears to 'capture'. The still image itself is a reduction as much as it is a reflection of subjects, objects and spaces. Taken out of the social space-time continuum, it produces a two-dimensional slice of social existence. Each mark on its surface represents but a trace of a once present entity. The image in all its vivid particularity reminds of its presence but also at the same time confirms its absence. It is not only the absence of what the two-dimensional mark represents that is negatively signified by the photograph. It is also the flattening of the context, the 'thick' experiential context of the lived continuum. In this sense, the image is like the word in the potential estrangement from immediacy. It stands in the place of what it represents on the axis of metaphor and metonymy whereby one thing always stands for something else and opens up a gap or lack in the moment of representation. The word represents the thing in the sense that it stands *for* the thing. It also stands *in the place of* the thing as a kind of mediating metaphor on the one hand but also as the death of the thing on the other.[40] The same logic applies to the pictorial, photographic and filmic image and is part of the fascination with which we often view these things.

The visual image then, although often assumed to work with a greater immediacy than the word, must always be *activated* within discourse to make sense. The visual image exists in visual discourse. This means that we can speak of a visual language, visual codes that make sense within a social practice, that occur within specific contexts in specific situations. One of the processes that is evident in much of what follows is the painstaking task of locating images, visual texts within the context of their production, within the context, too, of their reception. This same logic applies to pictures constructed through

---

40   See T. Eagleton, *William Shakespeare* (Oxford: Basil Blackwell, 1986) on Lacan, pp. 97, 106, 107; and J. Derrida, *The Ear of the Other* (Lincoln: University of Nebraska Press, 1988), pp. 3–38.

other technologies and to the moving image in film. It is the work of recreating contexts and meanings, those other necessary dimensions, that the writing on images in this collection represents.

If the image threatens to disturb a certain order of things in the domain of history, there may remain a question as to whether or not this disruption should be seen as positive or negative intervention. In the domain of the history of education some of these arguments have been rehearsed in *Paedagogica Historica*, where various contributors seek to make the case for establishing the visual.[41] The current volume does not attempt to address this debate systematically. It rather enacts a series of engagements that sometimes raise theoretical issues and that sometimes activate questions of the rights of the visual and the nature of the archive. Catteeuw, Dams, Depaepe and Simon in this collection argue strongly for a circumspect approach, wary of a modish displacement of conventional histories and the fetishization of the visual as a uniquely privileged form of archive (chapter 9). None of the pieces here shares Jean Baudrillard's sense that the order of simulation has somehow displaced our contact with the real.[42] In any case, that position depends on forgetting that signs have always played a part in mediating and determining our relations with 'the real' and forgets also that the sign is the absolute condition of the concept of reality coming into being.

Neither this book nor this introduction is an argument for luxuriating in the proliferation of interpretation afforded by the visual. On the contrary, its essays engage with the visual in the history of education with quite specific ideas, purposes and intentions. The visual here is used as both a source and a resource for engagement with the history of education, not to reveal the (impossible) singular truth of the evidential nature of visual material. Visual material can only be one element in the ongoing attempt to represent the truth (albeit always already understood to be provisional and positioned) of

41   Op. cit.
42   J. Baudrillard, *In the Shadow of the Silent Majorities* (New York: Semiotexte, 1983); *Simulations* (New York: Semiotexte, 1983); *The Illusion of the End* (Cambridge: Polity Press, 1994).

an interpretation, a position, an idea. In this attempt the visual may provide a different purchase, access to another dimension, a different way of apprehending the relations between subjects and objects. The visual may be seen and deployed as another mode of engagement with the social spaces and social relations of education. The visual can also offer access to the rhetorics of education as they move between different domains of representation (see Jones and Vuorio-Lehti, chapters 7 and 5). The visions encapsulated in policy documents, for example, and reform legislation are transposed onto the celluloid productions of documentary looking forward to bright new educational futures. Those futures now past, we view the pictures, photographs, film in terms of its realization of the ideal it represents, finding a method for further specifying the particular formation of ideas in the public domain.

In emphasizing aspects of representation in this collection, there is a recognition of the significance of the semiotic in relation to the production of knowledge. We hope it is clear, however, that this does not mean a negation of the idea of 'reality' as being the proper goal of historical studies, displaced by the playful engagement with myth. But engaging with visual materials in these ways seems to demand some account of the inescapable role of signs in knowledge. In the domain of semiotics reality and myth cannot be severely separated from one another. It seems necessary to engage constantly with this problematic, precisely in order to engage and re-engage with social realities. As historians of education this project seems to us necessary and productive.

KEVIN MYERS

1 Image, Inner Eye and T. C. Horsfall's Picture Loan Scheme

Introduction

In many accounts of late-nineteenth-century Britain the power of elementary schools in shaping subjectivities is near proverbial. Schools are casually cited as key institutions in the remaking of the working class and as central to the development of national identity and popular patriotism.[1] They are routinely ascribed a causal role in the formation of clearly delineated gender identities and frequently used to explain changes in the manners, morals and general behaviour of a whole society.[2] Yet in historical writing the precise operation of this power often remains obscure. Schools are assumed to be influential but there are relatively few empirical accounts of *how* schools managed to produce particular kinds of subjects.

Even in the specialized field of the history of education there have been apparently few attempts to ponder quite *how* the routines of schooling contribute to the production of subjects. Whilst there have been numerous studies of some aspect of the material cultures of

---

1 E. J. Hobsbawm, *Nations and Nationalism since 1780: Programme, Myth, Reality* (Cambridge: Cambridge University Press, 1990), pp. 92–3, 96–7; G. Steadman Jones, *Languages of Class: Studies in English Working Class History, 1832–1982* (Cambridge: Cambridge University Press), pp. 219, 221–2. J. Bourke, *Working Class Cultures in Britain, 1890–1960: Gender, Class and Ethnicity* (London: Routledge, 1994), pp. 185–6.

2 F. M. L. Thompson, *The Rise of Respectable Society* (London: Fontana Press, 1988), pp. 137–51; F. Bedarida, *A Social History of England, 1851–1990* (London: Routledge, 1991), pp. 153–8; P. Horn, *The Victorian Town Child* (Stroud: Sutton, 1997), pp. 70–98.

schools, these rarely explicate quite *how* school curricula and text-books were related to subjectivity. All too often the working assumption is that children passively absorbed the attitudes, values and myths promoted in lessons and in books.[3] Seldom are there detailed attempts to analyse just *how* the material culture of schooling – how the very classroom and its textures of desks, books, wallcharts and lessons – went about shaping the subjectivities of their pupils. Moreover, of those more recent texts that give greater attention to this question, many derive their method from Foucault and, as a result, inherit a weakness for saying rather little about either ideology or the actual processes through which subjects fill particular roles.[4] This chapter is an attempt to explore that question.

The point of departure is an apparently trivial moment in the history of schooling: the introduction and use of mounted images in the elementary schools of late-nineteenth-century Manchester. Launched by the local philanthropist T. C. Horsfall in 1887, the Schools' Picture Loan Scheme eventually consisted of some 237 collections of pictures that were distributed to over half the elementary schools of Manchester.

Each collection consisted of twelve frames that depicted a variable number of scenes – from Nature and the Bible or from History and Geography – and each school received a new set of pictures for display annually. The scheme was widely supported and popular and it led directly to a change in the school code that allowed time spent in museums to count towards the total attendance time of pupils. Interesting as this may be, it hardly establishes the Schools' Picture Loan Scheme as an important moment in the history of schooling. Nor is it obvious how it helps illuminate the relationship between schooling and subjectivity. In order to understand what this

---

3   P. McCann (ed.), *Popular Education and Socialisation in the Nineteenth Century* (London: Methuen & Co., 1977), p. xii; R. Lowe, *History of Education: Major Themes Volume III: Studies in Teaching and Learning* (London: RoutledgeFalmer, 2000), p. ix.

4   See, for example, I. Copeland, *The Making of the Backward Pupil in Education in England, 1870–1914* (London: Woburn, 1999).

historical moment might reveal about the organisation of subjectivity it will be helpful to draw on some theory.

Whilst it attends to the concrete historical detail of the Schools' Picture Loan Scheme, therefore, this chapter also draws on a deliberately 'loose' reading of Althusser's theory of ideology.[5] This is attractive primarily because, in providing a class-based theory of ideology and outlining a theory of interpellation, it helps make sense of a particular historical moment. It is also helpful, however, because it suggests a method for avoiding the error that seems to plague historians: the uncritical adoption of a socialization model.[6] Instead of describing the content of the images mounted on the wall and relating these to particular forms of consciousness, this chapter tries to explore how the images were designed and used to secure deep or unconscious structures that made pupils responsive to particular ideologies. In other words, this chapter can be partly read as a schematic attempt to apply Althusser's theory of interpellation to an empirical case study. No doubt this is at least partly because the issues that this kind of approach raises pose difficult questions regarding sources, methods and disciplinary boundaries. Yet the difficulty of the task should not deter its exploration and, leaving aside these wider theoretical and methodological questions, it is time to return to the case study in hand and to the philanthropist T. C. Horsfall.

---

5   L. Althusser, 'Ideology and ideological state apparatuses (notes towards an investigation)' in *Lenin and Philosophy and Other Essays* (London: New Left Books, 1971), pp. 121–73.

6   The criticism is not novel but continues to be pertinent. See J. Donald, *Sentimental Education: Schooling, Popular Culture and the Regulation of Liberty* (London: Verso, 1992), p. 47. An earlier and longer version of the same paper, helpful in terms of preparing this chapter, can be found in V. Beechey and J. Donald, *Subjectivity and Social Relations: a Reader* (Milton Keynes, Open University Press, 1985), pp. 214–49.

'Admiration, Hope and Love'

It is well known by historians that many late-nineteenth-century philanthropists regarded the industrial town as a dangerous artifice and an offence to nature.[7] T. C. Horsfall was certainly convinced that the new cityscape, containing new modes of living and working, had produced new personalities, attitudes and relationships. His view of his beloved Manchester was, for example, dominated by its 'foul air and gloom', by its 'small and filthy houses … the filthy street' and its 'soot-begrimed parks' all of which resulted in 'smoke-spoiled, dull and drunken lives'. Such lives were characterized by 'brutality and drunkenness', were experienced as 'small and monotonous', 'dull and silent', and were lived in the complete absence of culture and civilization.[8] Like other middle-class liberal reformers, Horsfall was genuinely committed to the ideal of social improvement and saw himself as a member of those 'guiding classes' whose duty was to teach, improve and civilize Manchester society.[9] Whilst fearful of the consequences of failing to improve the degraded lives of the working-class people he retained, a little unusually for the later part of the nineteenth century, a humanist belief in the innate goodness and potential of each individual. So despite sometimes employing the language of race, and despite devising some punitive-sounding solutions for the problem of the residuum, he did not exhibit a sustained interest in the degeneration theories that were popular with social imperialists. His rather different aim was the liberation (or the control) of human potential through changes in both the physical and cultural

---

7   See, for example, H. J. Dyos and M. Wolff, *The Victorian City: Images and Realities* (London: Routledge and Kegan Paul, 1976); E. Timms and D. Kelly (eds.), *Unreal City: Urban Experience in Modern European Literature and Art* (Manchester: Manchester University Press, 1985).

8   T. C. Horsfall, *An Art Museum for Manchester* (Manchester: A. Ireland and Co., 1877), pp. 7, 9, 10, 17–21.

9   M. Harrison, *Social Reform in late Victorian and Edwardian Manchester with Special Reference to T. C. Horsfall*, unpublished PhD thesis (University of Manchester, 1987), pp. 5–7.

environment of the nineteenth-century industrial working class.[10] Three mechanisms of this liberation need to be noted here.

First, there is the view of Nature and the countryside as a repository for all that is beautiful and true. The idea that the countryside allowed for the full development of human potential – a corollary to the panics that accompanied the development of the town – is elegantly expressed in correspondence that Horsfall received from Alfred Marshall in 1900:

> I am entirely in agreement with your claim that the community is bound to see to it that town dwellers have opportunities to [sic] knowing what a full and healthy life is. Country folk are less dependent on training and on inspirations derived from their fellow men. The fresh air and light and sunshine strengthen and stimulate [...] and the beauty of everchanging nature offers an invitation to reverent and religious feeling [...]. But town life, with its ever increasing density and extension shrouds the individual away from himself, and from the Infinite. It keeps up an incessant strain on his nervous strength, and tends to make him forget the blessedness of repose. He is always on the move, and therefore he is seldom entirely himself: he is scarcely ever completely refreshed and therefore he is apt to seek for excitement the path of least resistance, and the excitements to which they lead are seldom altogether pure and healthy.[11]

This passage also helps illuminate a second aspect of Horsfall's schemes for improvement; his view of improving culture. The density, anonymity and the frenetic speed of life in industrial cities offer no occasion for rest or repose, no stimulus to reverent feelings and, in short, no opportunity to be fully human. What is absent, in other words, is the core value of liberal romanticism – *Bildung* – or (very roughly) the chance to become oneself.[12] Marx, of course, developed

---

10   A. J. Kidd, 'Introduction: The Middle Class in Nineteenth-Century Manchester', in A. J. Kidd (ed.), *City, Class and Culture: Studies of Cultural Production and Social Policy in Victorian Manchester* (Manchester: Manchester University Press, 1985).

11   Manchester Public Library Archives, Horsfall Collection, correspondence files: letter 244, Marshall to Horsfall, 8 March 1900.

12   M. Berman, *Adventures in Marxism* (London: Verso, 1999), pp. 9–10 notes that there is no adequate translation in English, but the term Bildung 'embraces a family of ideas like subjectivity, finding yourself, growing up, identity, self-development and becoming who you are'.

the theory of alienation to explain precisely this phenomenon and advocated revolutionary changes in economic relations that would recover the 'loss of self' and the dignity and humanity of the worker.[13] Though both Alfred Marshall and T. C. Horsfall seem to agree on the problem of alienation in the town, their solution was rather more consistent with the philosophy of German Romanticism. It was in the healing power of Nature, in the feelings and thoughts that an awareness of Nature inspired, that the urban population could find a more noble and a happier future.[14]

The third element of Horsfall's reforms that needs to be noted here was his view of the children as naturally innocent with 'innate good qualities' that made them 'possible heroes or saints'.[15] It was in childhood that 'the hearts and minds, the physical, mental and moral habits of the people are influenced permanently and very deeply'.[16] After the introduction of compulsory elementary education in 1880, an increasing amount of that childhood was to be experienced in schools. Such schools were widely seen as offering the hope of a revolution in social manners but Horsfall consistently argued that the reality was of an inefficient and failing system that produced few discernible results. Not only were the aims of late-nineteenth-century English schooling excessively utilitarian, its methods were positively harmful.

Unlike that army of Victorian philanthropists and social commentators, who professed a simple belief in efficacy of rote learning, Horsfall was fiercely critical of elementary school pedagogy. 'We no longer believe', Horsfall told the Manchester Teachers Guild in 1897, 'that telling in words [to] unprepared ears and minds has very much

---

13   K. Marx, 'Economic and Philosophical Manuscripts' (1844) in *Early Writings* (Penguin, 1992), pp. 279–400 (p. 327).

14   D. A. Reeder, 'Predicaments of city children: late Victorian and Edwardian perspectives on education and urban society', in D. A. Reeder (ed.), *Urban Education in the 19th Century* (London: Taylor and Francis, 1977) offers an overview of the problems associated with the city and the kinds of educational activity that it stimulated.

15   M. Harrison, *Social Reform in Late Victorian and Edwardian Manchester*, p. 359.

16   T. C. Horsfall, *Reforms Needed in our System of Elementary Education*, (Manchester: J. E. Cornish, 1897), p. 2.

value.'[17] Or in 1895, 'lessons in words' could 'give no idea' of the beautiful and interesting things that Horsfall wanted to introduce to schoolchildren.[18] This kind of rote instruction 'bids defiance to all psychology', Horsfall claimed, and ignored both the nature and needs of the child.[19] If the school wanted to have a permanently good influence on the life, aims and habits of its pupils it had to be more ambitious and to concern itself with shaping the very character and feeling of children. Transmitting useful knowledge and doling out vicious punishment was not enough.

Schools' Picture Loan Scheme

Much has been written about the disciplinary function of elementary schools. Studies of educational rhetoric, school architecture and teaching materials have revealed much about the widespread desire in late-nineteenth-century Britain to reform and moralise the working class.[20] Somewhat surprisingly, however, it is only fairly recently that serious consideration has been given to the space of the classroom in this programme of reform. According to two leading historians of education, for example, the classroom remains the black box of educational history; a complex but mysterious space unwilling to give up its secrets and yielding only slowly to critical enquiry.[21] As a result the question of how schooling works – and, here, the role that it plays

---

17   Op. cit., p. 11.

18   T. C. Horsfall, *A Description of the Work of the Manchester Art Museum* (Manchester: A. Ireland & Co., 1895), p. 17.

19   Cited in M. Harrison, *Social Reform in Late Victorian and Edwardian Manchester*, p. 385.

20   See, for example, D. Hogan, 'The market revolution and disciplinary power: Joseph Lancaster and the psychology of the early classroom system' in *History of Education Quarterly*, 29. 3 (1989), 381–417.

21   M. Depaepe and F. Simon, 'Is there any place for the history of "education" in the "history of education"? A plea for the history of educational reality in and outside schools', *Paedagogica Historica*, 31. 1 (1995), 9–16.

in shaping subjectivity – is one that remains open. A consideration of T. C. Horsfall's work can provide some possible lines of enquiry precisely because he saw the elementary-school classroom as *the* crucial space in the new industrial towns. It offered the hope of a newly civilized Manchester, making good the 'deficiencies of the home and the general environment' and inspiring in children a Wordsworthian feeling for 'Admiration, Hope and Love'.[22]

Horsfall's Romanticism – his view of Nature and the country-side, his belief in the didactic power of culture and his ideas on the innocence of childhood – came together in the schools' picture loan scheme. Though this rather stuttered into existence in the 1880s it had, by December 1895, established and distributed 237 collections of pictures to over half the elementary schools of Manchester. Each collection consisted of twelve frames that were produced using a variety of reproductive techniques including chromolithographs, photographs and etchings. Each collection also featured images from a number of selected themes including Nature (flowers, animals, birds, trees, general landscape); History and Geography (scenery of the Lake District, architecture of Egypt, Greece, Rome and Mediaeval Europe, events in the history of England and other countries); and the Bible (scenery of the Holy Land).[23] In the absence of a surviving collection of these images a more detailed analysis of their content and their production and distribution must, for the moment at least, remain elusive.[24] Nevertheless judging by the notes and sketches that Horsfall made for the scheme, it seems safe to assert that along with images of nature and landscape, pictures of religious subjects and scenes, historical episodes and geographical locations adorned the walls of elementary schools in late-nineteenth-century Manchester. At first glance this may appear as a decorative and essentially trivial moment in the history of schooling. Yet when set against the wider changes wrought by the development of modern industrial capitalism, and

---

22   T. C. Horsfall, *Reforms Needed in our System of Elementary Education*, pp. 9, 12.

23   Horsfall, *The Manchester Art Museum*, p. 11.

24   A significant number were produced by local publishing entrepreneur and temperance campaigner John Cassell.

viewed in conjunction with the thought of Walter Benjamin, it can be thought of as a significant episode in the making of modern subjects.

It has already been noted that Horsfall's picture loan scheme was dependent on the use of relatively new reproductive technologies. Photography and lithography were the means through which school-children were to be introduced to nature, beauty and history. The work of the Marxist cultural theorist Walter Benjamin is potentially useful here because much of his writing was taken up with examining the relationship between human subjectivity and these reproductive technologies. As Esther Leslie puts it:

> Benjamin explores how human subjectivity might correspond to the contemporary exigencies of existence and how technological art – artworks that are produced by mechanical means and are reproduced in numerous copies – translates and retransmits contemporary existence.[25]

Technological art made possible the translation or retransmission of contemporary existence. It did so because when works of art or nature were reproduced for popular consumption they began to lose both their authenticity and their aura. No longer unique and no longer tied to specific locations (in churches and art galleries for example), the reproduced object is detached from the domain of tradition.[26] In doing so, the meaning of the image becomes fluid rather than fixed. It circulates around societies and may be seen and consumed in a variety of locations and contexts. In the process it becomes just another source of information that may be either used or ignored but whose meaning is never settled.[27] Benjamin thought that this technological culture had revolutionary potential because it offered new and more democratic ways of organising perception. In the sites of 'low culture' (or those public places of working-class leisure), for example, elite art,

---

25   E. Leslie, *Walter Benjamin: Overpowering Conformism* (London: Pluto Press, 2000), p. 42.

26   W. Benjamin, 'The work of art in an age of mechanical reproduction', in *Illuminations* (London: Jonathan Cape, 1970), pp. 219–240, (p. 223). J. Berger, *Ways of Seeing* (Harmondsworth: Penguin, 1972), pp. 7–34, provides an accessible introduction to, and application of, the ideas that Benjamin outlines in this essay.

27   Berger, *Ways of Seeing*, p. 24.

literature and music could easily be overlooked or its time-honoured meaning subverted. And whilst the revolutionary Benjamin may have welcomed the liberating potential of mass produced images, most members of the late-nineteenth-century elite were alarmed by what they saw as the linked decline in morality and piety. Indeed, the very development of compulsory state education owed more than a little to the attempts of the bourgeois elite to reassert their cultural authority over the seemingly debauched and degraded working class.

Alarmed by the emergence of urban popular culture – in the public house and the gin palace, the music hall and the temptations to be found in the street – Horsfall saw elementary schools as sites for the promotion of elite culture. In one sense his picture loan scheme simply seeks to recreate or hold onto what Benjamin, writing some forty years later, thinks has disappeared; namely the ritualistic consumption of images. Hanging pictures of Nature and of biblical or historical scenes in schools attempts to render present the civilization and values of a lost and much-lamented society. Moreover, the school, and more specifically the teacher, is used to reintroduce a form of collective and ritual consumption. The purpose of all this, as the following label attached to landscape pictures makes clear, is to fix the meaning and significance of the selected scenes:

> Everyone should learn to enjoy the beautiful scenery. The enjoyment of it is one of the greatest and most wholesome pleasures we can have. It gives us countless pleasant feelings and thoughts to keep our hearts and minds in healthy activity; it helps us to gain wholesome pleasure from books many of the best which describe scenery, from pictures which represent it, and from many other things [...]. The world is full of beauty, and the perception of it is necessary for our welfare. It is as foolish not to learn to see it as it would be, if we had money in the savings bank which we needed for the purchase of food, not to learn how to draw it out.[28]

At the very historical moment that images are beginning to proliferate – in the popular press and in the early advertising industry for example – there is a definite attempt to impose an order of meaning on those images. Since after 1880 all children had to attend elementary school,

28   *The Manchester Art Museum: Annual Report 1897–98*, (Manchester: William Darbyshire, 1898), pp. 24–5.

these images were consumed as a matter of compulsion and in a way that attempted to determine their symbolic value. It is worth pausing here and reflecting in a little more detail on just how these images worked.

It may help to begin by recalling, along with many other studies, that the dominant ideology shaping late-nineteenth-century elementary schooling was nationalism.[29] It is the idea of the nation that is articulated in the practices and rituals of the school and, importantly, in the organization and use of classroom space. In this sense the wall was part of a classroom technology and its purpose was to communicate the central tenets of a newly constituted national culture.[30] The individual elements of this culture are 'natural' in as much they consist of all the phenomena of the natural world and, most obviously, plants, flowers, animals and landscapes. Selected and cumulatively displayed in the schoolroom, however, it was the ideology of Englishness that appropriated these natural elements and turned them into cultural forms. This happens partly because of the display of the images in particular places and of the positions that seeing subjects then necessarily occupy. As has already been suggested, schoolroom images were grounded in a set of power relations – they meant what the teacher said – and in an institution that served particular social and political purposes. So in the schoolroom reproductions of Turner, Holman Hunt, Madox Brown and Everett Millais the landscape became a cultural and social construction and the birthplace of national identity. As W. J. T. Mitchell argues, images of 'landscape represented an artificial world as if it were simply given and inevitable', and made those images 'operational by interpellating its beholder in some more or less determinate relation to its givenness as sight and site'.[31]

---

29   I. Grosvenor, 'There's no place like home: education and the making of national identity', *History of Education*, 23 (1999), 235–50; A. O'Shea, 'English subjects of modernity', in M. Nava and A. O'Shea (eds.), *Modern Times: Reflections on a Century of English Modernity* (London: Routledge, 1991).

30   Generally, see R. Colls and P. Dodd (eds.), *Englishness, Politics and Culture, 1880–1920* (Beckenham: Croom Helm, 1986).

31   W. J. T. Mitchell (ed.), *Landscape and Power* (University of Chicago: University of Chicago Press, 1994), p. 2.

The label quoted above hints at the operation of this process of interpellation. It makes explicit, because it was novel, a process that subsequently became a matter of 'common sense'. Though the author of the label is not specified, the position of the image on the school wall encourages the individual to understand that some knowing authority is addressing them as a pupil. It is not only a descriptive piece of language but also an injunction to action. It addresses the individual and urges them to see this image not functionally but in a particularly contemplative way. The individual pupil is also encouraged to recognize themselves as part of a larger collectivity (as 'we' and 'our'), a single and homogeneous community whose happiness can be secured by learning to see particular things in particular kinds of ways. As well as addressing children as pupils – as individuals in need of education – this kind of aesthetic geography introduced those pupils to the ideas of national space and identity. Similarly, the illustrated images of history rendered the past into a national story.[32] All this begins to account both for the construction of the images and suggests ways that the process of signification might be unravelled. It hints at how a full set of the images might be read as a body of symbolic codes that enable people to live in 'an imaginary relationship their real conditions of existence'.[33] Yet the codes that the images sought to signify are, of course, complex and their communication to groups of children widely regarded as uncivilized was understood to present real pedagogical challenges that Horsfall spent a good deal of time and energy trying to solve.

Not least of the pedagogical problems posed by the images were the deficiencies that the images allegedly exposed in the cultural values and training of elementary-school teachers. In order to use the images successfully teachers needed to disclose their symbolic meanings but this required, in turn, an understanding of iconography. Yet, as Horsfall saw it, teachers were drawn from the 'class of scantiest culture' and the pupil-teacher system had deprived them of their

32   S. Bann, 'The sense of the past: image, text and object in the formation of historical consciousness in nineteenth century Britain', in H. Aram Veeser (ed.), *The New Historicism* (London: Routledge, 1989), pp. 101–15.

33   L. Althusser, 'Ideology and ideological state apparatuses', p. 153.

childhood.[34] They were incapable, therefore, of teaching about these images because they did not understand them; nor could they respond to them. Horsfall came up with short-term solutions for these problems – courses and study visits for teachers and the labels quoted above – but his reference to missing childhood indicates something very important both about his approach both to the images and to the wider questions of pedagogy.

Horsfall took a sustained interest in debates about pedagogy. He discussed and corresponded, for example, with both Sadler and Findlay, the two professors of education at Manchester University. He was a lifelong friend of J. M. D. Meiklejohn, a Professor of Education at St. Andrew's University, and had family connections in Germany, where he travelled regularly in order to see at first hand the famous pedagogical experiments being conducted by Kerschensteiner, Rein and others. With such a range of contacts and influences it is perhaps not surprising to find that Horsfall championed innovative classroom practices with a vigour entirely characteristic of those publicists for nineteenth-century sciences.

Horsfall was particularly interested in the work of Wilhelm Rein and shared his ambition to develop the ideal human personality.[35] The method of this transformation was a moral-historical curriculum that concentrated on teaching religious and profane history because this had 'the greatest influence on character and life'.[36] Such a method gave relatively little attention to formal instruction but worked instead to develop empirical, speculative, aesthetic, social and religious 'interests' that formed the key elements of rounded character. The first stage of this programme sought to prepare the pupil for learning by stimulating powers of thought, imagination and expression. Its purpose was to create something like a permanent disposition towards learning and the appreciation of 'high' culture. Moreover, its philosophy and its methods are to be found in the work of an expanding body of experts in psychology and physiology that claimed to be

---

34   Horsfall, *Reforms Needed in Our System of Elementary Education*, pp. 26–8.
35   See, for example, T. C. Horsfall, *Professor Rein's System of Religious Instruction for Schools* (London: Sherratt & Hughes, 1905).
36   Horsfall, *Reforms Needed in our System of Elementary Education*, p. 26.

making significant strides in understanding the processes of sensation, perception and memory.[37] It is in recalling the general arguments of these practitioners that the methods and significance of Horsfall's Picture Loan Scheme becomes clear.

Attending the Educational Conference held at the 1884 Health Exhibition, Horsfall can be found discussing the importance of teaching children to appreciate colours. Lamenting the absence of 'a Helmholtz to show us the physical basis of pleasant colour' he argued:

> The fact is, that susceptibility to rightness of colour depends entirely upon the early training of children before their nervous system had formed the bad habit of not noticing differences between good and bad colour. It is a question to be dealt with in elementary schools and there the opportunity is shockingly neglected.[38]

Helmholtz is significant here because he was a famous scholar of the processes of sensory perception. His famous treatise on the *On the Sensations of Tone as a Physiological Basis for a Theory of Music*, first published in English in 1875, argued that there were physical laws that governed the stimulation of nerve energies in humans.[39] In discovering these laws it became possible to stimulate sensations – or conscious awareness of stimuli – that produced, in turn, mental images of determinate external objects. Precisely how the sensations resulted in mental images was a matter for hotly contested debate amongst practitioners of the human sciences but there was an emerging con-

---

37   D. Pick, 'Stories of the eye', in R. Porter (ed.), *Rewriting the Self: Histories from the Renaissance to the Present* (London: Routledge, 1997), pp. 186–99. A schematic but suggestive outline of the troubled historical relationship between psychology and physiology can be found in B. Simon, *Intelligence, Psychology, Education: a Marxist Critique* (London: Lawrence and Wishart, 1971), pp. 125–38.

38   E. Cooke, 'Our art teaching and child nature: a review of the discussion – Art Section, International Conference, Health Exhibition, 1884', *Journal of Education* (December 1885), 462–5.

39   R. H. Wozniak, *Classics in Psychology, 1855–1914: Historical Essays* (Bristol: Thoemmes Press, 1999).

sensus around the idea that this was a psychological process involving the perception and organization of signs.[40]

Attempting to apply Helmholtz's theory to visual perception, Horsfall argued at the 1884 conference that there existed certain forms, colours and combinations guaranteed to stimulate nerve energies. 'The relation existing between our brains, or the whole of our nervous system, and colours and forms' must, he argued, 'be of the same kind as those fixed relations between sounds and our nervous systems.'[41] This helps explain Horsfall's repeated emphasis on the form and colour in those images selected for display.[42] The forms of the images were, in other words, shaped by physiology, as well as by aesthetics, and by the desire to systematically stimulate the appropriate nerve energies. Once this was achieved, the aim of the teacher was not so much to transmit a set of empirical facts but rather to establish particular symbolic codes that could be later used to categorize environmental stimuli. Horsfall is never explicit about how or where such symbolic codes were established but it was a commonplace of nineteenth-century psychological thought to speak of the deposit of sense impressions in the child's unconscious. What physiology and psychology jointly offered, in other words, was the apparent opportunity to establish modified forms of subjectivity by promoting particular classifications of knowledge and culture. In more Althusserian terms, what happens is the structuring of the unconscious.

In attempting to explain how individuals come to inhabit definite subject positions, Althusser turned to psychoanalysis for potential answers and devised a theory of interpellation or positioning derived from Jacques Lacan. For the purposes of this chapter it is perhaps only the mirror phase of development that needs brief elaboration. This is the moment when the infant, who has previously no self-image or co-

---

40   Pick, 'Stories of the eye', pp. 197–9. See also C. Steedman, *Childhood, Culture and Class in Britain: Margaret McMillan, 1860–1931* (London: Virago Press, 1990), pp. 203–5.

41   T. C. Horsfall, *The Use of Pictures and Other Works of Art in Elementary Schools: Paper Read to the International Conference on Education, London, 1884* (Manchester: Heywood, 1884).

42   T. C. Horsfall, *Art in Everyday Life* (London: C. F. Hodgson & Son, n.d.); *An Art Museum for Manchester*, pp. 11–12.

ordination, sees or imagines itself reflected – either literally in the mirror or in the mirror of the other's look – as a whole person. Yet this experience of wholeness is a fantasy. Indeed, the moment when the self is formed is characterized by a series of unresolved feelings and breaks – towards both mother and father, between the good and the bad parts of the self or in the disavowal of the masculine/feminine – that leave the subject unconsciously divided for life. As a result, when the child enters into various systems of symbolic representation the process of identity formation is not complete but active. In fact, precisely what is achieved in these primary psychoanalytical processes is not clear and Althusser is vague on this himself. Such ambiguity was undoubtedly problematic for Althusser's overall theory of ideology but here it opens up a space for some reasoned speculation about the legacy of the mirror stage.[43]

First, there is good reason to suppose that the process is important in terms of fixing gender identities.[44] Second, there seems to be enough evidence to cautiously support the supposition that the mirror stage establishes a kind of psychological predisposition to be called by specific ideologies. The basis of this lies in what Lacan calls the Imaginary. This is the dimension or realm of dreamy images that form the basis of the early and fragmentary identity that consists of material – of other children, pictures, adults and so on – that is external and alien to the child. The very creation of the self consists of a sense of absence, a feeling of 'misrecognition', and a desire for completion from the outside. Third, and importantly for this chapter, when children are finally called into language systems that help to name them, the early and pre-linguistic fragments of identity of the

---

43   The ambiguity is frequently noted in S. Hall *et al.*, *Culture, Language, Media and Society: Working Papers in Cultural Studies, 1972–79* (London: Hutchinson, 1980). See also Michele Barrett's reading of 'Althusser's Lacan' in *The Politics of Truth: from Marx to Foucault* (Oxford: Polity Press, 1991), pp. 81–120.

44   S. Alexander, 'Women, class and sexual differences in the 1830s and 1840s: some reflections on the writing of a feminist history', *History Workshop Journal*, 17 (1984), 125–49.

Imaginary become unconscious.[45] Existing outside language these fragments cannot be rationally expressed but emerge only in the form of dreams and fantasy. Put simply, each subject has a need, an unconscious yearning, to be hailed or positioned in particular kinds of ways as a result of these primary psychoanalytical processes. Moreover, rather than being blank, the unconscious already has a set of images that relate to the very early stages of identity formation. In this, admittedly rather crude and certainly minimal reading, the legacy of the mirror stage is a subject who both desires to be positioned and a set of pre-linguistic images or fantasies that exist partly at the level of the unconscious.

Horsfall's Schools' Picture Loan Scheme might, therefore, be explained in terms of its (particularly effective) address to the unconscious need posited by Lacan. Images may be able to address a kind of prelingusitic yearning for wholeness, a potentially powerful way of organizing perception and of establishing unconscious codes within which signs are made to mean. The function of the school, and of the images more specifically, was to hail the individual as a male or female pupil with specific identities and duties within wider codes of the family, the community and the nation. Yet all this remains at the level of the abstract and is useful only to the extent that it illuminates the concrete historical question; the introduction of images on school walls.

There is no shortage of anecdotal or autobiographical material that these kind of images had a significant influence on school-children. The former elementary school pupils who so brilliantly conveyed their classroom experiences in Ian Hislop's television series *School Rules* vividly recalled, for example, the images of Empire and moral living that hung on the wall. Similarly Daisy Cowper's memories of her infant school in Liverpool were dominated by a

> linen-faced picture of a lush Autumn hayfield: but like everything else in that school, it was old and shabby, and one bit of glazed-linen sky had dried and curled back, revealing the dirty, plain cotton backing. Our teacher was called

45 M. Jay, *Downcast Eyes: the Denigration of Vision in 20th Century French Thought* (Berkeley: University of California Press, 1994), pp. 349–51.

away, and left the room saying no one was to speak in her absence. All was silence, until I found myself [saying] 'That's God, peeping out of heaven.'[46]

This extract provides clues as to how pupils, using a set of attitudes or beliefs that they already lived, read into or made images mean. The relief that Daisy went on to express at escaping punishment for transgressing the classroom silence might be taken as a reward for reading 'correctly', or picturing despite its absence, the imagined moving force behind the painting. Yet this still does not address the prior or deeper question of how images helped to structure agency. In order to do this, it is important to note how the testimony cited here suggests that the images hung on walls had a powerful and memorable impact on some pupils. Certainly more empirical work is needed to establish the extent of this impact, but there is at least some indication that the images on school walls had a specific kind of power or immediacy for children. Even where there is no precise meaning attached to them, and even when they are dismissed as 'sentimental and dull', images seem to have been memorable.[47] Stuart Hall has suggested that one of the reasons for this is that, unlike the linguistic sign, images have the power to operate at the 'symbolic and psychic level of the unconscious' and to 'touch levels of experience that seem remote or archaic'.[48] In this reading, the power of the visual lay in its ability to reach into and shape the unconscious.

'Symbols of noble order, directors of feeling'

This chapter began with one general and one specific task. The general task was a consideration of the power of late-nineteenth-century elementary schools in shaping subjectivity; the specific an exploration

46   J. Burnett (ed.), *Destiny Obscure: Autobiographies of Childhood, Education and Family from the 1820s to the 1920s* (London: Routledge, 1994), p. 201.
47   Burnett (ed.), *Destiny Obscure*, p. 210.
48   S. Hall, 'Introduction: looking and subjectivity' in J. Evans and S. Hall (eds.), *Visual Culture: the Reader* (London: Sage, 1999), p. 311.

of T. C. Horsfall's project for hanging images on school walls. It is hoped that these dual aims have turned out to be complementary and have revealed something about both a particular historical moment and raised some more general theoretical and methodological issues for further discussion.

T. C. Horsfall's project of introducing images into schools was motivated by the familiar philanthropic desire to make urban living more bearable and the working classes more cultured and civilized. The philosophy and principles of the scheme were worked out on the basis of a sustained interest in pedagogical sciences and were far from the naive humanism that is often associated with educational philanthropy. Whilst much remains to be discovered about the production and distribution of the images, it is already clear that their content was related to particular social values and their form to particular kinds of scientific knowledge. Whether the bright colours and different textures succeeded in stimulating nerve energies, tapping the unconscious and depositing there new visual codes is, by its very nature, difficult to assess. Yet understanding the growing interest in perception certainly helps promote an understanding of the classroom as a designed space and can be seen as significant in a number of ways.

First, attention to the question of form raises an issue that seems to have been strangely underdeveloped; the school, its pupils and its staff as sites or bodies of consumption. The penetration of the classroom by an early form of commodity capitalism – by goods that were themselves not intrinsically valued but were invested with some sign value – was an innovation of considerable importance and might be seen as the beginning of the schooling of the consumer citizen. Indeed, Horsfall's expressed desire was to encourage children to purchase cheap replications of the images hung on school walls, and the enduring popularity of landscaped visions of rural England hints at the successful operation of this scheme.[49]

Second, if the images helped create the demand for the rural scenes that are now an embedded feature of English popular culture it

---

49   For a brief discussion on this point see J. Paxman, *The English: A Portrait of a People* (London: Penguin, 1998), pp. 145–7.

would be sensible to investigate why. In other words, a sustained assessment of the impact of the images is required. Horsfall was clearly convinced that the form of images held the key to reaching into the unconscious, or what he sometimes called the inner eye, and promoting an emotional response or affinity there. In this respect it is intriguing to note that in describing the content of working-class autobiographies Burnett *et al.* explicitly refer to both 'memories associated with the first realisation of the self' and to 'fantasies of childhood imagination'.[50] Whether these features hint at the operation of Lacan's mirror stage is a matter for debate but the resemblance is clear and worthy of further investigation.

Third, this chapter has attempted to make sense of Horsfall's Schools' Picture Loan Scheme by loosely drawing on the theories of Althusser and Lacan. In doing so such theories are not uncritically accepted but selectively employed in order to explain one element in the pedagogy of the late nineteenth century and in an attempt to understand its role in shaping subjectivity. This should not be taken to imply a wholesale acceptance of these theories but rather a willingness to be open to new ideas that may extend the explanatory power of historical studies.[51] If such theory has helped in the examination of the principles governing the use of images in elementary schools, it also raises another set of questions about the space for agency and resistance. There is no space to explore these here except to offer some hope against the determinist-sounding structuring of the unconscious. Indeed, the idea that there exists a pre-linguistic realm of experience with the power to touch raw levels of emotion perhaps offers a way out of the more pessimistic accounts of the way that language speaks subjects.

50   J. Burnett, D. Vincent, D. Mayall, *The Autobiography of the Working Class: an Annotated, Critical Bibliograpy: Volume I: 1790–1900* (Brighton: Harvester Press, 1984), p. xxiii.

51   P. Burke, *History and Social Theory* (Cambridge: Polity Press, 1992), p. 165.

SIRKE HAPPONEN

2 On Representation, Modality and Movement in Picture Books for Children

Pictures and words appear together on multiple and variable occasions, and yet they are various means of narration: showing and telling. These two forms of representation are not simply formal matters, two different instruments, but convey deeper aesthetic and cultural meaning. This chapter discusses the relationship between the visual and verbal representation in picture books for children focusing on some basic elements of the multi-modal art of the picture book: its representational and narrative characteristics, variations in modality, and the ways of how movement is implied in the 'composite text'.

According to Richard Rorty the enlightened contemporary philosophical scene is mostly concerned with words. This 'linguistic turn' is the final stage in Rorty's history of philosophy.[1] Rorty's remarks, beginning from the late 1960s, still seem pertinent in the human sciences of our era. Recent narrative research within education, for instance, is a vital example of this emphasis. Society, culture, art, education, as well as human life in general, are considered as texts and thus structured like a language. Many researchers of the visual arts speak about 'reading pictures', emphasizing the conventional character of visual signs, and the narrative and ideological implications of how we interpret them.[2]

---

1   R. Rorty, *Philosophy and the Mirror of Nature* (Princeton: Princeton University Press, 1979), p. 263.

2   N. Goodman, *Languages of Art* (Indianapolis: Hackett, 1968); M. Bal, *Reading Rembrandt; Beyond the Word-Image Opposition* (Cambridge: Cambridge University Press, 1991) and *Narratology: Introduction to the Theory of Narrative* (Toronto: University of Toronto Press, 1997), pp. 162–3; K. Jenkins, *On 'What is History?': from Carr and Elton to Rorty and White* (London: Routledge, 1995), pp. 10, 23–4.

Some scholars, however, see signs of a new shift emerging both in the human sciences and in the sphere of public culture. W. J. T. Mitchell calls this shift 'the pictorial turn'.[3] He sees several indications of this emphasis, such as Peirce's semiotic and phenomenological inquiry into imagination and visual experience, Derrida's grammatology, and Foucault's claim for a theory of power/knowledge that exposes the gap between the 'seeable and sayable'. These investigations either emphasize the non-linguistic symbol systems, decentre the model of language or, most importantly, do not assume that language is paradigmatic for meaning. In the field of education, Max van Manen's idea of *pathic experience*, non-conceptual knowledge, a kind of sensibility where eye, ear and body are involved with pedagogical understanding, might also serve as a possible complement to Mitchell's list.[4]

Side by side with the current interest in visual and non-linguistic meaning, however, is another attitude, which could be called 'the fear of the image'. For the Frankfurt school, for instance, the regime of the visual is associated with the mass media and the threat of a manipulative and industrially produced culture.[5] In contrast to words, images and pictures are seen as simple, naive, and easily accessible forms of information. We can also examine our attitude to the growing amount of visual influence that surrounds us daily through multimedia, television, videos, the Internet, and various kinds of commercials. Instead of rejection, or leaving the question completely unconsidered, Mitchell suggests a critique of visual culture that is alert to the power of images. Moreover, because most media are mixed, and words and images frequently appear together but also possess each

3   W. J. T. Mitchell, *Picture Theory: Essays on Verbal and Visual Representation* (Chicago: University of Chicago Press, 1994), pp. 11–15.

4   Pathic derives from the Greek word *pathos* 'to experience, suffer', which both refers to stirring emotion and to emotions themselves. Van Manen connects pathic to the 'general mood, sensibility and felt sense of being in the world'. See M. Van Manen, 'The pathic of pedagogical practice' in P. Kansanen (ed.), *Discussions on Some Educational Issues*, VIII (University of Helsinki: Department of Teacher Education, Research Report 204, 1999), pp. 75–96.

5   W. J. T. Mitchell, *Picture Theory*, pp. 3–5.

other's characteristics, the interaction between visual and verbal representations becomes a significant subject of study.[6]

Children's picture books have developed a variety of conventions of presenting pictorial and verbal semiosis side by side. In doing this they illuminate not only the differences and the similarities between the two forms of representation, but demonstrate how pictures and words give meaning and tell stories in co-operation. Although picture books have their own specific art of story-telling, they are good at revealing aesthetic, cultural and ideological relationships between the two forms of representation in general. This chapter discusses three intertwined bases of the multi-modal art of the picture book: its representational and narrative characteristics, modal attributes, and the ways in which movement is implied in the 'composite text'.[7] Over the course of time, these qualities have experienced some variations and shifts: the visual meaning has challenged the narrative dominance of verbal representation, a single story has begun to be told from several viewpoints (including both variable visual angles and narrational positions implied in the verbal text), and the depiction of spatiotemporal movement has become more and more apparent. Drawing on previous semiotically grounded picture-book research, especially Moebius (1986), Nodelman (1988, 1991), Doonan (1993), Thiele (2000), Bradford (1993) and Stephens (2000), I intend to discuss these visual-verbal tensions and composite constructions of meaning by

6   W. J. T. Mitchell, *Picture Theory*, p. 95.
7   Here I am using the same terminology as J. Schwarcz, *Ways of the Illustrator: Visual Communication in Children's Literature* (Chicago: American Library Association, 1982) and, in particular, J. Doonan's definition of composite text as a union of what the words say and what the pictures show, and which properly exists only in the reader/beholder's head. See J. Doonan, *Looking at Pictures in Picture Books* (South Woodchester: Thimble Press, 1993), p. 83. Other possible terms for combinations of visual and verbal representations are 'imagetext', adopted by Mitchell in *Picture Theory*, and 'ikonotext' (iconotext), the latter being used in Scandinavian research on picture books, and discussed in K. Hallberg, 'Litteraturvetenskapen och bilderboksforskningen', in *Tidskrift för Litteraturvetenskap*, 3–4 (1982), 163–8.

analysing four picture books published during the last thirty years in three different Western countries.[8]

From reading with pictures into reading pictures

The old idea of book illustration as something addressed to children is linked to the conception that pictures give children both pleasure and easily approachable information.[9] As E. H. Gombrich puts it, 'the visual image is supreme in its capacity of arousal.'[10] It is difficult not to take account of a picture on the wall, whether it is a painting or an advertisement. This fact has a connection with the presumed educational significance of children's books: from J. A. Comenius's *Orbis Pictus* (1658) onwards, illustrations have often been regarded as tools for getting children closer to words and reading.

In many picture books the narrative power of the visual images can, however, be prior to the verbal text; in other words, the story cannot be understood unless the pictures are 'read' as well. In some books, there are no words at all, just the continuum of pictures that convey the story to the beholder. Ordinarily, reading a picture book means switching between two forms of communication: the reader may begin with the visual and then move to the verbal, or read the text

8   W. Moebius, 'Introduction to picture book codes', *Word & Image*, 2.2 (1986), 141–58; P. Nodelman, *Words About Pictures: The Narrative Art of Children's Picture Books* (Athens, Georgia: University of Georgia Press, 1988) and 'The Eye and the I: identification and first-person narratives in picture books', *Children's Literature*, 19.2 (1991); J. Doonan, *Looking at Pictures in Picture Books*; J. Thiele, *Das Bilderbuch: Ästhetik, Theorie, Analyse, Didaktik, Rezeption*. With contributions by J. Doonan, E. Hohmeister, D. Reske and R. Tabbert (Oldenburg: Isensee, 2000); C. Bradford, 'The picture book: some postmodern tensions', in *Papers: Explorations into Children's Literature*, 4.3 (1993), 10–14; J. Stephens, 'Modality and space in picture book art: Allen Say's "Emma's Rug"', *CREArTA*, 1.1 (2000), 44–59.
9   P. Nodelman, *Words About Pictures*, pp. 2–5.
10   E. H. Gombrich, 'Visual image', *Scientific American*, 227 (September, 1972), 82–94.

first and then look at the pictures. In fact, many good picture books make the reader/beholder move back and forth between the both forms of communication and relate not only the knowledge received from the picture to the expressions in the text but also to previous pages with texts and illustrations.[11] This applies especially to postmodern picture books which often make use of the text-image relationship by presenting contradictory information in words and pictures within a single opening.

Playing with and questioning the idea of meaning is particularly characteristic for so-called metafictive picture books, which self-consciously draw attention to their conventions of communication.[12] However, the oldest picture-book tradition – 'epic picture books', in which the illustrations mostly decorate and illustrate the turning point of the story or important actions described in the text – is still very powerful.[13] For instance, the majority of picture books published in Finland in 2000 had text-driven narratives, and a large amount of text in relation to the proportion of pictures. These picture books converge with the concept of illustrated books, in which reading and under-standing the story does not depend on the pictures, which are often made long after the verbal text is written, and incorporated to the text without any co-operation of the writer and illustrator taking place. In contemporary picture books there are, however, more and more examples of what Ulla Rhedin calls 'genuine picture books': Maurice Sendak's *Where the Wild Things Are* (1967) being a classic example of the simultaneously contradictory and intertwined relationship be-

---

11   J. Doonan, 'Stimmen im Park und Stimmen im Schulzimmer: Rezeptions-bezogene Analyse von Anthony Brownes "Stimmen im Park" ("Voices in the Park", 1998)', in J. Thiele, *Das Bilderbuch: Ästhetik, Theorie, Analyse, Didaktik, Rezeption*, pp. 142–56; L. R. Sipe, 'How Picture Books Work: a semiotically framed theory of text-picture relationships', *Children's Literature in Education*, 29.2 (1998), 97–107 (p. 101).

12   R. McCallum, 'Metafiction and experimental fiction', in P. Hunt (ed.), *International Companion Encyclopedia of Children's Literature* (London: Routledge, 1996), pp. 397–409 (pp. 397, 400).

13   U. Rhedin, *Bilderboken: På väg mot en teori* (Stockholm: Alfabeta, 1992), pp. 79–81.

tween the illustration and the verbal text. When reading the text only, the story is both different and more frightening.[14]

Play with meanings and boundaries of seeing – a postmodern picture book

David McKee's picture book *I Hate My Teddy Bear* (1982) presents an ambiguous example of the interplay between visual and verbal from the early 80s (Figures 1 and 2). It is one of the earliest post-modern picture books that reflect some of the directions taken in post-modernist fiction and art. It mixes genres and modes of pictorial representation, intermingles high and popular culture, concentrates on flat rather than deep narrative planes, and combines art and life instead of separating them from each other.[15] In addition, the presence of an overt narrator is minimal, representing one of the strategies of modernist children's fiction that evoked the rise of postmodernism.[16] The verbal narrator in McKee's book is most impersonal, opening the story with two sentences set on separate pages: 'On Thursday, Brenda's mother came to see John's mother' / 'Brenda came to play with John.' The rest is for the most part a dialogue between the two children, which makes the reader recognize the two protagonists and focus on them while viewing the pictures. In the pictorial com-positions, however, the quarrelling children and their teddy bears stay on the periphery, and their cryptic settings filled with peculiar people and enormous hands seem to be at least as salient. Building a contra-dictory and enigmatic relationship between the words and images,

---

14   P. Nodelman, *Words About Pictures*, pp. 245–6.
15   L. Hutcheon, *A Poetics of Postmodernism* (London: Routledge, 1988), pp. 5–13; J. Stephens, 'Modernism to postmodernism or the line from Insk to Onsk: William Mayne's "Tiger's Railway"', *Papers: Explorations into Children's Literature*, 3.2, (1992), 51–9 (p. 53); C. Bradford, 'The picture book: some postmodern tensions'.
16   J. Stephens, 'Modernism to postmodernism', p. 53.

McKee's book teases its reader/beholder with multiple meaning and demands active contemplation when reading its composite text.

 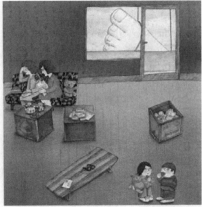

On Thursday Brenda's mother came to visit John's mother.   Brenda came to play with John.

Figures 1 and 2: David McKee's *I Hate My Teddy Bear* (London: Andersen, 1982): ©David McKee.

The modes of representation in *I Hate My Teddy Bear* draw attention to the positions offered for the viewer/reader: what we see and hear (through the dialogue) and what we cannot see and hear and thus not understand.[17] The flat-surfaced pictures convey surreal elements such as the sculptures that depict enormous hands (and a foot), and the variety of people seem to represent various cultures, lifestyles and nationalities, even epochs. Some of these elements get more clarification as they recur on later openings, but some remain mysterious until the end of the book. We can only make assumptions about the people in each setting and move back and forth between illustrations to find recurring motifs or causality for their behaviour. For instance, on the left-hand page of the first opening (Figure 1), what are Brenda and the men who carry the sculpture looking at?

17   D. McKee, *I Hate My Teddy Bear*. (London: Andersen, 1982). Copyright illustrations and texts ©David McKee.

What does the dark-haired woman see in her hand? Looking at the right-hand side of the next page: what has happened to Brenda's mother? Why has John's mother so little furniture? Every conclusion the reader/viewer makes about those scenes reflects his or her own way of viewing the world and interpreting social relationships. Since there is no coherent narrative implied by a narrator who organizes and evaluates the depicted incidents, we become distanced and surprisingly aware of our own ways of structuring both fiction and the world it mirrors.

"My teddy can count backwards," said John.   "So can mine," said Brenda.

Figures 3 and 4: David McKee's *I Hate My Teddy Bear* (London: Andersen, 1982): ©David McKee.

Although McKee's book is not overtly metafictive, his pictures draw attention to their constructed nature by means of flat surfaces, non-shortening of perspective, and sometimes rotating perceptual angles within a single picture (Figures 1, 2, 3 and 4). In doing this they play with the confusion and curiosity of the reader, and raise awareness of the constructedness of illusion by pointing at the differences between meanings that are given by various forms of representation. In each setting, McKee has also radically truncated some objects with a visual frame which again emphasizes the limitations of our view, questioning the possibility of making objective statements about both the fictive world, and indirectly, the world we ourselves live in. As John Stephens has pointed out, the act of reading postmodern fiction becomes often analogical to the act of interpreting human situations.[18] Presenting various perspectives on a single incident and setting, McKee's book suggests that making meaning is never self-evident and free from ideological notions.

Picture books as representational art

Moreover, McKee's ambiguous book exposes the *dual readership* characteristic of children's literature in general.[19] The social event of reading a picture book often implies an adult and a child; the adult usually concentrates on reading aloud the text while the child looks at the pictures. The argument often posed in relation to postmodern picture books as well as metafictive children's fiction that 'this is not a children's book' can also highlight the unease felt by the adult who, after reading the text, cannot grasp the narrative as a whole and might have difficulties in answering the questions posed by the child beholder/listener. This type of duality and uncertainty are, however, natural for picture books, since they offer 'so many multiple possibilities for ironic interplay and multiple construction of meaning that

---

18   J. Stephens, 'Metafiction and interpretation: William Mayne's "Salt River Times", "Winter Quarters", and "Drift"', *Children's Literature*, 21 (1993), 101–17 (pp. 102–3).

19   B. Wall, *The Narrator's Voice: The Dilemma of Children's Fiction* (London: Macmillan, 1991) makes a distinction between single, double and dual addresses (see pp. 35–6), depending if the narrator addresses – overtly or covertly – only a child audience, or a *double* audience possibly making jokes on the expense of an ignorant child narratee, or a *dual* audience which applies the same 'tone of seriousness' as for adult readership, addressing the child narratee and simultaneously satisfying the adult audience. Here, it is a matter of interpretation whether McKee's book has a double or a dual address. In relation to Wall's definition I see the address closer to a dual audience.

they inevitably cross the boundaries between both younger and older readers, between children's and adult's fiction'.[20] Moreover, irony is embedded in the very form of the picture book, because words and pictures signify in different ways and have a competing but complementary relationship.[21]

Jens Thiele writes about picture books as a controlled medium with a fixed framework for representation, maintained by the conservative children's book market and supported by publishers, writers, illustrators, critics and customers.[22] Experiments in the use of abstract art in children's book illustrations show the limitations created by this consensus: the art of illustration is essentially 'Gebrauchskunst', art for usage, which has to make compromises to please the common taste. For instance, the avant-garde picture book by El Lissitzky, *Suprematische Erzählungen von zwei Quadraten in sechs Konstruktionen* (1922), which was based on plain geometric forms, was found too abstract for a child reader. On the other hand, more than thirty years later, Leo Lionni's *Little Blue and Little Yellow* (1959), whose visual language was also grounded on abstract forms, made a breakthrough because its text pointed at the relationships between the characters and gave causality to the story.[23]

Thiele stresses that the art of illustration for children has always had a representational emphasis, and the occasional non-representational experiments in the area carried out by artists such as Kandinsky, Picasso, Matisse and Miro have only managed to give some new impulses to the picture book scene and point at its narrowness.[24] That representational art is the favoured means of expression in picture books may also explain why some picture books

20   C. Bradford, 'The picture book: Some postmodern tensions', p. 11.

21   P. Nodelman, *Words about Pictures*, p. 221.

22   J. Thiele, 'Wurzelkinder und Honigpumpe. Zum Verhältnis von Kunstmoderne und Bilderbuch', in H.-H. Ewers, M. Lypp, U. Nassen (eds.), *Kinderliteratur und der Moderne: ästhetische Herausforderungen für die Kinderliteratur im 20. Jahrhundert* (Weinheim und München: Juventa, 1990), pp. 141–74 (pp. 172–3) and *Das Bilderbuch*, p. 35.

23   J. Thiele, 'Wurzelkinder und Honigpumpe', pp. 163–167 and *Das Bilderbuch*, pp. 23–32.

24   J. Thiele, 'Wurzelkinder und Honigpumpe', pp. 158, 172.

inspired by the pop art of the 1960s and 1970s, and especially picture books of the postmodern era – with parodic citations to well-known paintings as in Anthony Browne's work – have been a lot more successful. Their emphasis is on representation itself: they borrow, blend and deconstruct the meaning but their art always stays closer to life, culture and society, even when subverting and disillusioning them. Moreover, it should also be remembered that some postmodern features have already long been evident in children's literature. The boundaries between high and popular culture were never so clear as in 'adult' literature. There was already a tendency for flat narrative planes, and fantasy as a kindred for postmodern forms of narration was one of the appreciated genres.[25]

Narrative notions on pictures and words

If the traditional emphasis of picture books is on representational expression, what kind of a theoretical frame would explain both visual and verbal representations? Images can never exactly present what words do or vice versa, and in addition to this representational difference they have ideological divisions, linked with things like the difference between the one *who speaks* and the one *who is looked at* (or *observed*), in other words, the *self* and the *other*.[26] Picture-book analysis is often rooted in semiotic ideas, seeking to take both visual and verbal codes into consideration, and drawing on Roland Barthes's notion of the textuality of all processes of signification. Furthermore, narrative theories, or more precisely narratology based on the thinking of Gérard Genette, Seymour Chatman and Mieke Bal, have been shown to be a fruitful application for the purpose of relating and combining the narrative meaning of both visual and verbal repre-

25   J. Stephens, 'Modernism to postmodernism', pp. 52–3.
26   W. J. T. Mitchell, *Picture Theory*, p. 5.

sentations. Here I am referring to researchers such as Moebius, Nodelman, Stephens and Nikolajeva and Scott.[27]

By means of narratology, for instance, it is possible to illuminate the complicated role of the narrator in various picture books. Is there a different narrator in the pictures from the one in the text? In fact, many picture books tell the verbal story in a first-person narrative; in the illustration, however, the narrative is in the third person.[28] For example, the book *O meu avô*, 1990 (My Grandfather) by the Portuguese author and illustrator Manuela Bacelar, may seem very simple, but a closer look at the pages reveals how advanced the reader/beholder actually should be.[29] In some double-spreads the first person narrator, the little boy speaking in the text, is depicted in the picture; in others it seems to be him who is looking at his grandfather from various perspectives. When reading and viewing this book, we occasionally share the viewpoint of the protagonist, the boy, while sometimes we view him from above or seem to look at his actions from the same level, as if we were one of his companions. This picture book, presumably aimed at younger readers, combines not only two different forms of focalization (*who sees?* and *who speaks?*), but also two different combinations of them.[30]

27   W. Moebius, 'Introduction to picture book codes'; P. Nodelman, *Words about Pictures* and 'The Eye and the I'; J. Stephens, 'Modality and space in picture book art: Allen Say's "Emma's Rug"', *CREArTA*, 1.1 (2000), 44–59; M. Nikolajeva, and C. Scott,. *How Picturebooks Work* (New York & London: Garland, 2001).

28   P. Nodelman, 'The Eye and the I', pp. 3–4.

29   M. Bacelar, *O meu avô* ('My Grandfather', Porto: Edições Afrontamento 1990). Copyright illustrations and texts ©Manuela Bacelar and Edições Afrontamento.

30   G. Genette, *Narrative Discourse: An Essay in Method.* (Ithaka, New York: Cornell University Press, 1983), pp. 189–91.

Por vezes o meu Avô fica muito chateado,

Figure 5: First-person visual and verbal perspective. Translation of the text: 'Sometimes my grandfather gets rather upset,' *O meu avô* (1990, 'My Grandfather') by Manuela Bacelar. ©Manuela Bacelar & Edições Afrontamento.

The two openings in Bacelar's book also expose the division of narrative and representational content in picture books. Although both pictures and texts can represent similar things and ideas, such as the feelings and personae of the characters, words are better at depicting *time*, while pictures express *spatial* meaning more effectively.[31] In picture books the emphasis of the verbal text is often on the continuity and causality of the narrative, whereas pictures concentrate on portraying the relationships between characters and objects in a spatial composition. In *O meu avô*, the text on the subsequent opening reveals why the grandfather is upset ('because he forgets to go to the kitchen'), while the picture alone implies the boy's reaction and delight in relation to what has happened.

31   B. Uspensky, *A Poetics of Composition* (Berkeley: University of California Press, 1973), pp. 76–7; P. Nodelman, *Words about Pictures,* p. 198.

Figure 6: Third-person visual perspective and first-person verbal narration. Translation of the text: 'because he forgets to go to the kitchen and the jam boils out of the
pots.' *O meu avô* (1990, 'My Grandfather') by Manuela Bacelar. ©Manuela Bacelar
and Edições Afrontamento.

Bacelar's book, however, is a good example of narrative suspension built between the two pictures themselves: to a reader/beholder
the 'cloud' or 'patch' on the right-hand page in the previous opening
(Figure 5) – which is cut by the page frame and continues on the next
page (Figure 6) – can imply anything from an abstract depiction of
grandfather's displeased mood to a colourful balloon or a wallpainting
done by the young protagonist. The division of the sentence into two
separate openings creates an end-focus, redoubling the visual surprise
that takes place when turning the page.[32] When observing the composite text, both words and pictures in this opening, we may well think
that the grandfather is annoyed because of the boy whom he is
viewing from above. The reciprocal gaze between grandfather and
viewer, and the visual angle he is depicted from, positions viewers on
the same low level as the non-visualized little boy, the first-person

32   C. McMillan, 'Metafiction and humour in "*Great Escape from City Zoo*"',
     Papers: Explorations into Children's Literature, 10.2 (2000), 5–11, (p. 10).

visual focalizer of the opening, and makes us share his visual view-point. Because of the direction of the grandfather's gaze it is possible for the viewer to conclude that the cloud has a connection with the recipient of this gaze. The text which begins with the word 'sometimes' may as well imply that, at times, this could be the case. However, the next opening discloses that *this time* the boy has caused neither the grandfather's mood nor the boiling jam – he only takes advantage of the overwhelming but delightful mess. In actuality, then, by means of text-image interaction, which is here simultaneously both contradictory and complementary, functioning in several possible combinations in these two openings, we face a challenging and humorous depiction of a complex human situation.

Within research on composite texts the narrative interest has also addressed opposing and supplementary perspectives. It has been acknowledged that the 'linguistic imperialism' (Mitchell's phrase) linked with the idea of 'reading pictures' undermines the originality of the visual signs and their receiving processes, and exposes the images only in relation to their narrative attributes and characteristics commensurable with verbal representation. Jane Doonan, for instance, takes a stand on this problem by using the word 'beholder' constantly together with or instead of the word 'reader'.[33] These two words also expose the division of the reading and viewing process between the child and the adult: the traditional view is that the text, because of its symbolic form, requires a more sophisticated reading. The syntactic and semantic differences between images and words that Goodman pointed out – 'continuity' and 'density' of the images vs. 'differentiation' of the words – might in part explain why the verbal text, much easier to separate into single units for an analysis, becomes the starting point even in considering the composite text as a whole.[34] When looking at a picture we tend to 'narrativize' it, says John Stephens. Picture-book readers often concentrate on the represented content of the pictures, which 'reduces them to elements of story and their function as visual semiosis disappears'. Furthermore, with all nar-

---

33   J. Doonan, *Looking at Pictures in Picture Books*, p. 9.
34   N. Goodman, *Languages of Art*.

ratives we tend to privilege representation over abstraction, and temporality over spatiality.[35]

In relation to *O meu avô* it would be relevant, for instance, to talk about the use of negative space throughout the book, particularly in relation to the depiction of the grandfather and the 'cloud' or 'patch', which is a fragment cut out of the patch on the next page. Here, the relationship between the figure of the grandfather and the 'patch' is accentuated by the distance between them: the larger the negative space, the more tension there is in the relationship. Also the interplay between the visual forms suggests that the man is indeed connected to the 'patch' although he looks the other way. The round shape of the figure that presents the grandfather is parallel to the patch but vertical, and both of the shapes are cut by the page frame and have a clear contour line. Everything in the grandfather is round, accentuated by the curving contours which outline his body parts and his clothes. Furthermore, the horizontally elliptic shape of the grandfather's head parallels the shape of the patch. The unfinished, cut shape of the peculiar patch directs the viewer's curious gaze to the next opening (Figure 6), where it travels across the page and reaches its 'origin', the pot.

The arched, abstract form of this gigantic jam cloud builds a vector which is echoed by the boy's curved and reaching posture, nearly fusing with it, and creating a humorous effect in combining an abstract form with material, concrete pleasure. The boy's posture, however, bounces the viewer's gaze back to the left: to the realistic direction in which the jam is flowing, adding to the temporal suspension between the two openings. This right-to-left vector is against the general flow of the composite text and against the direction of verbal text and visual movement usually implied in Western picture books. The stream of the colourful jam is certainly the dominant visual image of the opening, and the overwhelming feelings it stimulates in both of the two characters are embodied in its visual weight. In the second opening, this overruns not only the boy but also the verbal text. Here the text offers an exclusive explanation of the grandfather's reaction only (although focalized by the boy): 'because

35   J. Stephens, 'Modality and space in picture book art', pp. 44–5.

he forgets [...] and the jam boils out of the pots'. This textual layout might be interpreted as a kind of an intangible depiction of the grandfather, situated beside the boy, and virtually present through the speaker of the text.

Modality and its paradoxes

McKee's and Bacelar's books give us opportunities to discuss what is implied by the images and words and how this is actualized. If the illustrations and the texts present radically contradictory information we may encounter the problem of which one to believe, which one to take as a normal reference point. More likely, if there is any 'truth' as such, it seems to lie *between* the two forms of representation, because the pictures may offer another perceptual and attitudinal viewpoint than the verbal narrative does, as we noticed in the latter opening of *O meu avô* (Figure 6). However, in both books the illustrations and words seem to relate to reality in different ways. In other words, they have diverse modal qualities of expression. Modality, which 'refers to the truth value or credibility of statements about the world', is a concept which characterizes both visual and verbal texts and their relationship to each other.[36]

The first opening of *I Hate My Teddy Bear* (Figures 1 and 2) presents a text with a higher modality than the illustrations in the same opening. The two sentences are factual expressions, reminiscent of a summarized report in their brevity, while the exaggerated flatness and surreal contents of the pictures display a lower credibility and break any illusion. The temporal qualification – 'On Thursday' – emphasizes the narrative function of the text, but because the text completely lacks nuances which would make the move from factual to the attitudinal, we start to seek the information from the pictures. Later on, as the text consists of direct quotations of the children's dialogue (see Figures 3

---

36   G. Kress and T. van Leeuwen, *Reading Images: The Grammar of Visual Design* (London: Routledge, 1996), p. 160.

and 4), its modality decreases slightly but the reader learns to approach the pictures even more, since the narrative content of the text shrinks to a monotone arguing ('My teddy can count backwards' – 'So can mine') which mostly signifies a passage of time elapsing during this quarrelling.

Although Western picture-book art resists non-representational abstraction, the base modality of picture books is, as John Stephens argues, some degree of abstraction: exaggerated or attenuated representation.[37] Generally, the highest modality in visual images in general is close to a 35mm colour photograph and its perspective – high in colour saturation, detail and depth.[38] As Stephens states, in children's picture books photo-realism seems hyper-real because of the low average modality. Interestingly, children thus learn that for picture books, a lower modality than a photograph is the norm. The photograph seems to present normal base modality only in information books, which portray, for example, the life of plants and animals. The degrees of picture book-modality also vary in different countries and cultures, whilst the preferred techniques, materials and traditions (watercolour, guache, crayon, ink, pencil, lithography, collage) and the use of frame and decorative detail, all tend towards distinctive modalities.

Manuela Bacelar's *O meu avô* demonstrates just how relative and dependent on the cultural context the modal qualities in picture books can be. In this book, the pictorial style gives an impression of a child's own drawing with its flat, unmodulated colours and incomplete settings. This is, of course, a lower modality, as is the first-person narrated verbal text, which implies a limited point of view, especially in the case of a small child as a narrator. However, since this book is a story of 'my grandfather', the credibility of the multi-modal text

---

37   J. Stephens, 'Modality and space in picture book art', p. 47; see also D. Lewis, *Reading Contemporary Picturebooks: Picturing Text* (London: Routledge-Falmer), p. 164. Not all picture-book researchers follow Kress and van Leeuwen in their discussion of modality. Nikolajeva and Scott, for instance, focus their attention on the narrative aspects of picture books and categorize picture-book modalities as indicative, dubitative, or optative (*How Picturebooks Work*, pp. 173–93).

38   G. Kress and T. van Leeuwen, *Reading Images*, pp. 163–7.

increases because this is seen as a depiction of *his* truth. Indeed, in a culture that emphasizes the originality of a childhood experience and at least covertly believes that the truth is not only spoken by an innocent child but also possibly depicted visually by her or him, the effect is powerful. Moreover, the modal paradox is further nuanced by the fact that an adult, the illustrator and writer Manuela Bacelar, is behind these naive expressions and viewpoints, conveyed both visually and verbally.

In McKee's book the modal qualities can vary within a single picture, as can be seen in Figures 1, 2, 3 and 4. People's faces have been depicted using different styles. For instance, the man with the guitar has a face with a plastic quality and shadings, while the faces of John and Brenda, and the two red-cheeked dancers, are depicted as two-dimensional and flat. The same opening also draws attention to the attributes of two-dimensionality versus three-dimensionality by other means. The bold man leaning on the balustrade adopts the distorted posture familiar in Auguste Rodin's sculptures. The lions, as the actual sculptures of this picture, presented in the same visual plane, seem to possess anthropomorphic qualities. These, in turn, are opposed by a representation of a gathering of some literally flat human shapes in the right foreground.

The modal characteristics between words and pictures in the eclectic *I Hate My Teddy Bear* also deserve some attention. The surreal characteristics in the images seem to suggest a low modality, and before the last picture of the book it is possible to think that the big portable hands signify a modality of a dream. The report-like text with its direct quotations of character speech seems to express a higher modality than the pictures, but its terseness and a certain kind of detachment in relation to the images makes us search for deeper meaning and credibility in the pictures. Just as John and Brenda seem to be a fragment of a collage of interpersonal relationships in variable settings, in which both the people and their relationships and settings are intermingled but still separated from each other, the text is only a part of the collage, a 'voice over' implying a presentation of the dialogue. However, applying the Bakhtinian concept of voices as ideologues that present different character world-views, this voice is not the dominant voice in the narrative.[39] In McKee's book the verbal voices, the dialogue between the two children and their alter egos, the teddy bears, make these characters more salient in regard to the composite text. However, it is significant that this is the only voice we can 'hear', whereas the other implied voices, the other characters and their situations, are presented only visually. For me, the modal qualities of the verbal text in relation to the pictures here signify the absurdity of representation and interpretation of interrelationships in general: the text gives a focus to contemplate the pictures but at the same time it implies how narrow this focus can be.

The base modalities of visual and verbal representations in children's picture books are variable, and have changed over time. The development of reproduction techniques has enabled higher modalities in illustrations: full saturated colours instead of black and white illustrations and three-colour printing, from xylography to computer assisted illustrative techniques. Other composite texts such as cartoons, animations, cinema, video games, advertisements and the Internet have indirectly influenced both the visual and verbal ways of representing reality (and fantasy) in picture books. One of the obvious changes is a strengthened illusion of movement in illustrations which develops when pictorial representations of movement are combined with other, rather new illustrative means such as saturated colour or radical visual angles. Yet it should be stressed that the idea of movement is already embedded in the narrative form of the picture book, and the word 'movement' is used very differently in various connections.

39   M. M. Bakhtin, *The Dialogic Imagination* (Austin: University of Texas Press, 1981).

Fear and praise of movement

One of the obvious things that causes 'fear of the image' as well as general opposition to moving images, is the visual bombardment we face in our society. This is usually created by electronic images, which seem to change and move more and more rapidly. Compared to the images of television and music videos, for instance, one might consider illustrated books a rather static medium. Generally speaking, however, illustrations in children's books seem to present more motion, action, and turmoil than they have done before. It is not necessarily the mimetic depictions of movement (e.g. dynamic postures of characters that imply a possible direction of movement) that have increased, but rather that the intensifying and contrasting of colour, dynamic lay-outs, and varying perspectives between various perspectives that together create a stronger impression of kinesis and motion. This combination of illustrative means suggests a tendency in the contemporary picture book that implies a higher modality than ever before. Movement suggests higher modality not only because life is commonly equated with movement and energy, but also because in everyday experience we encounter an abundance of representations of movement created by various visual media. The underlying attitudinal assumption might be that dynamic (i.e. not static and boring) illustrations will persuade present-day children, especially boys, to approach books more easily. Books with dynamic illustrations are considered to be closer to the media children are more used to, such as television, computer games, and the Internet. Actually, the situation has some similarity to the case of *Orbis Pictus*. This time movement and action presented in pictures will serve as the manipulative medium to make (or should we say keep) children interested in words and reading.

The words 'movement', or 'motion' are quite often used to express the characteristics of a picture or a series of them. Its concept, however, remains rather abstract and vague. We mostly talk about an illusion, whose origin is difficult to express precisely. In research literature on children's books, the remarks on movement link with the dynamics of a story, depicting action, alternating situations, and the liveliness and diversity of the book as a whole. Pictorial art can convey movement in various ways. In addition to *depicted action* movement serves as a *compositional element*, for instance in visual rhythm. Verbal language in turn produces dynamic impressions through intransitive verbs (opposing the static verb 'to be'), emphasizing causality, and by means of rhythmic changes. Because movement takes place both in time and space, the words and images in picture books often share their capabilities and generate the illusion together. Since pictures present only still images of motion, the impression of movement is created together with the flow of the words that the verbal story conveys.

The direction of reading a picture book, which in Western culture proceeds from left to right, usually fuses with the impression of the character(s) moving in the same course. In most of the illustrations a protagonist's posture points in the same direction that we read the verbal text: forwards to the next situation or adventure, to the next opening. Moreover, in picture books the succession of pictures and words also creates an illusion of movement, in which continuum the *place between the pages*, the reader's anticipations and expectations while he/she turns the page, become significant. In this continuum, the conventions between the *left and right* sides of the picture, which often demonstrate closeness and unfamiliarity, as well as the 'glance curve', a certain path that our eyes follow when looking at a picture, have a special forwarding and dramatic meaning.[40] In western culture the hero usually progresses from left to right, and the barriers, physical or psychological, entering from the right, must be both faced and overcome. In other cultures this direction, the depiction of the action, is converse. In many Japanese picture books, for example, the story unfolds from right to left.

---

40   P. Nodelman, *Words About Pictures*, pp. 135–6; U. Rhedin, *Bilderboken*, p. 169; M. Gaffron, 'Right and Left in pictures', *Art Quarterly*, 13 (1950), 312–31 (pp. 313–15, 321).

Figure 7: Movement and stasis within various figures. Tove Jansson: *Vem ska trösta knyttet?* (1960, 'Who Will Comfort Toffle?', Helsinki: Schildts ©Moomin Characters™, Tove Jansson).

A picture book opening by the Finnish author and illustrator Tove Jansson from 1960 is a good example of the left-to-right movement in an overtly static scene (Figure 7, 'Who Will Comfort Toffle?').[41] It also illuminates *movement within a figure*, arising from the visual forms depicted in this opening.[42] These can be either closed or open, with or without a specific direction, and possibly emphasized by other lines and figures depicted in the picture. Some characters just expend energy in various directions, while others appear static and slow. In this doublespread one can find these opposites in the same

41   T. Jansson, *Vem ska trösta knyttet?* 'Who Will Comfort Toffle?' (Helsinki: Schildts, 1960).

42   G. Cavallius, 'Bilderbok och bildanalys', in L. Fridell (ed.) *Bilden i Barnboken.* (Göteborg: Stegelands, 1977), pp. 31–60 (pp. 40–2); S. Happonen, 'Choreography of characters: movement and posture in illustrated texts for children', *Reading*, 35.3, (November, 2001), 99–105.

picture. On the left, the protagonist performs a war-like dance – rapid and energetic, so light that he does not even touch the ground. On the right stands the terrible monster, heavy and solid in appearance, with her hands hanging inertly. One would not expect this character to immediately start moving anywhere. The energy of the little protagonist is emphasized by the negative space around him, and echoed by the clouds above the monster that express movement in the same direction as pointed by his bristling dance. Remarkably, this is all the visual movement in the opening – in spite of the typography of the text which also suggests visual movement with its handwritten, forward-leaning style – everything else expresses a moment of stagnation: a frozen moment of horror and anticipation.

The text freezes the moment using a historical present tense instead of the past tense which dominates the narration elsewhere in the book. The poetic language is full of dramatic expressions and visual emphasis: 'now everything becomes silent, now all the lights die down […] even the moon loses all its colours'. The verbal and visual representation of stasis go hand in hand in relation to the first half of the verbal text, but after this the text switches rapidly to the past tense again. It describes the protagonist's attacking action and its implications in which temporal adverbs (*first –, then –, so that –*) express causality, and a sense of acceleration is implied by an increase in the number of syllables. The first six lines are iambic pentameter, and the second six are 14-syllabled rhyming couplets. This evokes an illusion of a gathering of tempo because it might encourage the reader to speed up in the second half, accentuating keywords and running more quickly over function words in order to fit the verse within the same time span as before. Hence the second six lines of the text parallel the visual dynamics implied in the protagonist's angular and prickly form, making a contrast with both the heaviness and fixity of the monster's solid shape and the formal, measured and grandiloquent register of the first six lines of the text.

When Gustaf Cavallius charted the concept of movement in picture books in the late 1970s, he dedicated most of his attention to movement within a figure.[43] This still needs greater elaboration,

43   G. Cavallius, 'Bilderbok och bildanalys', pp. 40–2.

although his remarks on the *varying perspectives*, *angles* and *distances* from which the pictures are depicted and the *changing scenes* of page openings that follow each other have also become more and more visible in picture books of our time. Further, the *transfer* type of movement, which Cavallius only briefly discussed, has become more prominent in recent picture-book illustrations. Transfer refers to a practice whereby vigorous motion, such as when a car suddenly accelerates, is signified by lines drawn behind the speeding object to highlight its speed. My last example is the second last opening of a Finnish picture book published in 2000, Aino Havukainen's and Sami Toivonen's *Veera ja Menopelit* ('Vera and the Moving Vehicles').[44]

The visual settings of this book present many variations of depicted movement, especially transfer, intensified by the use of colours and diagonal lines, which often cross each other (Figure 8). The human-powered vehicles and the paths on which they move dominate this scene and create sloping vectors crossing the pictorial plane in several directions. The emphasis on closeness and remoteness in the double-spread also creates an illusion of movement, as do the contrasts between highly saturated, bright colours that give energy to the scene. The visually more salient characters of this opening, the girl with two plaits who is connected by reciprocal gaze with the gigantic baby on the left foreground, are not the main characters of the book. The protagonists are the silhouetted figures in the right distant background – the three figures who ride their bikes against the sunset and in the direction of the picture book's general narrative movement.

Transfer type of movement is more characteristic of cartoons and animations than picture books, but in this opening we even have a visual depiction of exhaust puffs, a typical indexical sign in the composite text of comics. The clouds are 'caused' by the board-skating boy in the centre and the roller-skating male on the right, and they give an impression of a rapid change of place. These small effects, however, receive only a minor emphasis in this opening, whereas the much bigger clouds bisecting the rays of the setting sun

---

44   A. Havukainen and S. Toivonen, *Veera ja Menopelit* ('Vera and the Moving Vehicles', Helsinki: Otava, 2000). Copyright illustrations and texts ©Aino Havukainen and Sami Toivonen.

have more salience and draw attention to the bipartite modal qualities in this picture. At this point this doublespread interweaves the ideas of multi-modal representation, modality, and movement: concepts that have been the focus of this chapter. The kinetic impression, which is created by the representation of the sunrays and the pink candyfloss-like clouds floating over the artificially actualized perspective depth, varies from the modality of the rest of the picture. The depiction of the sky alludes to pop art, while as the way the three protagonists are represented riding against the sun implies a connection to the end of the movie *ET*, or alternatively to some westerns where the heroes ride against the sunset in the end of the film.

Figure 8: Movement, modality and estranging from the protagonists. Aino Havukainen and Sami Toivonen, *Veera ja Menopelit*. ('Vera and the Moving Vehicles', Helsinki: Otava, 2000.) ©Aino Havukainen and Sami Toivonen.

As is traditional in picture books, the verbal text has a temporal and specifying accent as it expresses where the main characters are heading (back to the town). At the same time, it also represents the thoughts of two of the characters which would be difficult to itemize in a single pictorial setting, focusing on estranging the reader from the characters and adding a slightly utopian, comically heroic halo around them before ending the story. The modality of the text is closer to realism and does not aspire to the two-fold construction of modal representation conveyed by the picture. Although this is not a radical, avantgarde picture book, this type of text-picture relationship might imply a kind of 'compromise' as suggested by Jens Thiele because the text offers both narrative continuity and characterisation as a contrast to the metafictive and experimental representations of reality in the picture, which in turn draws attention to its manner of presentation and distances the reader from the protagonists.

The idea of breaking the illusion and ending a story in this picture has an especially interesting implementation in relation to the previous illustrations in this book. This pictorial setting plays with the idea of movement and the positioning of the viewer: the protagonists have gradually moved to the background of the stage after appearing on bicycles in the forefront of the visual scene for most of the book. So far we have more or less looked at the openings behind their back, partly sharing their viewpoints, but now we as viewers have approached the moving people and their moving vehicles, as if we would have been drawn into their world and at the same time separated from the protagonists. Havukainen and Toivonen's book ends its celebration of the depiction of visual movement by repositioning its readers and beholders themselves, and shifting the given subject position in order to bring the flow of the picture-book narrative to the final opening of the book.

Concluding remarks

The intention of this chapter was to show some brief examples of how picture books demonstrate the rather general juxtaposition and co-existence of words and pictures in our culture. Even though picture books do provide tools for the development of visual and verbal literacy, their profundity emerges more effectively when considered as aesthetic and cultural objects. The intertwined ideas of representation, modality and movement invite us to take both words and images into consideration, and discuss their aesthetic, cultural and ideological characteristics. All the chosen picture-book examples somehow accentuate the impossibility of one fixed meaning, and, as in picture books in general, their composite text is worth more than the sum of their visual and verbal signs alone. However, as the coexistence of words and pictures constantly displays both interaction and juxtaposition, harmony and dissonance, picture books can be seen as performers of this overarching complementary but agonistic relationship of visual and verbal expressions, especially in the lives of children and their parents. Characteristic of the picture-book type of composite text is a greater degree of abstraction and intangible expression. The pace of this narrative flow is set by the alternating rhythm of the adult reading aloud and the visual movement conveyed by the pictures. This continuity may, however, be interrupted at anytime: making a stop and perhaps talking more about a certain opening, or riffling back and forth between texts and pictures on previous and forthcoming openings.

Despite certain conventional characteristics of visual images, and the vocabulary for the visual offered by for instance Kress and van Leeuwen's book, pictures seem to be difficult to talk about, and in doing this we commonly use words, thus subsuming pictures under the system of verbal language.[45] This task does not become any smoother if images are accompanied by words, since the ways of discussing both visual and verbal semiosis and their relationship are only at a developing stage. The tendency to approach images from the dominant of the more conventional type of text, the verbal representation, has not directly been avoided in this present paper either. On the other hand, in analysing picture books the pictures, because of their facility in expressing intangible feelings and ideas, tend to become the more exciting and expressive half of the composite text, whereas the verbal component seems to descend to a more concrete and dry level, as a factual servant of the exuberance of the images –

---

45   G. Kress and T. van Leeuwen, *Reading Images*.

even in cases where the verbal expression is nuanced, ambiguous and rich in meanings.

A closer look at picture books illuminates not only the differences but also the similarities between images and words and their ways of representation. W. J. T. Mitchell (who after all engages himself with Goodman's conventionalism) states that their ways of communication are eventually intermingled and hybrid: pictures can be textual and narrative, and texts can convey visual meaning.[46] These aspects fall beyond the scope of this article but not of picture books. The ideas of modality and movement may give rise to the notion of these intermingled qualities of words and pictures – although nothing prevents us widening the gap between the two forms of representation with these two interwoven concepts. What Cheryl McMillan calls 'the marriage of dual codes at varying degrees of independence, interdependence and dependence' characterizes not only the alternating representational balance between pictures and words in children's picture books in various traditions and periods of time, but also the varying perspectives and emphases in the research of composite texts, which often struggle to do justice to this duality of expression by analysing them either one by one or in interaction.[47]

46   W. J. T. Mitchell, *Picture Theory*, chapters 2 and 3.
47   C. McMillan, 'Metafiction and humour in "*Great Escape from City Zoo*"', *Papers: Explorations into Children's Literature*, 10.2 (2000), 5–11.

IAN GROSVENOR AND MARTIN LAWN

3   Portraying the School: Silence in the Photographic Archive

Introduction

This chapter contains an exploration of a rare photographic study of schooling at Eton, undertaken by László Moholy-Nagy (1895–1946) in the late 1930s. The study of Eton through these images, produced for a book on the school by an ex-pupil, creates a very intimate portrait; yet the vision of the photographer is radical and is close to the modernizing gaze of the time. However, this chapter's interests stretch beyond Eton into the portrayal of common schooling, the primary and secondary schools of the land. The absence of school images, undertaken as a form of thick description of the school, and not just as incidental illustrations, is a major loss to historians studying classrooms, school technologies or work practices. This chapter, through the study of a particular case, raises the problems of image-based data on schools and the cultural and social context in which images are produced.

Portrayal and the school

Schools are constructed by, and exist within, a text-based context. Texts commanding the school, describing its functions or recording it administratively were produced by local-authority councillors, inspectors, personnel and maintenance staff, parents and head teachers (in logbooks). Most of this textual positioning of the school was produced outside it by the auditing, recording, listing, checking, measuring, numbering and counting of it by the local authority across its departments and functions (education, buildings, meals service, personnel, etc.). Few of the texts about a school were produced within it, and if they were, probably only from one room within it – the head teacher's office. It was unusual for schools to exist within an image-based context, that is, within images produced to describe or record the school. It was even rarer for these images to be produced by the school itself. This paper makes observations about an exceptional case to illuminate the Eton case and the problem of school images.

Although there has been an extensive proliferation of images about education since the 1950s, in common with the rise of image-based magazines, films and television, images are often disconnected from their context. Images of classrooms, of technology, of 'learning' or 'teaching', of school buildings are plentiful but they are often an illustration of schooling and education; they are used to illustrate a history, an idealized present or a projected future. They are rarely used as an exploration of an idea or of the site from which they are extracted. Of course, an historian can use these images for other purposes, for example, a series on classroom organization over time, but they cannot substitute for a 'thick description' of aspects of the schooling site. It is rare for a school to be a source of images about itself; schools were plundered for their visual information or were sometimes audited via images by their local authorities. Since these images rarely dealt with schooling but with a symbolic or illustrative aspect, the daily work of the school, its use or creation of material artefacts and its social relations over time emerges incidentally.

A distinction has to be drawn between images produced by the local authority or state about its schools and images produced by/ with/from schools themselves. In the first case, there may be collections of school images, often produced for special opening ceremonies of the whole school or an annexe, and these may be linked to images/plans taken by the architect's department in the construction of the school. In the second case, self-production by a school, there are a number of possibilities which have emerged: private schools producing visual information to attract customers (positive images of buildings, pupils, pleasure, etc.) and 'progressive schools', with similar needs but with different kinds of visual information.[1] A third category, emerging in the 1970s, was the deliberate creation of school visual information through the need to illustrate teaching texts or training courses about schooling; for example, in the UK the Open University in conjunction with the British Broadcasting Corporation created many still and moving images of schooling as part of its programme materials. A growth in educational ethnography, with qualitative researchers entering and studying classrooms, created a further image source in which small cameras were used to study school interactions. The state school was not a producer of images for external consumption as it was not its own manager; it was the servant of the local council. Informal production of visual information about its 'events' (curriculum, shows, classes, etc.) was produced but constitutes a temporary archive, often not officially collected within a school and existing on the margins.

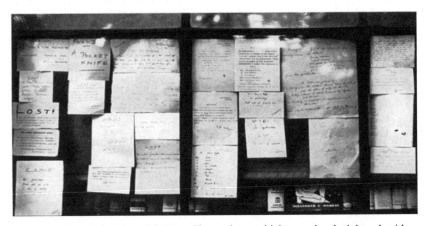

Figure 9: Spottiswoode's Window. The notices, which may be deciphered with a little patience, treat of everything from a lost pocket book to a Water Polo Match.

---

1   See, for example, H. Snitzer, *Summerhill: A Loving World* (Toronto: Macmillan, 1964) and A. and T. Malpas (eds.), *The Book of John Beddoes School* (Hereford: Davis Brothers, 1989).

Why would photographs of a school site be useful? Firstly, they would contextualize the text-based information about schooling, offering detail, particularity, and context to the other sources. Secondly, they would offer information which could not be produced in any other way; they would allow hypotheses to be generated and further research undertaken on aspects of overlooked schooling.

It is in this context that the Eton photographs, used as the basis for this paper, can be placed. They constitute a strong visual record of a school over a short period in the late 1930s. Even for a private school, even one of the most important elite schools, this set of photographs is unique. They were produced with the consent of an elite institution; an outsider and a professional artist/designer created them; they were created in a compressed time period, with no clear mandate from the school about their purpose. They exist within their own right as a record of a particular school, and may be valued as a unique visual record of a school. They can also be used to raise questions about visual records and how they can be created, examined and planned. Before considering the photographs of Eton it is necessary to develop knowledge about their construction, about the gaze of the photographer.

The photographic gaze: Moholy-Nagy and photography

A photograph of a past event has both a temporal and a physical presence. It records what was real. What was in front of the camera existed and is captured as a moment. It is a moment open to historical scrutiny. It allows us, as historians, to become eyewitnesses of a historical event, to see the past as it was. The viewer is confronted by the appearance of history itself. The photograph acts as a bridge between the past and the present. It turns historical subjects into intimate contemporaries. However, while a photograph may capture the truth of a moment, the process of recording is never innocent. Photography constitutes a site of production and representation, a photograph is a product of cultural discourse and as such must be read not as an image but as a text, and as with any text it is open to a diversity of readings. Photographs, if they are to be used for 'knowledge' of a subject, require historians to engage critically with issues relating to their production.[2] So, what is known about László Moholy-Nagy, the photographer of Eton, and what was his approach to photography?[3]

Moholy-Nagy wrote extensively about the nature of photography from the early 1920s until his death in 1946. In his earlier photographic work he preferred no captions and used oblique views, displaced proportions, light and dark, to intentionally disorientate the viewer. However, by the 1930s he shifted away from an abstract realism towards a realistic photography for the mass media with its concerns for aspects of contemporary life. In an essay in 1932 he described the camera as 'a new instrument of vision' which afforded eight different ways of seeing the world:

The Eight Varieties of Photographic Vision
1. Abstract seeing by means of direct records of forms produced by light: the photogram.
2. Exact seeing by means of the normal fixation of the appearance of things: reportage.
3. Rapid seeing by means of the fixation of movements in the shortest possible time: snapshots.

2   See I. Grosvenor, 'On Visualising Past Classrooms' in I. Grosvenor, M. Lawn and K. Rousmaniere (eds.) *Silences and Images: The Social History of the Classroom* (New York: Peter Lang, 1999) pp. 83–104.
3   Moholy-Nagy was born in Hungary, and moved to Germany in 1919 where he became associated with the Russian and Hungarian Futurist circle, the Berlin Dadaists and the Russian Constructivists. In the 1920s Moholy-Nagy joined the staff of the Bauhaus and produced photographic work, drawings, sculptures and constructions. Moholy-Nagy was the most active photo-monteur in Weimar Germany and was involved in poster art drawing on both Bauhaus and Russian design principles to create what he described in 1925 as 'typo-photo: visual communication represented with maximum accuracy'. He also worked on designs for ballet and theatre and made experimental films. Moholy-Nagy became one of the leaders and main shapers of the *Neue Sachlichkeit* or New Realism movement. With the rise of Nazism, Moholy-Nagy left Germany for Amsterdam in 1934.

4. Slow seeing by means of the fixation of movements spread over a period of time: prolonged time exposures.
5. Intensified seeing by means of: a) micro-photography; b) filter photography.
6. Penetrative seeing by means of X-rays: radiography.
7. Simultaneous seeing by means of transparent superimposition.
8. Distorted seeing: optical jokes. [4]

For Moholy-Nagy the role of the photographer was not 'to make photography an "art" in the old sense of the word'. On the contrary, 'the real photographer' had 'a great social responsibility'. Using this new instrument of vision, the work of the photographer was 'the exact reproduction of everyday facts, without distortion or adulteration', and the quality of the image produced had to be measured 'not merely by the photographic aesthetics, but by the human-social intensity of the optical representation'.[5] It was through the agency of the photographer that 'humanity [...] acquired the power of perceiving its surroundings, and its very existence, with new eyes.'[6] Photography imparted 'a heightened, or increased power of sight in terms of time and space'.[7] Moholy-Nagy recognized the subjectivity of the image-maker, but accepted this as a consequence of engaging with society:

> the photographer has to focus his [*sic*] attention on the facts which give an adequate record of the actions and ideas of his time. As he cannot do this without participating fully in life, consciously or intuitively his specialised field must be integrated with social reality. So naturally his visual selections will be coloured by his attitude toward life. This relationship to society may have the power of rising to objective heights of expressing the constructive framework of our civilisation instead of drowning in the chaos of a million details. Then the photographer will bring to the masses a new and creative vision. This will be his social significance. For culture is not the work of a few outstanding

4   L. Moholy-Nagy, 'A New Instrument of Vision', written 1932, published in Telehor Brno, 1936. Reprinted in R. Kostelanetz (ed.), *Moholy-Nagy* (London: Allen Lane Penguin Press, 1970), p. 52.
5   L. Moholy-Nagy, 'Photography in a flash', *Industrial Arts*, 1.4 (Winter, 1936). Reprinted in R. Kostelanetz, op. cit., p. 56.
6   L. Moholy-Nagy, 'How photography revolutionises vision', *The Listener* (November, 1933), 690.
7   L. Moholy-Nagy, 'A New Instrument of Vision', p. 52.

people. To benefit society their theories have to penetrate into everybody's daily routine.[8]

In a world of proliferating images it was essential that people developed an understanding of how images were created: 'a knowledge of photography is just as important as a knowledge of the alphabet. The illiterates of the future will be ignorant of the use of camera and pen alike.'[9] In sum, Moholy-Nagy the photographer was both a theorist and a practitioner.

Eton, Moholy-Nagy and the construction of the record

Moholy-Nagy made three short exploratory visits to London, before moving there in May 1935 as a refugee from Nazism.[10] For Moholy-Nagy England was, as Senter observes, 'a refuge to establish himself afresh'. It was also an 'unfamiliar setting', with formidable language problems for him. Herbert Read sponsored Moholy-Nagy's arrival and he received assistance from the Artists International Association's Artists' Refugee Committee and the Modern Architectural Research Group (Mars).[11] Moholy-Nagy, on his arrival, found he was best known in England for his photographic work and within a month he was commissioned to illustrate Mary Benedetta's *The Street Markets of London*, Bernard Fergusson's *Eton Portrait* and John Betjeman's *An Oxford University Chest*, for publication over the following three

8   L. Moholy-Nagy, 'Space-Time and the Photographer', *American Annual of Photography* (1942). Reprinted in R. Kostelanetz, op. cit., p. 64.

9   L. Moholy-Nagy, 'Photography in a flash', pp. 56–7.

10   T. Senter, 'Moholy-Nagy's English photography', *Burlington Magazine*, 944 (November 1981), 659.

11   Moholy-Nagy (1970), op. cit., p. xvii; L. Morris and R. Radford, *The Story of the Artists International Association, 1933–1953* (Oxford: Museum of Modern Art, 1983), pp. 29, 52; Senter, op. cit., p. 659.

years.[12] These commissions emerged through his contacts with Leslie Martin, J. M. Richards and Betjeman, who were all involved with Mars. It was Betjeman who recommended him to the publisher Harry F. Pariossien.[13] Through Ashley Havinden, head of department at the advertising agents W. S. Crawford and a devotee of Bauhaus, Moholy-Nagy also gained a lucrative design consultancy with Simpsons' new menswear store in Piccadilly.[14] On his arrival in London, Moholy-Nagy renewed contact with fellow Hungarian exile, Frederick Antal, an art historian. Antal's approach to art history provided a theoretical model for the New Realism in England, encouraging artists to deal with the social and political realities of their own times.[15] Moholy-Nagy also joined the network around the documentary film-maker John Grierson, who along with his collaborators elaborated in their films what Colls and Dodd have termed a 'national-collectivist myth' of Britain which celebrated the interconnectedness of the nation.[16] Late in 1935 Moholy-Nagy began a documentary film on lobster fishing, which presented a journey to the fishing grounds, the catch and natural hazards as ingredients of a dramatised 'ocean tale'.

12   M. Benedetta, *The Street Markets of London* (London: John Miles, 1936); B.
      Fergusson, *Eton Portrait* (London: John Miles, 1937); J. Betjeman, *An Oxford
      University Chest* (London: John Miles, 1939).
13   Op. cit., p. 670.
14   Op. cit., p. 659.
15   Morris and Radford (1983), op. cit., pp. 23–5.
16   R. Colls and P. Dodd, 'Representing the nation: British documentary film,
      1930–1945', *Screen*, 26.1 (1985), 21–33. Grierson saw documentary realism as
      an instrument 'because the citizen, under modern conditions, could not know
      everything about everything all the time, democratic citizenship was therefore
      impossible. We set to think how a dramatic apprehension of the modern scene
      might solve the problem, and we turned to the new wide-reaching instruments
      of radio and cinema as necessary instruments in both the practice of
      government and the enjoyment of citizenship' (J. Grierson, 'The course of
      realism' (1937) in F. Hardy (ed.), *Grierson on Documentary* (London: Faber &
      Faber, 1966), p. 78).

Figure 10: Rafts. Froggie superintends the embarkation.

Figure 11: Absence. From one of the windows of the Provost's Lodge.

The *Eton Portrait* commission was undertaken alongside the two other commissions, and the images were compiled in 1936 with extraordinary speed. For *Eton Portrait* he took over 400 photographs, only fifty-seven of which were later used. Moholy-Nagy took all of the photographs for the Oxford book in two days.[17] The three texts constitute a thematic series, linked by their narrative expressions of scenes, persons and incidents. Hight has described the photographs for these commissions as 'illustrative and conventional' in comparison to Moholy-Nagy's earlier work, commissions that were driven by expediency. Moholy-Nagy moved back and forth between commercial and experimental photography. The flexibility of photography, and of Moholy-Nagy too, enabled him to make the most of exile and support himself and family.[18] However, while Moholy-Nagy saw potential for photography in the revelation of social and economic conditions, Jeffrey has argued that in *The Street Markets of London*, he combined 'British interests in character with modernist dispositions'. His market traders

> dress and act like figures in a pantomime, but they work in arranged settings – stacked, piled and heaped. Although talkative enough for Dickens, they are also artisans and constructors in a modified Bauhaus style.

The folk-speech of the traders reported by Benedetta 'situated its photographed subjects within the discursive, everyday milieu in which they were scanned and received'.[19]

The Street Markets of London (1936) consisted of a long essay by Mary Benedetta and sixty-four photographs by Moholy-Nagy interspersed within, and subordinate to, the text. Moholy-Nagy's preface to the book reflects his concern with the possibility of using photography to provide documentary realism, to reveal social and economic conditions. It also offers valuable insights into how he

---

17 B. Fergusson, *Portrait of Eton* (London 1949: Muller), p. 63.
18 E. M. Hight, *Picturing Modernism: Moholoy-Nagy and Photography in Weimar Germany* (Cambridge: Cambridge University Press, 1995), p. 211.
19 I. Jeffrey, 'The way life goes' in M. Frizot (ed.), *A New History of Photography* (Koln: Könemann, 1998), p. 517.

approached his documentary subjects and therefore is worth quoting at
length:

> The photographer can scarcely find a more fascinating task than that of
> providing a pictorial record of modern city life. It is not, however, a task to
> which the purely aesthetic principle of pictorial composition (which many
> readers may expect in my work) can be applied, for from its very nature it
> requires the use of the pictorial sequence and thus of a more effective technique
> approximating to that of the film. I am convinced that the days of the merely
> 'beautiful' photograph are numbered and that we shall be increasingly
> interested in providing a truthful record of objectively determined fact.
>
> To many people's minds the street markets still suggest romantic notions of
> showmen, unorganised trade, bargains and the sale of stolen goods. The photo-
> graphic report can either encourage or correct these ideas. I consider the latter
> to be the more important task, since in my opinion these markets are primarily
> to be regarded as a social necessity, the shopping centre, in fact, for a large part
> of the working class.
>
> The subject is a vast one, comprising problems of history, sociology, eco-
> nomics and town planning. It is approached in this book by means of literary
> and impressionistic photo-reportage. This method of studying a fragment of
> present-day reality from a social and economic point of view has a wide general
> appeal. The text provides considerable opportunities for this study, and it was
> my aim to underline these opportunities through the pictorial record.
>
> For those interested in the technical aspects of photography I should add
> that as a rule I prefer to work with a large camera in order to obtain the
> minutely graded black-white-grey photo-values of the contact print, impossible
> to achieve in enlargements. But unfortunately the large camera is much too
> clumsy for taking rapid shots without being observed. The whole street
> immediately crowds around the photographer, the natural life of the scene is
> paralysed and the characteristic features of the traders, their happy-go-lucky
> behaviour, their elementary actor's skill, their impetuosity, are lost.
>
> Thus after several attempts with a large camera I always returned to the
> Leica, with which one can work rapidly, unobserved and (even in the London
> atmosphere, or in interiors) with a reliable degree of precision.

Moholy-Nagy concludes the preface with a plea to the reader to
condone any 'defect incompatible with the standard of photographic
quality demanded in theory [...] in view of the rapid and unprepared
fixation of lively scenes that never have been posed'.[20]

---

20   *The Street Markets of London* (1936), op. cit., pp. vii–viii.

Eton College, when approached by John Miles publishers, suggested Bernard Fergusson, a regular contributor to the magazine
Punch and an Old Etonian of eight years standing, as the author for
Eton Portrait. Fergusson visited the College with Moholy-Nagy on six
occasions, each time for between three and four hours.[21] While
Fergusson referred to Moholy-Nagy in the 1949 book *Portrait of Eton*
as being 'my photographer', and years later remembered meeting with
him to 'more or less suggest what he should take', it also is evident
that the photographer exercised freedom of action to create his own
record. A freedom of action captured by Fergusson in his introduction
to the 1949 text where he describes how Moholy-Nagy, 'with his
superb tactical eye'

> plunged into Mr. Hope-Jones's house, dashed upstairs to a first floor window
> and began work. I stood nervously between the window and the door of the
> room. Mr. Hope-Jones's dame, summoned by a suspicious boy's-maid, swept
> in, ignored me, tugged Moholy by the tails of his mackintosh and asked what he
> was doing and how dared he. He paid no attention to her tugs, but continued to
> kneel on the ottoman and take photographs. Only when he had finished did he
> turn to face her [....]. He began an explanation in broken English. 'Are you a
> German, or what?' she said; and then I had to overcome my shyness and
> intervene. He and I were escorted from the house by the bootboy, he
> triumphant, I red as beetroot; but we had our photographs.[22]

Moholy-Nagy, according to Fergusson, excelled in seizing the moment, and it was 'a lively experience to see him at work'. He 'did not
give a hoot for anybody' and became involved in a confrontation
outside Chambers with 'a furious Eton Master' who challenged is
invasion of privacy.[23] Moholy-Nagy also visited Eton by himself on
one occasion to take photographs. The photographs were taken before
Fergusson completed the text of *Eton Portrait*. Sibyl, Moholy-Nagy's
wife, later recalled that Fergusson and Betjeman dominated their lives
'while the pictures were taken', but 'not that they themselves took
the initiative'. Further, the success of the books was determined by

21   T. A. Senter, 'Moholy-Nagy in England: May 1935 – July 1937', unpublished
      MPhil thesis (Nottingham, 1975), pp. 82–3.
22   Fergusson (1949), op. cit., pp. 9–10; Senter (1975), op. cit., p. 83.
23   Fergusson (1949), op. cit., p. 10; Senter (1975), op. cit., p. 84.

'the extent to which Moholy had decided to see England through their eyes'.[24]

At Eton, Moholy-Nagy was creating a pictorial record 'of a fragment of present-day reality', a record created by impressionistic photo-reportage. Bringing his own image aesthetics, which he had written about, and a view of Englishness, which is harder to discern, he constructed a view of Eton which opened it outward and generated further myths about it, so necessary to such a symbolic institution.

Eton – an Unusual Case

The photographs of Eton are unusual. They were published twice as a record of a school for outsiders and for Etonians, especially past pupils. *Eton Portrait*, published in 1937, consists of 187 pages, made up of fourteen chapters, interspersed with fifty-eight photographs, fifty-seven taken by Moholy-Nagy. There is a list of illustrations with captions like 'Books in Chapel', 'Spottiswoode's Window: A Study in Emotions', 'Fourth of June: Today the wall suffers the indignity of being sat by the common herd', and 'Joby: "Not till you've paid for that flake you 'ad on Thursday, you don't get no tick, Sir".' The 1949 *Portrait of Eton* consists of eighty numbered pages: a list of the same illustrations with some minor adjustments to the captions, a short introductory essay which offers an account of the original book, the same fifty-eight photographs each on a single page, a two-page gloss-ary and seven unnumbered pages blank except for a single word: 'Autograph'. It is clear that this edition, with the Autograph pages, and the Glossary's sub-heading 'Strictly for the non-Etonian reader' is aimed primarily at Old Etonians. It celebrates the Eton of the 'thirties' which the writer attended before the Second World War. The aim of this second volume is self-evident in Fergusson's text:

24   Senter (1975), op. cit., pp. 79–80.

Moholy's pictures have therefore been a talisman to me these twelve or thirteen years, the next best thing to a pilgrimage in person. I see more than they portray; they serve as a starting point for much mental rambling. [25]

Figure 12: The Bill. Two hats left outside the door, one with books in it – the victim's – and the other without – the Praepostor's – alone hint at the drama within.

25   Fergusson (1949), op. cit., p. 13.

Figure 13: Practising for Certificate A. Seen from an upper window of the Drill Hall Schools.

Figure 14: The Biter Bit. This boy has been put on to write on the board and translate for the rest of the division.

The book is a reminder, a memento-mori, for lost days.

The photographs are not formal images of an institution but taken as a form of social documentary in which the formal and informal aspects of the school, its routines, its people and work are recorded.

Eton Portrait and the photographs were celebrated on publication, according to newspaper reviews, as an accurate depiction of Eton life:

> the portrayal of Eton as it appears to Etonians and not, as it may appear to the Sunday newspapers, in search of feature and scoop [...]
> a description of the ordinary life of the School, no one can misunderstand what Eton can mean to those who pass normally through it [...]
> a book which is not about the history and architecture of Eton, but about the life of Etonians [...]
> a valuable handbook, giving as it does a comprehensive, and comprehensible, outline of what the boy has to look forward to during his five years' progress [...]

The *Eton College Chronicle*, in particular, commented on the involvement of the photographer: 'The name of Moholy-Nagy is sufficient guarantee for the excellence of the photographs which are in the fullest sense of the word illustrations.' The book was chosen by the First Edition Club as 'one of the fifty best produced books of the year'.[26]

It is not clear why a renowned European photographer, known for his experimental interests and avant-garde connections, should be working on producing a portfolio of pictures about the grand institution of Eton, a boy's boarding school known for its traditions and its powerful elite. Nor why the book on Eton was chosen to be one of his three book contracts in his short time in England. Why did this powerful institution open itself to this person, the consequence of which was to project Eton as a human environment captured in a particular time?

As a social-visual document of a school, the photographs are unusual. They are intimate, social and non-hierarchical. They view the school in the round, looking into many of its public spaces and also recording intimate moments of school life. The pictures appear 'natural', a stylistic break with school photographs of the time. These images do not look rehearsed or collective or representative. They are also recognizably realistic, representing the new style of documentary film, in which lightweight cameras are used to explore common spaces of life and represent them within new forms of popular media.

---

26   These extracts are quoted on the flyleaf of the third commissioned book, *An Oxford University Chest* (1939).

They stand with the coming approach of *Picture Post* in the UK, and so create a contrast between the new style of the work and the old tradition and site of the subject. They humanize and make familiar the strange and powerful ways of the elite: yet there is no loss of social power here. It is as if this 'private' document has been made 'public' for a purpose: it is a family picture which others are allowed to see. In this period, this can be seen as very opportunistic – the elite school reveals itself to be a friendly place, very human in scale, and shifts attention away from its powerful discursive position in society. It tries to stop appearing as the remote training ground for the ruling class and wanting to become another common social space in which people live their lives. Even if quaint, Eton's unseen nature is apparently revealed and democratized.

Of the fifty-seven photographs published, the majority of the pictures were taken outside in the yards, streets and riverbank used by the school. The remainder of the photographs, roughly a third, were of inside spaces, the specialist curriculum spaces, the classroom (only two images), the halls and rooms in which the pupils, their artefacts and their traces were present. Buildings featured in seven external shots, mainly without pupils in the frame. About ten of the photographs showed the clothing, books and notices belonging to the pupils, in their absence. The pupils dominated the images, dressed in the varied hierarchical or sport clothing which carry powerful signification in the school. In addition, there were images with about ten adults in them, usually service staff in the school, rarely tutors and once or twice parents; the latter included the only pictures of women. Most of the photographs (approximately forty) were taken at face level or about 500cms above; a handful of photographs were taken down onto the subjects, either at an angle of 45 or 90 degrees to the horizontal.

Although few pictures were of the tutors, there were several of other adults working in the school. Often referred to in the captions by their name rather than role, it is likely that they include a boatman, a rowing coach, an army cadet officer, a porter, a tailor and/or laundryman, and a school messenger. Tutors were called masters, 'M'Tutor', the Lower Master and Head Master, sometimes by their formal address, Mr ... . The other college employees were called by their first name or a diminutive – Alf, Froggie and Joby – or by their function at Eton – the School Messenger, the Colleger. Of the classroom scenes, and of the same lesson probably, the photographs are taken from the middle of the classroom, looking forward and then back. Individuals are shown working in specialist curriculum areas engaging in painting, potting, boat-building and metalwork or playing sport (fives, cricket, rowing). The pictures of the school artefacts offer an additional source of information about the school; they include a desk (or 'burry'), a window, lecterns and wall panels. The desk image shows a lamp, a framed photograph of a dog, an alarm clock, a pencil sharpener, ink bottles, loose papers, a paper pad and a thin book. In another photograph, a line of top hats, some with books in or on them, have been placed on the floor outside rooms. The window of a bookshop has displays of notices covering it; the notices are about sports events and lost and found articles. The image captions generally place the image; they do not explain it. It is assumed that the viewer will know what 'Between Schools', 'The Bill' or 'Absence' means, or who 'Alf' is, or the significance of the 'Fourth of June'. A glossary is produced at the back of the book 'strictly for the non-Etonian reader'.

Although there are a number of images lacking – for instance, teaching or tutor rooms, a plan of the school and its environs, a meeting of tutors, a library, etc. – the images of the school are useful. A variety of angles upon the working of the school are revealed: across the curriculum, especially sports; between lessons; school employees; walls and spaces; routines and ceremonies; social relations; signs and symbols. A lot is learnt about the school and its operations: for the old Etonian these images are particular spurs of memory, but for the outsider they offer information about elite education. More importantly for historians, they offer a way of seeing and thinking about the investigation of schools through the visual.

In the 1949 text the book of photographs is organized in the new way of the time; the pictures drive the story, the story of the school, and they are created and placed in a way which will tell 'the story' transparently. It is an expression of the way in which the new photography magazines in the UK told their popular stories of 'national life', of 'us', which was made possible by the new technology from Germany and the artistic and design advances in Germany and the

USSR. The photographs and their teasing captions are immediately recognizable to any student of post-war magazines. It is a particular kind of realism which now appears dated. Realism in a visual sense organizes space, producing order and stability (not its opposite). Photographs in this paradigm

> often have a before and after outside the specific moment captured in the frame. They are episodes in a story and imply the rest of the narrative in the nature of their images and the meanings that these construct. The meaning of the picture is given by its place in an implied narrative.[27]

Portrait of Eton accords more closely than the original text to Moholy-Nagy's idea of the 'phototext', in which photographs replace text as an objective sequence of communication arising from inherent visual, associative, conceptual and synthetic interrelationships.[28]

The story of Eton is then a specific construction, produced by a selection of images, the framing of the visual, the editing and the caption. This is not the Eton of powerful Ministers of State, famous as the training ground of the great public elite which runs Britain, but a place of curious rituals, of ordered lives, of a British institution, of something to be saved in times of trouble, of social solidity and continuing strength. It is part of the reassuring series which reveals the curiosities and eccentricities of the British; it is neither ironic nor subtle, its realism is in the technique. It presents itself as if it was not constructed, as if there was no author, making us passive observers. So, there is a social accord operating at this level as well. When schools are beginning to be revealed visually, they are 'opened' out by means of a realistic paradigm in which they appear to contain a series of stories about ordinary human beings working, creating stability about the enterprise and its time, creating rules of operation in times of instability. In this way, the Eton archive will echo the later series of

---

27 N. Abercrombie, S. Lash, and B. Longhurst, 'Popular representation: recasting realism' in S. Lash and F. Friedman (eds.) *Modernity and Identity* (Oxford: Blackwell, 1996), p. 121.

28 L. Moholy-Nagy, *Malerei, Fotografie, Film*, Bauhaus-Buch No. 8, Munich 1925. English translation: *Painting, Photography, Film* (Cambridge; Massachusetts: MIT Press, 1987).

pictures in the 1970s in which all kinds of attempts are made to capture the nature of schools and learning in realistic ways, a process intensified by the new market context of education which relies upon the creation and selection of images about the school.

Portrayal and the school revisited

Although the Eton study was a commission, a necessity for survival, it is the conduit for a radical approach to photography as part of a social observation movement of the time. It was an intervention in 'social consciousness' as the Mass Observation put it, as people became the subject of study. It seems odd to describe the powerful and rich public school Eton as part of an 'anthropology of ourselves' as M-O put it, but by revealing the commonplaces of the site and the institution, in a way that *Picture Post* would soon do, it was a significant intervention in the Britain of the time and since. The necessity for power to wrap itself in mystery and obscure and opaque ritual allowed its institutions to flourish. In the 1930s a new social commentary coexisted with revelations of curiosities or traditional cultures; yet here they are combined with an intimacy about the subject, the place and the artefacts and revealed in new combinations and angles, so that Eton appears to be a set of unexplained questions. It was not that Moholy-Nagy was using the idea of the stranger or outsider, a common idea in social observation of the time, but that he *was* an outsider. A 'foreigner' exploring the halls of the mighty, through an anthropological interest and an eye for form and juxtaposition, produces surprising information about how this world is constructed, how it communicates and interacts, who supports its existence and what material objects it leaves its traces upon.

Looking again at this school, in these pictures, there appears a frozen image of a time gone, 'remembered' as a set of traditions and objects, and as a form of past Englishness. But there exists within these pictures an opportunity for a cultural historian of schooling to offer questions, drawn from comparison, contemporary school studies and cultural theory, about the way in which schools reproduce themselves, offer recognizable aspects across culture and time, and insights into their social and material cultures.

An extended use of images in history of education would be very useful to aid the formation of a more complex reading of schooling. It would test the documentary approach as it would both enhance the reading, producing a deeper context about the particularities of classrooms, their relations, spaces and technologies, but it would also challenge the documents, their points of construction and their usage. Images are not just illustrations of the text but have their own coded information, produced by context, gaze, framing and use. A greater use of images would bring its own methodological problems for historians. The same care taken about the document needs to be taken with the image. It is not neutral, waiting for interpretation; it is an actor, bearing messages.

The production of school records which include images would further extend the search for postdocumentary history of education, which has taken place with the growth of oral history and the postmodern discursive turn. The use of images would become part of the widening historiography of schooling. Like any form of documentary analysis, image analysis will offer some new insights about the history of schooling but, like documentary analysis, the document or image cannot be taken on trust. It is a new step, but it has its own problems.

ULRIKE MIETZNER AND ULRIKE PILARCZYK

4 Methods of Image Analysis in Research in Educational and Social Sciences[1]

God is in the detail. (Aby Warburg)[2]

The 'pictorial turn' and 'visual anthropology'

We live in a world of images. Paintings, sculptures, drawings, prints, photographs and films provide views of the social, cultural and anthropological phenomena of an age. The importance of visual media has increased significantly over recent decades. We are all more than ever exposed to information and communication technologies that are visually based.[3]

One of the 'primary' technologies, photography, spread round the world immediately after its invention in the first half of the nineteenth century. Scholars refer to a new age of changed per-

---

1 Translation by Richard Holmes.

2 For the origins of this variation of the phrase 'The Devil is in the detail', see E. H. Gombrich, *Aby Warburg: Eine intellektuelle Biografie* (Hamburg: Eva, 1992), p. 28.

3 See B. Fuhs, 'Fotografien und qualitative Forschung. Zur Verwendung fotografischer Quellen in den Erziehungswissenschaften', in B. Friebertshäuser and A. Prengel, (Eds.), *Handbuch Qualitative Forschungsmethoden in der Erziehungswissenschaft* (Weinheim: München, 1997), pp. 265–85, (p. 265); V. Burgin, *Thinking Photography* (London: MacMillan, 1982) and *In/Different Space: Place and Memory in Visual Culture* (Berkeley and Los Angeles: University of California Press, 1996).

ceptions.[4] Now, at the beginning of the twenty-first century and the end of classical photography, the boundaries are disappearing between world and image, reality and simulation; the dimensions of time and space seem relative; the distinctions blur between the signifier and the signified. Science reacts to this with the 'pictorial turn', demanding a discursive science of images with less of a linguistic basis, and which makes use of the social qualities of the image, the visibility of 'the other'.[5] New approaches to the methods of image science and the interpretation of photographs are probably also connected to developments in the social sciences over the past two decades. Photographs allow the integration of new approaches in gender history, for example, or the anthropology of symbols.

In order to decode the information in pictures, historical science of culture and images was initiated by Aby Warburg at the beginning of the twentieth century which still provides the basis for all image analysis. Disciplines such as anthropology,[6] history, and more recently educational science have begun to adapt the contributions of art history and art science and to develop these as 'visual anthropology'.[7] Klaus Mollenhauer (1983), Horst Schiffler and Rolf Winkeler (1985)

---

4   Jonathan Crary sees the transformation in full flow in 1820, and he also suspects the model of perspective set in the Renaissance was already undergoing change at this time. See *Techniken des Betrachters: Sehen und Moderne im 19. Jahrhundert* (Dresden/Basel: Verlag der Kunst, 1996), pp. 14–16.

5   Mitchell comments that 'whatever the pictorial turn is, then, it should be clear that it is not a return to naive mimesis, copy or correspondence theories of representation, or a renewed metaphysics of pictorial "presence": it is rather a postlinguistic, postsemiotic rediscovery of the picture as a complex interplay between visuality, apparatus, institutions, discourse, bodies, and figurality.' See W. J. Mitchell, *Picture Theory* (Chicago/London: University of Chicago Press, 1994), p. 36.

6   Early uses of photography and film in ethnology are not dealt with here. See J. Collier, Jr. and M. Collier, *Visual Anthropology: Photography as a Research Method* (Albuquerque: University of New Mexico Press, 1986); M. Banks and H. Morphy (eds.), *Rethinking Visual Anthropology* (New Haven: Yale University Press, 1997); E. Edwards (ed.), *Anthropology and Photography 1860–1920* (New Haven: Yale University Press, 1992).

7   See P. Hockings (ed.), *Principles of Visual Anthropology* (Paris: Mouton, 1975).

and Konrad Wünsche (1991) were among the first to begin to investigate images systematically as a source for educational history.[8] Photographs are now also used for contemporary empirical investigations in educational science.[9]

Educational scientists are turning their attention to the materialisation and embodiment of culture. Bodily posture, as well as all sorts of artefacts, and thus also the media, are seen as an expression of culture. Photographs record and transport visual aspects of culture, so that they therefore repeatedly *reconstitute* culture in both public and private spheres. The images contain coded information about the relationships between generations, or about long-term transformations, that seem to be in opposition to all political changes. In contrast to literary works, which usually record the untypical, photographs preserve the everyday and the trivial.

However, we still know little about what photographs actually show, and the complex structure of the source rules out any quick, slick interpretations.[10] A key question is whether photographs are documents or produced arrangements.[11] However, for educational and

8   See also: M. Parmentier, 'Jenseits von Idylle und Allegorie – die Konstruktion des ästhetisch Subjekts in Bruegels "Kinderspielen"', *Pädagogische Korrespondenz*, 5 (1989), 75–88; H. Schmitt, J.-W. Link, F. Tosch (eds.), *Bilder als Quellen der Erziehungsgeschichte* (Bad Heilbrunn: Klinkhart, 1997); H.-G. Herrlitz and C. Rittelmeyer (eds.), *Exakte Phantasie: Pädagogische Erkundungen Bildender Wirkungen in Kunst und Kultur* (Munich: Juventa, 1993).

9   M. Schratz and U. Steiner-Löffler, 'Pupils using photographs in school self-evaluation' in J. Prosser (ed.), *Image-based Research: A Sourcebook for Qualitative Researchers* (London: Falmer Press 1998), pp. 235–51; I. Grosvenor, M. Lawn and K. Rousmaniere, *Silences and Images: the Social History of the Classroom* (New York: Peter Lang, 1999). See semiotic-sociological investigations, for example, on gestures in C. Müller, *Redebegleitende Gesten: Kulturgeschichte – Theorie – Sprachvergleich* (Berlin: Arno Spitz, 1998).

10   The authors were able to spend six years researching the problems of photography as a source as part of a DFG-funded research project on 'Dealing with indoctrination – educational intentions, forms and effects in German "Erziehungsstaaten",' led by Heinz-Elmar Tenorth and Konrad Wünsche. The support and stimulation of all those involved made it possible to open up a form of critical qualitative research.

11   E. H. Gombrich, *Bild und Auge: Neue Studien zur Psychologie der bildlichen Darstellung* (Stuttgart: Klett-Cotta, 1984), pp. 240–73.

social scientists, photographs are all the more valuable because they are never only one or the other – so that it is not only possible to interpret the arranged elements, but also any unintended and coincidental aspects. Photographic images contain traces of political, cultural, social, and subjective life. But the camera notes what is in front of the lens, which might be something accidental and unintended. Sometimes it is precisely these elements of an image, such as the slightest of body movements, that comment on an event. Photographs always direct attention to the non-verbal aspects of every communication because they restrict reality to its visual elements.

On the basis of our research findings, we will go on in section two to consider specific aspects of photography as a source, its relationship to reality, the role of coincidence and the unintended and the importance of camera technology. In section three we then review the value of photography as a source and describe the effects of interplay of the intended and unintended image contents for the educational and social sciences, before going on in section five to present the methodology for analysing individual photographs and large photographic collections. Finally, section five we discuss the future potential and limitations of the method.

Photography as a source: a medium between authenticity, arrangement and coincidence

Doubts are raised about the suitability of photographs as a source for social historians either when they are used simply as illustrations or when they are advanced as evidence without the necessary scrutiny of the source.[12] The fascination of photography, however, is the tension

---

12   See J. Hannig, 'Bilder, die Geschichte Machen: Anmerkungen zum Umgang mit "Dokumentarfotos" in Geschichtslehrbüchern' *Geschichte in Wissenschaft und Unterricht* (GWU), 40 (1989), 10–32. For critical analysis of sources of historical photographs see D. Barnouw, *Germany 1945: Views of War and Violence* (Bloomington: Indiana University Press, 1996); C. Brink, *Ikonen der*

that exists between the authentic and the arranged. A photograph creates the impression that things were the way they seem, so that since the development of photography the photographer can play with the possibility of producing an apparent reality.

There are two characteristics that explain why people call into question the value of even classical photography as a source (where the photograph is intended to be documentary, with no manipulation, or digitalization), namely its relationship to reality and the role of coincidence.[13]

Photography and reality

If we take as an example the photographic illustrations in the West German journal *Pädagogik* in the 1980s, then it might be thought that the teacher had completely disappeared from the classroom. The photographs almost all show only schoolchildren. Now, we know that there would have been a teacher somewhere, even in the 1980s, so does this make the photographs useless as a source? Certainly not, but it does mean that we cannot use the photos in the journal to draw conclusions about real teaching situations. In general, photographs do not relate so directly to reality, because they do not document a one-to-one reflection, but present a point of view. In terms of the optical perception, the camera is indeed unbiased, and whatever appears on the photograph must also have been visible in front of the camera lens when the shutter fell. But where and how it appears is largely a matter for the photographer to decide. The photographic image is a reduction of reality, a selection. In the course of being photographed, the things of objective reality not only lose their spatial, acoustic, tactile and

---

Vernichtung: Öffentlicher Gebrauch von Fotografien aus nationalsozial-istischen Konzentrationslagern nach 1945 (Berlin: Akademie, 1998).

13 This has been widely discussed. See from an art-historical viewpoint: E. H. Gombrich, *Bild und Auge: Neue Studien zur Psychologie der bildlichen Darstellung* (Stuttgart: Kletta-Cotta, 1984), pp. 240–73; or photo-theoretically: A. Sekula, 'On the invention of photographic meaning' in Burgin (1982), op. cit., pp. 84–109; S. Sontag, *On Photography* (Harmondsworth: Penguin, 1984); and from the historical position Hannig (1989), op. cit., pp. 10–32.

olfactory properties: the object is also, to paraphrase Aaron Siskind, torn from its normal surroundings, alienated from its neighbours, and forced into new relationships.[14] The photographs of the journal *Pädagogik* are not suited as a source for describing what happens during teaching, but they can be used to describe pedagogical intentions, editorial policies and social trends – for example the emphasis on the learning role of the children by the editors of *Pädagogik* in the 1980s, as opposed to the teaching role of the teacher.

Intention and coincidence

In contrast to painting, photography is not essentially a physical creative process, so that it is not possible to interpret every element of the photograph as intentional. On the contrary, it appears as if from year to year photographers are coming to rely more and more on their camera, and thus on coincidence. Can photographs be interpreted at all if they are not the product of intention? There are two replies to this. Firstly, the effect of an image is independent of the original intention and the nature of the production process. It works according to formal aesthetic criteria, which can be analysed and described. Secondly, it is in the nature of photography that the effect of the image is realized initially in the selection and composition of the motif and the technical implementation, and then again in the decision to develop the film, print a negative and preserve or utilize the final photograph. This means that photographers usually decide whether they think that a picture has turned out well or not. A similar decision is taken when the editor of a publication chooses or rejects a photograph.

The ways of dealing with the coincidental in photography differ from genre to genre. Artistic photographers often work with coincidence as a creative element, generating other perspectives, new ideas, and breaks with convention.[15] Professional photographers also work

14   A. Siskind, 'Was ist moderne Fotografie?' (1950), in W. Kemp, *Theorie der Photographie*, 3 vols. (Munich: Schirmer/Mosel, 1979–83), vol. 3, p. 71.
15   Of course, automatic cameras can now often achieve results that not long ago were the preserve of professionals. When assessing the skill of a photographer

with coincidence and the accidental. However, in relatively static motifs such as class photos or formal events they try to eliminate this as far as possible. For interpretation, the element of the unforeseen can be very useful, since it is these unintended, unpredictable details that often reveal key information about how individuals react to reality.

A third characteristic of photography is responsible for the special relationship of photography with reality. From the very early days, the capacity of the camera to capture the optical 'truth', the interaction of chemical and physical laws in photography, have led people to view photographs as being generally 'true'. It was only some time later it was realized that the technical procedure can be modulated, so that without altering the photographic situation, the effect of an image could be constructed, accentuated, and interpreted simply by appropriate technical intervention.

Camera technology offers the photographer certain options such as the variation of the aperture, exposure time, and focus that allow the motif to be selected in front of the camera. Through the viewfinder it is possible to determine the main aspects of the composition and the main motif, to centre the photograph and to determine the vanishing point. It is possible to obtain completely different photos of one and the same object depending on whether it is photographed from a bird's eye view, at eye-level, from level with the object, or from below. By focusing on a particular area or adjusting the depth of focus it is possible to alter the relationships of time and space, and thus also the significance of an object. Further processing is also possible in the darkroom, and often whole areas of a picture are touched up to produce the desired effects, especially in press photography. The form of the final photograph is influenced by the function it is to be used for. If it has been taken for publication in a newspaper, certain aesthetic arrangements might be out of the question. Some uses call for specific camera perspectives: for example, a child-centred approach frequently leads to the photographer holding the camera at the child's eye level so as to simulate their equal standing. Obviously, the difference between professionals, hobby photographers and naive lay-

it is always important to take account of the photographic technology that was available at the time.

photographers at the mercy of the technology in their hands plays a major role in the production process. Nor should the cost of producing a photograph be neglected. A work of art is something valuable, but for many decades photographs have been cheap – so that many 'snaps' are taken without much thought. They are also readily reproducible. They do not need to depict anything unique. It is particularly their ability 'to capture the fleeting shadow of the present in its flight' that make them so valuable for historians.[16]

The value of photographs as a source

What do photographs actually show? What do they show that other sources do not show, or what are they a source for?

1. Photographs depict what was in front of the lens when the film was exposed, whether this was specially arranged, or came into the picture unintentionally.
2. Whereas the fine arts, literature, or even diaries and the minutes of a meeting concentrate on the particular rather than the ordinary, photographs preserve not only the photographed event, but also the familiar, unnoticed details, ritualized normalities, and unrecalled bodily postures. They show things that have been long forgotten because of their banality, such as the appearance of a room, or someone's posture and facial mannerisms.
3. A photograph has many meanings. In this it is comparable with the fine arts, and like all historical sources it is over-determined. The reason for this lies in the multitude of visual signs that are brought together in a picture, in the fact that a picture mediates both in its details and as a whole, in the aesthetic quality (which means that contents and form are seen together inseparably as a picture), and also in the rules of visual perception.

16   Friedrich von Raumer (1840), cited in Kracauer, (1973), op.cit., p. 75.

4. Photographs *can* be understood as acts of self-representation of the photographer, or as representations of the wishes of the client or of an ideology. Photographs produced by a press photographer give a view of school that differs markedly from the snap-shots of schoolchildren. The Government Press Agency in Bonn did not distribute the same pictures about school lessons as the East German ADN-Picture Agency or the Ullstein Service in West Berlin. A photographer for a news magazine would not take the same pictures as a disillusioned teacher.
5. The subjects can also influence the photograph to a certain extent, so that it is always necessary to determine the relationship between the (self)-presentation of the photographer and the self-presentation of the subjects.

In summary, the value of a photograph as a source for research derives from its complexity. This corresponds to the ambiguity of phenomena in the experienced world; the way a photograph is constructed suggests construction patterns of pedagogic and social situations and relationships. The concealed perspectives of the photographer and subject correspond to the multiperspectivity that would be expected on the basis of sociological and historical research. It would be wrong to limit the historical analysis of visual sources merely to the contents of the image. The aesthetic quality of a picture is inseparably linked with the contents and must be handled equally when it comes to determining the significance of a photograph.

Methods of interpreting photographs

The fine arts have been well researched, and frequently art historians have also studied genre painting and the educational aspects of motifs.[17] This has produced a methodological repertoire and detailed background information. This literature can help educational scientists without training in art history to interpret sources from visual media appropriately. However, no works were dedicated specifically to the use of photographs. Despite increasing numbers of publications on all aspects of photography, there have been relatively few studies of the genres relevant for educational science such as youth photography, family photography, etc.[18] Although the important aspects of photographic theory have now been covered,[19] there is still no widely tested and recognized method for the interpretation of photographs within the framework of historical or empirical research.[20] Photographs can

17   On the uses of paintings and drawings see K. Mollenhauer, 'Methoden erziehungswissenschaftlicher Bildinterpretation', in B. Friebertshäuser and A. Prengel (eds.), *Handbuch Qualitative Forschungsmethoden in der Erziehungswissenschaft* (Munich: Juventa, 1997), pp. 247–64; K. Wünsche, 'Das Wissen im Bild: Zur Ikonographie des Pädagogischen', in the 27th Supplement of *Zeitschrift für Pädagogik*, 1991, 273–90.

18   Such works are more common in the literature written in English. For example: M. Hirsch (ed.), *The Familial Gaze* (London: University Press of New England, 1999); S. Isherwood, *The Family Album* (London: Broadcasting Support Services, 1988).

19   See W. Kemp (1979–83), op. cit.; H. Amelunxen, *Theorie der Fotografie Bd. 4. 1980–1995* (München: Schirmer/Mosel, 2000).

20   Some discussion of this exists. See Fuhs (1997), op. cit., pp. 265–85; R. Lehberger, 'Das Fotoarchiv des Hamburger Schulmuseums zur Dokumentation der Reformpädagogik in Hamburg der Weimarer Republik', in Schmitt *et al.* (1997), op. cit., pp. 125–48; B. Schonig, 'Mädchen und Junge, Lehrerinnen und Lehrer auf Schulfotografien 1928–1961 – Ein Versuch zur Evokation pädagogischen Erinnerungsvermögens als Einstieg in eine historische Bildkunde', in Schmitt *et al.* (1997), op. cit. The theoretical discussion in visual anthropology, ethnology and the social sciences has made more progress, but has not yet lead to well-developed methods. For a history see J. Jäger, *Photographie: Bilder der Neuzeit Einführung in die Historische Bildforschung* (Tübingen: Edition Diskord, 2000).

be used and interpreted in a variety of ways, but this cannot be done arbitrarily. The results must be plausible, and capable of confirmation. The interpretation of photography offers the opportunity to be guided not only by hypotheses or questions raised by research projects, but also to identify and take account of the questions raised by the images themselves. There are two ways of clarifying research questions and generating hypotheses: the analysis of large quantities of photographs; and the analysis of individual images. The interpretation of individual images also requires the examination of larger comparable groups of photographs. The interpretation of individual images and the analysis of large numbers of photographs therefore do not represent an alternative, but are inter-dependent.

The analysis of large quantities of photographs: sorting photographs as a source – classification, ordering, categorisation

One of the advantages of photographic image analysis is that photographs form genres, can have motifs in common and similarities of style, and there are also conventions that are usually typical of a certain era. In order to be able to recognize these, it is necessary to have a large number of images from various authors and different historical phases. As they gain the character of a mass medium, photographs become available in numbers and with such heterogeneity that it is necessary to sort these in terms of contents and historical criteria, rather than investigate arbitrary individual photographs or series of pictures. Because of the complexity and ambiguity of images, the photographs must first be placed in some external context. The first step is therefore to archive the photographs in terms of their origin and time of production. For scientific work with large collections, and for the comparison and contrasting of series of photographs, however, this is not enough. The photographs must also be classified in terms of standard criteria that ensure that at least the minimum amount of information about context is available without which the photographs could neither be correctly interpreted nor effectively processed and structured in large numbers.

The classification of photographs. Each individual photograph is classified by assigning standardized text formulations about origin, use, and collection context. The relevant information is either taken from the picture itself, so that it is internal (topics, motifs and style) or it is external, that is not included in the picture (date, place, photographer, use). Date and place are the hard data of classification, and without these it is rarely possible to evaluate a photograph properly. In addition, the classification of the photographs also involves entering keywords into an image database. In general, it will be necessary to set up a reference catalogue based on these criteria for every type of social-scientific investigation, involving large numbers of photographs. The image database should also include all the information known about the photograph.

The external classification factors relate to historical or sociological facts about the photograph, that is:

(1) *Date.* For empirical investigations it is usually sufficient to be able to assign a photograph to a decade or a certain limited time period. Uncertainties of a few years are not much of a problem for investigations in educational science on transitions of form, because changes usually take place over longer periods anyway.

(2) *Place.* In addition to the date, the place where a photograph was taken is important, above all for the allocation of the photograph to a political era, a social system, or a specific culture.

(3) *Authorship.* For the analysis of both large numbers of photographs, and of individual photographs it is particularly important to know whether a photograph has been taken by a private individual, or by someone acting in a public function or with a specific assignment. A first rough subdivision is therefore between private and professional photography. Private photographers usually act in accordance with different rules from professionals, and there are also considerable differences in the photographic and artistic means, as well of course as the different conventions of each genre. Private photographers can be divided into the snap-shooters and hobby enthusiasts.[21] There are also

---

21   T. Starl, *Knipser: Die Bildgeschichte der privaten Fotografie in Deutschland und Österreich 1880 bis 1980* (Munich/Berlin: Verlag Koehler and Amelang, 1995), pp. 12–25.

considerable differences among professional photographers: for example between artistic and press photographers. Whereas the artistic photographer is exploring the possibilities of the medium, the press photographer is producing a comment on a current topic, usually with a specific group of viewers in mind. There is also a separate group, what we call semi-public photographs. This is usually the work of photographers with pedagogic ambitions, such as teachers, or parents, or also schoolchildren. All these photographers have intentions that differ from press photographers or official school photographers. Photographs from school or class chronicles belong to this group, as do many photographs from youth organisations.

(4) *Use.* This is closely linked with the photographer – we group together all information about the occasion when the picture was taken, and the original and subsequent uses. The questions here are: Why was a photograph taken? Did someone commission it? How was it used? Was a print made? How has it been passed on? As with the photographers we distinguish between public, semi-public and private purposes. Public here, for example, would imply use in a publication, but a photo in a family album would be private. Semi-public would be the use of a photograph in a school chronicle.

Internal factors of classification are relatively easy to obtain in comparison with external ones, because they relate exclusively to data which can be gained from the image itself, such as the topic, the photographic motif, and the style. The need to classify in accordance with internal criteria arises above all from problems of structuring large numbers of photographs, above all sorting in terms of motif allows series to be collected for comparison. However, the real categorization of the photographic material for an investigation takes place by linking the classification characteristics.

Structuring and ordering in accordance with classification patterns. Classified collections of photographs can be structured in various ways depending on the nature of the research and the topic of interest. This means that the classified archive can be rearranged in a different way for a new topic of investigation and new questions. In this way, a single photograph, or an archive, can be investigated for a variety of reasons. A photograph can be assigned to various groups under different headings. Before every investigation, the question is what photographs are suitable for inclusion, and what is their specific value as a source. The public image of schools and an education system are transported mainly by photographs that have been published; private snapshots taken by schoolchildren in class, in contrast, tend to give a private view of the same phenomenon.

Having decided what is to be investigated, it is necessary to define the selection criteria by classification characteristics. By linking internal and external classification characteristics, a selection grid can be set up – this can be done most effectively by means of an appropriate function of an electronic-image database. By applying the grid to the entire database, groups can be generated that are sorted in terms of historical criteria and contents, and which allow the necessary comparisons to be made for the study in question.

Analysing individual photographs

Various methods are available for the analysis of individual photographs, based on artistic and historical approaches.[22] One of the best-known analyses is by Roland Barthes.[23] Many artistic photographs, however, or private snap-shots, lack the unambiguous nature of the advertisements interpreted by Barthes. If it wishes to do justice to the photograph, interpretation always has to take account of:

1. The technical means available for the photography and the development of the film.
2. The genre (private or public photography).
3. The specific histories of style and motif.
4. The function and use of a photograph.

---

22   See H. Talkenberger, 'Historische Erkenntnis durch Bilder? Zur Methode und Praxis der Historischen Bildkunde', in Schmitt *et al.* (1997), op. cit.
23   R. Barthes, 'Rhetorik des Bildes' (1964), in Kemp (1979–83), op. cit., pp. 138–49.

It would belittle a source to reduce it merely to a depiction, interpreted only in terms of content without consideration of the aesthetics.

We have adapted iconographic-iconological image analysis for use specifically in the interpretation of photography. This has been developed in detail as historical methodology for the analysis of the cultural significance of images and other forms of visual expression, and has been well tested down to the individual procedural steps.[24] It seems well suited for use in educational-science studies. Panofsky, who developed the method and varied it many times, attached considerable importance to the analysis of forms, symbols, facial expression, gesture, body posture and minute details in their historical context.[25]

The aim of iconographic-iconological analysis of individual photographs is to treat the photograph in its details as a whole, with its historical technique, motif, and critical reception, and to take account of the function of the photograph in the interpretation, so that rather than just isolating single motifs from the picture and producing these as evidence, information is gained from the photograph itself in the sense of a 'grounded theory'.

In principle, all photographs are suitable for iconographic investigations if the key facts (date and place) are known. However, for iconographic analysis of individual photographs aimed at testing new research hypotheses, photographs should generally be selected that not only seem particularly relevant for the topic, but that also suggest a certain ambiguity, and create the impression that they could reveal information that is not apparent at first sight.

In a first step – the pre-iconographic description – an attempt is made to grasp the photograph in all its details. Details that are often overlooked in photographs include the spatial arrangement, the illumination, or details of gestures. At this level the formal structure of the picture is described. In the second step – the iconographic descrip-

24   J. K. Eberlein, 'Inhalt und Gestalt: die ikonographisch-ikonologische Methode', in H. Belting, *et al.* (eds.), *Kunstgeschichte: Eine Einführung* (Berlin: Reimer, 1985), pp. 169–90, (p. 169).

25   E. Panofsky, 'Ikonographie und Ikonologie: Eine Einführung in die Kunst der Renaissance', in E. Panofsky (ed.), *Sinn und Deutung in der bildenden Kunst* (Cologne: Dumont, 1978), pp. 36–67.

tion and interpretation – the information from the first step is related to the external knowledge about the photograph, and to other photographs. All the available information is used to research the function of the photograph, its use, and its critical reception. The type history of the photograph is investigated, so that it can be classified historically. It will be compared with other photographs that are related in terms of topic. Taking all this information together, a first attempt is then made to produce an interpretation of the intended meaning of the picture.

In a final step, aspects such as knowledge about context, arrangement, contradictions and unique features of the photograph, the role of the photographer and the photographed, the form and contents, are related to each other. Then, in a step referred to by Panofsky as 'synthetic intuition', an attempt is made to arrive at the 'real' meaning or the deep structure of the photograph by hermeneutic means. Whether the 'real' meaning of an individual photograph bears typical traits of a phenomenon must then be investigated using comparable photographs. In contrast to other products of the representational arts, the non-intended element plays a considerable role in photography. Nevertheless, for both the intended and the non-intended messages of a photograph there are formal reasons, elements of content, and precise methodological indicators than can be understood by others. Since a photograph presents a visual expression, it is always possible to show how something was expressed on the photograph. To this extent, this final step of the interpretation, which usually serves to formulate hypotheses, is scientifically precise and can be replicated with other photographs.

Possibilities and limitations of the method

Photographs are not simply depictions of the world or representations of objective facts, but offer a kaleidoscope of individual and collective perspectives. Therefore photographs in themselves cannot be taken as proof of social-historical developments. But the viewpoint of the photographer represents a reflection of this development. For example, the fragmentation of our lives and the volatility of our insights, which we attribute to modernisation of society in its post-modern phase, are presented metaphorically in photographs, and the photograph itself is the first medium of modern mass culture.

Photography has brought the world closer together. The same pictures are used to transmit information worldwide, although that does not mean that their effect is the same everywhere. Whatever the case, they form the world view of those that view them; they serve both information and manipulation. A critical school of viewing, along the lines of Alfred Lichtwark, Johannes Itten, Laszlo Moholy-Nagy or Paul Klee, seems to be more necessary than ever.

To be sure, in the case of social-historical investigations there is also a risk of cultural relativism. The apparent ambiguity of the photo-graph can lead to the viewer giving up all attempts of explanation. Transient images can then be seen as a metaphor for the transience of views.

The more one knows about photography, the more photographs one knows from different periods and regions, the more precisely one can interpret them, the more varied are the possible applications:

1. *The photograph as document.* The contents of the photographs as an archive of what actually existed. Like no other medium, photographs preserve the images of former times.
2. *Photographs as a source for studying environments and effects.* The material, physical, and aesthetic forms of expression shown in photographs can be interpreted as reactions to historical and experienced phenomena. Changes to these forms of expression can be described in the shorter or longer term. The postures and gestures of individuals, the presentations of occupational groups,

institutions, young people and society can be seen in the complex layering of continuity and change, of intention and effect, of external influences and internal logic.

3. *Photographs as a medium of visual communication.* It is not only what photographs depict that can supply information for investigations in educational science. It can also be profitable to investigate how photographs are employed and what types of image are preferred in order to present or illustrate pedagogically relevant topics.

4. *Photographs as evidence of a development process.* Photographs that children and young people take of each other, for example, can be interpreted as a source for the analysis of the process of self-realization of active subjects.

5. *Photographs as a source for intra-cultural and inter-cultural comparisons.* Photographic sources are linked to cultures, but they show elements of style that transcend an individual culture. For this reason, photographs are excellent as a source for example for intercultural research into childhood and youth.

6. *Photographs as a medium for intercultural projects.* Both existing and specially prepared photographs can be used to promote the intercultural communication within Europe, for example, between students, or between teachers.

In conclusion

The complexity of the medium corresponds to the complexity of the world we live in: the way photographs are set up indicates the patterns of pedagogic and social situations and relationships. The value of photographs as a source lies in the fact that the photographic medium provides both internal and external image representations. This is due firstly to the value attached to photographs in private and in public life, both historically and in the present. It also depends on the visual nature of photographs. They can be seen as a visual link between the external image of the society and the expressive image of individuals. The easier the technology is to use, then the more directly will an image represent a visual reaction to an impulse, the closer will it be as a source to the expressions of people about their life. This is comparable with recordings of speech. However, the direct nature of the visual does not mean that photographs are not coded. Personal experience is just as much a part of the visuality of photographs as image formulas that have developed historically. Photographs – like all images in art – show the central, the problematic, and the burning issues of an age.

MINNA VUORIO-LEHTI

5 Constructing Firm Faith in Education: Finnish Films in the 1930s and the 1940s

Introduction

There was strong faith in education in the Western world in the twentieth century. Education was seen as panacea for social and economic problems. It was believed that good education and culture would promote both the welfare of individuals and, eventually, the welfare of nations. Finland was not an exception in this process. At the end of the twentieth century education was taken as a part of building a nation-state in Finland. It was thought that with the help of education the common people would gradually become aware of their own state and identity. Education did not mean only schooling. It was believed that when the general educational level of the common people increased social and economic problems would necessarily decrease. As the first concrete steps towards a civilised nation the popular education system was created in the 1860s, and compulsory education was introduced in the 1920s.[1] The seeds of education fell on fruitful ground in Finland. It was said that in the twentieth century the Finns had an exceptionally strong faith in education which was seen particularly in the manner the working class realized the importance of education and was ready

---

1 A. Halila, *Suomen kansakoululaitoksen historia* (The history of Finnish primary education) (Porvoo-Helsinki: WSOY, 1949); T. Iisalo, *Kouluopetuksen vaiheita: Keskiajan katedraalikouluista nykyisiin kouluihin* (Education in Finland: from the medieval cathedral schools to today's school system) (Helsinki: Otava, 1991); O. Kivinen, *Koulutuksen järjestelmäkehitys. Peruskoulutus ja valtiollinen kouludoktriini Suomessa 1800–1900 – luvuilla* (The systematisation of education from the nineteenth to the twentieth century) (Turku: Turun Yliopisto, 1988).

to finance their children's schooling.[2] This growing faith in education became especially clear in the 1950s, when grammar schools had more pupils than they could teach. Families wanted a good education for their children and that was what grammar schools were believed to offer.[3] Later on strong faith in education was seen in the numbers of those pupils who wanted to continue their studies in the upper secondary school and in higher education.[4]

This faith in education has traditionally been examined by using written documents. Yet there is evidence to suggest that the very creation of this was achieved partly through visual means and, more specifically, through films.[5] This chapter will, therefore, examine what kind of educational space was constructed in two Finnish films in the 1930s and the 1940s.[6] The period is interesting precisely because it was the time when the outlines of mass education were constructed in

2   A. Karisto and S. Montén, *Lukioon vai ei: Tutkimus Alueellisista eroista helsinkiläisten lukionkäynnissä ja lukiolakkautusten vaikutuksesta* (To the Upper Secondary School or not?) (Helsinki: Paintmedia Oy, 1996).

3   K. Kiuasmaa, 1982, *Oppikoulu 1880–1980* (The grammar school in Finland 1880–1980); J. Salminen *et al., Yksityisoppikoulujen historia, 1872–1977* (The history of private grammar schools in Finland, 1872–1977) (Helsinki: Painatuskeskus, 1995); M. Vuorio-Lehti, 'Oppikoulun yhdestoista hetki?' (The eleventh hour of the Finnish grammar school?), *Kasvatus* (The Finnish Journal of Education), 30.2 (1999), 170–84.

4   M. Vuorio-Lehti, 'Œ Ylioppilastutkinto itsenäisessä Suomessa' (The matriculation examination system in Finland from the 1920s to 1990s), *Suomen kouluhistoriallisen seuran vuosikirja* (1997) (Saarijärvi: Gummerus, 1997), pp. 95–122. E.-M. Heikkilä, 'Ylioppilassuman synty Suomessa' (The flow of matriculated students in Finland) unpublished diploma work, University of Turku: Deparament of Education, 1991; O. Kivinen, *Koulutuksen järjestel-mäkehitys: Peruskoulutus ja valtiollinen kouludoktriini Suomessa 1800–1900 – luvuilla* (The systematisation of education from the 19th to the 20th century) (Turku: Turun Yliopisto, 1988).

5   The meaning of a picture and how it takes shape is a very complicated process where the image, viewers, time and place are in interaction. Meaning takes shape in interaction with private and public cultural experiences. See K. Saarinkangas, *Kuvasta tilaan* (From Picture to Space) (Tampere: Vasta-paino, 1999), p. 7.

6   For a parallel see P. Cunningham, 'Moving Images: Propaganda Film and British Education 1940–45', *Paedagogica Historica*, 36.1 (2000,) 389–406.

Finland. So there might be some 'hidden messages' in the films the function of which was to tell audience that education is worthwhile.

This chapter will ask how education is presented in two particular films. What kind of functions do these films give to education? And how is education spoken about in these films? What kinds of values are related to education? And how is education visualized in the films? In what follows the films are analysed on a narrative level whereby the cinema creates an illusion of a true story or true world.

The two full-length feature films addressed here tell a story of their own time and express an attitude to social problems. These films were chosen both because education is so clearly a part of them and because they were very popular in their own time. The films shared the discourse of the importance of education but they do so in very different ways.

Finland and Finnish national films in the 1930s and the 1940s

Finland gained her independence from Russia after the First World War in 1917. The next two decades were a time when this new nation-state was legitimized. In the 1920s relations with other European countries was very important. International agreements and new relations were established on many levels. In the 1930s the situation was different. Finland had its legitimated position in Europe and now it was time to turn the gaze to Finland's own questions. Of course, the world economy was behind everything. At the beginning of the decade worldwide depression has its impacts on Finland too. Firms went bankrupt, unemployment reached record figures and the mental atmosphere in society was one of despair. At the end of the decade the boom began. The 1930s were the time of right-wing parties in the Finnish Parliament. Left-wing parties were in opposition and the Communist Party was forbidden. It worked underground. The Second World War changed everything. Five hard war years consolidated the

Finnish people and healed the wounds of the Finnish Civil War of 1918. The left-wing parties even got a majority in Parliament. The hard times continued until the middle of the 1950s. There was a shortage of raw materials and food. The situation was made worse by the fact that Finland had to pay huge war indemnities to the Soviet Union. Until the 1950s there was a controlled economy in Finland, and as late as the 1950s about 60 per cent of Finland's population lived in the countryside.

The Finnish film industry had its 'Hollywood period' from the 1930s to the 1950s. Comparing the Finnish films to those of Hollywood sounds maybe a little bit amusing, but there are characteristics in the Finnish film industry which make this comparison understandable. First of all the American rational film production model was adopted in Finland as in so many other small European countries. The Hollywood period of Finnish national film was its hour of glory. Films and film-going were the most popular form of entertainment. The number of the cinemas was high and audiences reached new records all the time. In those days films spread to rural areas and more new national films were produced than ever before. Finnish audiences loved American films but national films were very popular too. In the 1930s and the 1940s there were two national film companies in Finland: Suomi-Filmi Oy (The Finnish Film Company) and Suomen Filmiteollisuus (The Finnish Film Industry).[7]

The two films described here are 'Hulda from Juurakko' and 'Olli's Surprise'. They were both produced during the Finnish Film Industry's 'Hollywood period'. 'Hulda from Juurakko' was based on Hella Wuolijoki's play. The film was directed in 1937 for the Suomi-

7   K. Laine, 'Elokuvateollisuutta Rakentamassa' (Constructing the Finnish film industry), in Teoksessa A. Honka-Hallila, K. Laine, M. Pantti (eds.), *Markan tähde:. Yli sata vuotta suomalaista elokuvahistoriaa* (Turku: Painosalama Oy, 1995), pp. 70–134 (p. 79); K. Laine, *'Pääosassa Suomen kansa': Suomi-filmi ja Suomen Filmiteollisuus kansallisen elokuvan rakentajina 1933–1939* ('Finnish people in the main role': Suomi-Filmi and Suomen Filmiteollisuus, the constructors of Finnish national films) (Helsinki: Gummerus, 1999); K. Uusitalo, *Suomalaisen Elokuvan Vuosikymmenet* (The decades of Finnish national film) (Helsinki: Otava, 1965), pp. 25–45.

Filmi Company by Valentin Vaala.[8] 'Olli's Surprise' was a Finnish Film Industry film and was directed in 1945 by Orvo Saarikivi.[9] Both films were very much of their own time. 'Hulda from Juurakko' told a story from 1930s Finland and 'Olli's Surprise' concerned the immediate aftermath of the Second World War. Social problems of the time were dealt with in the films, although they were not 'problem films'. Both films were very popular. It was said by critics of the film 'Hulda from Juurakko' that it was entertaining but that Hulda's education and social mobility from servant to a member of the educated middle class was a good example for the audience to see. The strength of 'Olli's Surprise' was that it tried to find answers to certain specific social problems that arose after the Second World War.

'I am Hulda from Juurakko'[10]

The film *Juurakon Hulda* (Hulda from Juurakko) was the most successful film of the Suomi-Filmi (the Finnish Film Company) in the 1930s. The film was released in the autumn 1937 and was based on Hella Wuolijoki's play which had premiered in the spring of that year. The author also offered her manuscript to Hollywood and had it accepted. In 1947 it was released under the title *Farmer's Daughter*.[11]

Hella Wuolijoki was a woman who knew what she wanted. She was born in Estonia but she moved to Finland in the beginning of the

8   Valentin Vaala (1909–76) worked for 28 years at the Suomi-Filmi Company. During his career he directed 39 films. He was one of the most famous film-directors in Finland and it is said that his professional skill was very high. He directed both comedies and dramas. *Juurakon Hulda* was regarded as one of his best films. See Uusitalo (1965), pp. 135–6.

9   Orvo Saarikivi (1905–70) directed 20 films during his career. He was famous for short films but he directed four full-length feature films too (Uusitalo, (1965,) 158–9).

10   The Finnish word 'Juurakko' means 'stump' in English.

11   K. Laine (1999), pp. 341–2.

twentieth century. She was a famous writer, businesswoman and politician. She was a member of parliament and later on managed the Finnish Broadcasting Corporation. Her political background was left-wing and that is why her opinions were sometimes silenced in the conservative-minded Finland of the 1930s. Her popularity was high, however, so that the conservatives knew that it was politically unwise to silence Wuolijoki. Wuolijoki had difficulties also because of her sex. In the 1930s it was very difficult to publish books or create a career if you were a woman,[12] and in fact Wuolijoki had to use a male pseudonym (Juhani Tervapää). Nevertheless, she had opportunities to publish her works. The pseudonym helped her to publish plays and other writings. In this way she could avoid a preventative censorship. The women in Wuolijoki's books and plays were always very strong-minded and brave.[13]

Hella Wuolijoki was the most successful playwright in Finland at the end of the 1930s. She wrote two 'servant stories'. 'Hulda from Juurakko' was one of them. Hulda's route from the poor Finnish countryside to Helsinki and to parliament was an unlikely event in the 1930s but not an impossible one. There were in fact two figures in parliament who had shown that working-class women could be successful. It is said that the play represented Finnish society in the 1930s very well. Through her plays Wuolijoki legitimated a totally new way to picture Finnish people. In the film social questions about rural life, class and gender were emphasized. Hulda, for instance, spoke to the members of parliament about the problems of the country people. This kind of scene had not been included in the stage version. The stage version also differed from the film in terms of language. In the theatre version Hulda used popular language and her speech included swearwords. In the film version Hulda's speech was very neutral by nature. Wuolijoki was famous for her rich characters in her plays. Audiences felt her characters were very real.

---

12   P. Karkama and H. Koivisto (eds.), *Ajan paintessa* (Pressure of Time) (Jyvaskyla: Gummerus, 1999), p. 12.

13   P. Koski, *Hella Wuolijoki: 1886–1954* (http: llhaku.kansallisbiografia.fi – 15.xi.2000), pp. 1–8.

The social effects of the film *Hulda from Juurakko* were extraordinary. To some extent the film exceeded the boundaries of its narrative space. The story and the actors seemed to be very real to the audience – and it appears that the film created the effect of non-fiction, although in reality it was really rare for a poor woman to educate herself in the 1930s. On the other hand the effects of the film spread to the social space of the audience too. Many a female viewer later reported (via a large national questionnaire) that the example of Hulda had opened her eyes. It was a totally new experience to the female audience to see how a poor uneducated girl from the country-side was so resolute and successful with her studies. It was amazing too that the girl's background was very 'low'. And a new dimension was that the film was situated in a city. Traditionally the countryside represented all good and real things in films; and cities were injurious places. But in this film the situation was totally different. It is said that the film *Juurakon Hulda* spoke to the audience in a new way and that, as a result, it was popular with women, the working class and the intelligentsia.[14]

From a poor girl to an educated member of parliament

What follows is a synopsis of the film *Hulda from Juurakko* that pays attention to the central messages of the film and provides an analysis of how these messages are conveyed.

Hulda, a young woman, has to leave her home in rural Finland because there are too many persons in her family to look after. She travels to Helsinki and wants to get a job. She does not find a place for the first night and she sits on a bench in a park in the middle of the night. A little group of men (they are members of parliament) come from a restaurant. They see Hulda and want to help her. They take Hulda with them and continue their evening at lawyer Soratie's flat. At the lawyer's home Hulda asks for a job and the lawyer's aunt,

14   Laine (1999), pp. 362–63.

Conny, takes her on as a housemaid. Hulda is happy with the job but faces several difficulties when she tries to adapt to the new environment. The most difficult thing is that she often does not understand what people are saying even though they speak the same Finnish language as herself. She feels herself uneducated and stupid and gets told as much. Lawyer Soratie informs her that in his home the housemaid must be invisible. Hulda accepts her position as an invisible housemaid but decides to go to evening school. She wants to learn to understand what people around her are talking about. Hulda begins grammar school studies at adults' evening school and after that she continues upper secondary school studies and finally graduates at the university. She studies very quickly and shows that she is not stupid at all. Lawyer Soratie does not know that his housemaid is educating herself; but aunt Conny and the other housemaid at the lawyer's home encourage Hulda to continue. Hulda interests herself in politics too and decides that one day she will be a member of parliament. Her dreams break down when the lawyer's rich female friends hear about Hulda's plans. They announce in public that Hulda was found seven years ago sitting on a bench in a park, implying that Hulda is nothing more than lawyer Soratie's mistress. The situation is very humiliating to Hulda but she shrugs it off. At the end lawyer Soratie wants to marry Hulda who initially opposes the suggestion but after all accepts it. 'Why did I fall in love with a dictator like you?' asks Hulda in the end of the film. With the help of her education and 'good' marriage she achieves a place in the upper middle class.[15]

'I want to study all subjects'

In *Hulda from Juurakko* education is a tool that helps people out of the quagmire of ignorance. In addition, education helps them reach better positions in society. The film has many levels. In relation to education questions of gender and social class were also examined.

15   *The Finnish National Filmography*, part 2 (1995), 153–160.

Hulda is a woman from a low-social-status family who wanted to educate herself. At the end of the film she had achieved a place in the upper middle class. This position was reached with the help of education and marriage. In the film education and culture were represented as absolutely good things – socially and personally transformative. The message was that education was not solely a privilege of the higher social classes. It was the right also of poor people.

Concrete things, places, spaces, events, time, other students and teachers represent education and schooling in the film. Places like school buildings are shown to the viewer. There are pictures of adults' evening school and pictures of the university. Hulda carries out her studies in different places. She is attending lessons, walking in school corridors, reading her books at home.

At lawyer Soratie's home there is a huge bookshelf in his library. This bookshelf is shown a couple of times in the film. First it is like a big monument which Hulda cannot reach. She cannot understand even the names of the books. Later Hulda borrows books from the shelf and reads books written in German. Books and maps, for example, are things which represent learning. They are signs which every viewer can understand as the paraphernalia of education.

Movement is one element which represents Hulda's education. There are scenes in the film where Hulda's feet on a stairs are shown. Hulda is mounting the stairs running, which is a symbol of her progress in her studies.

With the help of editing Hulda's double role as a housemaid and a student are represented. The pointer in Hulda's hand in one scene is changed into a carpet beater in the following scene. In one scene Hulda gives a lecture and in the following scene she serves evening tea to her master.

Time is a significant element in the film. A clock shows the viewer that Hulda reads every night very late. As time passes the number of books in Hulda's own bookshelf increases, and it is also shown how the seasons change.

Figure 15: *Hulda from Juurakko.*

The other students in those schools where Hulda studies are in a marginal position. They do not occupy an active role and their only duty is to fill the empty space. One teacher is pictured as Hulda's friend who encourages her in her studies. The teacher's role in the film is to show Hulda's eagerness to learn. Hulda's own family is also in a marginal position. She sends letters to them and writes how she works and studies very hard. Hulda is an uneducated girl from the countryside when the story begins. At the end of the film she is educated and very elegant. Education affects her whole being. She says many times in the film that her motive to learn is to help her family and other uneducated people.

'What will happen if all people want to educate themselves?'

In the film education is an instrument which helps Hulda to reach a position amidst the intelligentsia/educated people. Education and especially adult education is the route to a better life. In the 1930s it was certainly not very usual in Finland that a woman from the lower social class educated herself and became elected to parliament. As a matter of fact it was an illusion for most women. Hulda's education was such an exceptional matter in the 1930s that the scriptwriter has included Hulda's 'godfathers' talking about it in the film. There is an interesting scene in the film where those godfathers admire Hulda's achievements but wonder what happens in the future if all working-class people want to educate themselves. What will happen to the social structure of society and who is going to pay for all the schools and libraries that will be needed? Will housemaids become better educated than the gentry?

The message of the film is that education is absolutely valuable. It is a modern possibility to free oneself from the fetters of gender, social class and urban-rural division. Education offers the possibility of a radically new future.

Olli Suominen's surprise with a white cap[16]

The film *Suomisen Olli Yllättää* (Olli's Surprise) was released in 1945. *Olli's Surprise* was a very popular film in its own time. It received positive criticism and it was recommended especially to older people and parents. The film was the fourth part of a series which told about the life of the family Suominen. Actually the

---

16 In Finland a white velvet cap is a sign that you have passed the matriculation examination at the end of the upper secondary school. The cap is used always on the first of May.

Suominens premiered as a 'radio family' in the 1930s.[17] Because of its huge popularity on radio it was decided to bring the family to the screen. The Suominens was an ideal Finnish family which had the same problems in everyday life as real Finnish people.[18] The family was a middle-class family living in Helsinki. The family's father was a lawyer and the mother was a housewife. They had three children and, after the Second World War, adopted two more. There was a housemaid in their home though the mother was at home. The atmosphere at the Suominens was warm and it was represented as an exemplary family. This series was very popular in Finland from the 1930s to the 1950s.[19] Radio and television families similar to the Suominens appeared in other European countries too. The family Björk was the Swedish radio and television family in the 1930s and in the UK there were the Robinsons and the family saga *Mrs Dale's Diary.*[20]

It was said that the Suominens were an ordinary Finnish family. This was not true. For instance in the 1940s when the family Suominen lived in Helsinki most Finns lived in the countryside. The family's father was a lawyer who had an office in public administration. In reality only three per cent of the working population had the same social position as he had. Maybe it is better to say that family Suominen was a picture of an ideal family of its time.[21]

17   The name 'Suominen' refers to the word 'Finnish'.
18   A. Honka-Hallila, 'Suomisen Ollin 400 Kepposta' (Olli Suominen's 400 practical jokes), *Filmihullu*, 4 (1990), 32–37.
19   J. Sihvonen, 'Suomisen Perhe – Elokuvat' (The Family Suominen in film), *The Finnish National Filmography, part 2* (1995), p. 666.
20   D. Nordmark, 'Suomisen Perheen Sukulaisia Ruotsissa ja Maailmalla' (The Family Suominen's Swedish relatives), *Lähikuva*, 1 (1996), 7–18, p. 7.
21   J. Sihvonen (1995), p. 669.

I have to go back to school

Olli's Surprise tells about the problems of its own time. In the story the Second World War is over and Olli and his friends return home. The family is very happy because Olli survived the Second World War. But it is not so easy to adjust back to normal life. When Olli left to go to war he was a schoolboy. Now he is a man and he does not want his parents to control his life. Olli faces several problems. The worst of them is that he and his friend have to finish their upper-secondary-school studies. School does not feel to be the right place for them. The other students are younger than the ex-soldiers and during the wartime they have learnt habits which do not fit school life. Some teachers try to make the ex-soldier's life intolerable. Another problem is that Olli and his friend need more money than their parents can give. The answer to this problem is Mrs Johansson who offers the boys a possibility to earn money in a criminal way. After many difficulties Olli finishes his studies and decides to stay on the straight and narrow. Education will help him in the future.[22]

In the film *Olli's Surprise* schooling and education are represented in many ways. Education is connected to concrete places and everyday routines at school and at home. At home the family speaks all the time about school: Olli has to go back to school; Olli promises to do his best at school; Olli's sister Pipsa reads her English home-work; younger sister Maija asks if Olli is too old for school; and the whole family is nervous when Olli takes his matriculation examination.

Many scenes in the film occur in typical classrooms with desks, blackboards and maps. Teachers play an active role in the film. They discuss the problems of postwar Finland and the difficulties facing young people. There are two kinds of teachers in the film: those who understand young people and then those who do not. For instance, the mathematics teacher is a very strict old man and the history teacher is gentle. The headmaster is very fair to the young men and tries to explain to the other teachers that they must understand those who were in the war for many years.

22   *The Finnish National Filmography*, part 3 (1992), pp. 434–39.

Olli's school attendance is pictured quite a lot. There are scenes in the film where Olli reads his books at his desk at home. Very interesting (and historically valuable) is a scene where Olli is taking his matriculation examination.[23]

Olli's 'surprise' occurs at the end of the film: he has passed the examination and as a symbol of it he puts the white cap on his head. The last image of the film shows Olli and his girlfriend also wearing the white cap. This final sequence is full of Finnish national symbols. A young couple is sitting together. The sun is shining and beautiful nature surrounds them. They have finished their schooling – white caps are the sign of that – and the future is waiting for them. In *Olli's ‚Surprise* education represents triumph over adversity. In that last image Olli's troubles are clearly being related to postwar troubles of Finland in the 1940s.

Figure 16: *Olli's surprise.*

23   The matriculation examination is a nationwide exam taken at the end of the upper secondary school.

'A child of the gentry does not do casual work'

Education is one of the main themes in the film *Olli's Surprise*. It is mentioned for the first time in the first dialogue where Olli talks with his friends. Olli's family speaks of the importance of education all the time and also Olli's friends are aware of the value of education. Some of Olli's friends have interrupted their grammar school and it is interesting to see that these figures are pictured as thoughtless youngsters. It is self-evident to Olli's parents that he should study at grammar school. It belongs to the family's middle class 'habitus'. This comes very clearly to viewers' eyes in a scene where Olli borrows money from the family's housemaid. He is a little bit embarrassed and says that it would be better for him to look for a job. Hulda, the housemaid, immediately says that this is not right. Olli is from a good family and his place is at grammar school.

There is one 'advertising campaign' for vocational schooling in the film which is quite surprising. In one scene Olli meets a friend who belongs to a working-class family and who is now in vocational school. This young and vigorous man proudly presents his school and the camera follows this presentation. Olli admires his friend's school and its friendly teachers but it remains self-evident that his place is in grammar school. There is a clear division in the film between schools that are for middle-class students and those for working-class students.

But schooling is a trial for Olli. He really tries to do his best but it does not help. At the second half of the film the family understands Olli's problems with schooling and the father says that Olli can finish his education if he wants to. 'You need not become a matriculated student if you do not want to,' says father. 'What shall I do then?' asks Olli looking shocked. He makes the decision to try once again.

When watching *Olli's Surprise* it feels sometimes that the whole film is constructed as teaching material. It is true that *Olli's Surprise*, more than *Hulda from Juurakko*, is a film which deals with social problems of the time. That is why some social problems of young people (the dangers of alcohol, criminality and sexual relations before marriage) are taken into consideration. *Olli's Surprise* is black and

white in nature. Things are either good or bad; there is nothing between them. In the end, good triumphs and the ideal family manages
to achieve a proper upbringing for Olli who makes the decision his
parents approve of.

It is worth while to educate yourself!

Hulda from Juurakko and *Olli's Surprise* are both films where
education is presented as a positive and necessary social good. They
share the discourse of faith in education. But the elements of that faith
vary very much between them. Characteristics of the film *Olli's
Surprise* are stability, the present (the 1940s) and nationalism. In
Hulda from Juurakko key characteristics are change, the new future, a
new social order and changing gender identities.

The film *Olli's Surprise* is conventional in mode and effect. Its
narrative does not contain any other surprises than Olli's graduation.
The story is concerned to sustain traditional principles of its own time.
Even the filmic mode in *Olli's Surprise* was conventional and in the
Hulda from Juurakko unconventional. Its function is to preserve or
restore society, its structure and its good old values.

Hulda from Juurakko is more dynamic. It compels the viewer to
take an attitude to social and gender questions. Hulda's resolutions
are, in their context, very unconventional. Her studies and ideas are
atypical for a woman in the 1930s. Hulda's story is so unreal that it is
easy to believe that the viewers in the 1930s took her as the model of a
'modern woman'. It encouraged especially women and working-class
people to dream about education and imagine a life where they themselves could determine their own future. The picture presented is still
very powerful some seventy years after its premiere. Even now its
social and political message comes through.

Both films represent education via common elements: schools,
classrooms, teachers, homework, books and bookshelves, pencils,
pointers and maps. While the messages of the two films vary, above

all both represent education positively so that the audience could understand dominant if contradictory meanings: education unites the nation and it frees you from the fetters of gender, social class and the urban-rural division. So it is always worth while to educate yourself!

DAVID LIMOND

6 Keeping Your Head and Losing it in the Celluloid Classroom: (non)Sense and (Feminine) Sensibility in Two Films of Boarding School Life: *If…* and *Picnic at Hanging Rock*[1]

[M]y mother, when I misbehaved, wield[ed] the threat of sending me back … [from the US to Belgium] to boarding school, so that it came to seem like the awful final punishment. (The term [in French] for boarding school is *pension*, which happens to sound a lot like *punition*.)[2]

The rationale

David Geoffrey Smith considers the film *Menace II Society* 'brilliant'.[3] Viewing it 'As a former school teacher and now instructor in a university program for the preparation of teachers […]' in southern Alberta, Canada, far away from the ghetto of Compton, Los Angeles, in which it is set, what does he see?[4]

---

1 I am grateful to Dr Ian Grosvenor of the University of Birmingham who has never once quibbled at my pirating of his term 'celluloid classroom' and to the staff of the library of the University of Central Lancashire in Preston where this piece came to fruition in the summer of the year 2000. It is dedicated to Verity Ratel Tansy who also came to fruition around that time.

2 L. Sante, *The Factory of Facts* (London: Granta Books, 1998), p. 49.

3 D. G. Smith, 'Experimental hermeneutics: interpreting educational reality', in *Pedagon: Interdisciplinary Essays in the Human Sciences, Pedagogy, and Culture* (New York: Peter Lang, 1999), pp. 45–60 (p. 48).

4 Op. cit., p. 51.

> The film has pertinence [...] not only because it is about young people, African-Americans in this case, but because for an educator one of the most telling moments [...] occurs when Cain [the central character] openly declares: 'I didn't learn f___n' sh_t [*sic*] in high school.'[5]

Smith takes several personal lessons from the film. Not least of these is the following:

> As a teacher, I feel challenged to be more mindful of the cultures of difference that increasingly predominate in our classrooms. The film underscores the way knowledge-forms are connected to forms of life, so I cannot in any way pretend that what I teach is somehow value-free or not connected to the structures of power in my own society.[6]

What follows seeks to explore the way(s) in which I, like anyone involved in the study of history, necessarily more distant from that subject matter than ever Alberta could be from Compton, respond to and am moved by two films which depict distinctive educational communities in the past. Historians, whether of education or not, are often expected to comment on historical films solely in terms which 'focus on issues of authenticity, at times in relation to significant questions of interpretation'.[7] The authenticity of films is certainly a cause of outbreaks of popular disquiet and perhaps there is an expectation that historians will, or at least should, take some lead in this.[8] But to lead any such reaction against either of the pieces featured

5   Smith, 'Experimental hermeneutics', p. 48.
6   Op. cit., p. 51.
7   S. Higashi, 'Rethinking film as American history', *Rethinking History*, 2.1 (1998), 87–101 (p. 87). See, for example, K. Manners Smith, review of *Anna and the King*, in *American Historical Review*, 105.3 (2000), 1060–1. Typically, when historical films are reviewed in the *AHR* in these terms they are found wanting. In this case *Anna and the King* is judged no exception.
8   Random example: eight letters (more than half the total published that day) on *The Patriot* in *Daily Telegraph* (21 June 2000), 29. Further examples can be seen in the responses variously to *Joan of Arc*, S. Hayward, review, *Sight and Sound* (February, 2000), 30–3; *Saving Private Ryan,* C. Hastings 'D-Day hero fury at knighthood for Speilberg: film director's honour reignites anger among Normandy landing veterans', *Sunday Telegraph* (31 December 2000), 4; *Stalingrad,* J. Graffy, 'Stand until death', *Sight and Sound* (April 2001), 28–31; *Captain Corelli's Mandolin,* J. Farouky, 'Rhapsody in blah', *Time* (14 May 2001), 85; *Pearl Harbor,* C. Raven, 'Sunk without trace', *New Statesman* (11

here is not my intention. It is true that I am interested in the use of the semi-autobiographical *If...* for the purposes of teaching. In teaching a subject entitled 'Social History of the Classroom' I have used it to introduce students to aspects of the history of boys' public boarding schools in England but my intention is not to review its usefulness for that purpose by gauging any aspect(s) of its accuracy.[9] Rather, returning to the lead I take from Smith, I shall seek to see (and show) how I am 'challenged' by both *If...* and *Picnic at Hanging Rock* [hereafter *PHR*] when I think about the history of education as teacher/researcher. That is to say: I shall consider what *good* it does me to see and think about these films. I value *If...* and *PHR* not because they tell me about the (educational) past, but because they make me *think* about the past.

> Rather than opening a window directly onto the past [certain historical films can open] a window onto a different way of thinking about the past. The aim is not to tell everything about the past, but to point to past events, or to converse about history.[10]

What follows then is a kind of travelogue of my journey into these films. I shall concentrate on one scene from each in particular and attempt to show how it has prompted me to think about the work of 'doing' the history of education.

June 2001); and *Black Hawk Down,* M. Hubard, 'Not just a film', *Prospect* (March 2002), 64–66.

9   In passing however I cannot help but note that its claims to accuracy may run deep. Unremarked on by anyone else who has written on the film so far as I can establish is an intriguing fact identified by John Rae. Substantial portions of several of the key speeches of the headmaster in *If...* were taken, with a degree of fidelity sufficient to interest a copyright lawyer, from a contemporary book by a senior member of staff at Eton. See J. Rae, *The Public School Revolution: Britain's Independent Schools, 1964–1979* (London: Faber & Faber, 1981), p. 109 and J. D. R. McConnell, *Eton – How it Works* (London: Faber & Faber, 1967), pp. 123, 153–4, 161, 163–4 and 172.

10   R. A. Rosenstone, *Visions of the Past: The Challenge of Film to Our Idea of History* (Cambridge: Harvard University Press, 1996), p. 63.

The scenes in brief

In Lindsay Anderson's 1968 film *If...* several scenes are set in the gymnasium of the elite boys' boarding school which forms the backdrop to the action. 'Symbolic acts of love and war take place [...] the[re]'.[11] In one, a blond-haired new boy, in the 'arcane and self-perpetuating slang' of the school '(a) scum', watches in rapt fascination as an older pupil, a member of the final year/sixth form though significantly one who is not a power-wielding 'whip', executes gymnastic exercises.[12] This 'very romantic sequence' is the symbolic commencement of a love affair between these two.[13] In time the gymnasium will be the location in which the prefectorial whips beat Travis, Wallace and Knightly, the rebellious central characters, drawing from them the blood they will avenge in the film's apocalyptic conclusion. But for now it is a haven of peace, a place set out of time, filmed in languid slow motion. The new boy, Philips, dresses and watches his idol, Wallace, perform.

If... does not have a conventional narrative.[14] Thus it does not lend itself to summary. Its many absurdist devices defy easy explanation – which of course they are intended to do. It is an avowedly illogical film. There is no 'then' to complete the causal sequence; nothing follows anything else. Suffice it to say the following. The three main protagonists are senior pupils in their final year of schooling in England in the 1960s. Over the course of the film they engage in acts of resistance against its regime. These acts escalate until they culminate in what may or may not be the murder of a member of the school's staff. This in turn comes in retaliation for the

11   E. Sussex, *Lindsay Anderson* (London: Movie Magazine/Studio Vista, 1969), p. 80.
12   J. Richards and A. Aldgate, 'The Revolt of the Young: *If...*', in *The Best of British: Cinema and Society, 1930–1970* (Oxford, Basil Blackwell, 1983), pp. 147–61, (p. 147).
13   Sussex (1983), op. cit., p. 80.
14   It is literally a textbook example of unconventional narrative. See A. Rowe, 'Film form and narrative', in J. Nelmes (ed.), *An Introduction to Film Studies* (London: Routledge, 1999), pp. 92–128, Case Study 3, '*If...* – An Alternative Text' (pp. 124–6).

whips' beating of the three for their 'general attitude'. En route to the film's climax the three acquire two supporters – one the new boy described above and another, the Girl, encountered first during an episode of truancy from the school on the day of an important rugby match.[15] This handful of crusaders, having purged the school's symbolic unconscious mind, a storage space under the chapel, of its accumulated detritus make terrible use of a cache of arms they find there. It is with these that they rain down fire on the pupils, parents, staff and others who have gathered for Founder's Day, the centre of the school's ritual calendar. In the dying moments, the Girl fires a single shot to kill (execute? martyr? murder?) the headmaster as he attempts to reason with the rooftop protesters whom he still believes himself to 'understand'.

I turn now to my second selected scene – the last moment of contact between the character Irma and her schoolmates in Peter Weir's 1975 film *Picnic at Hanging Rock*, an adaptation of Joan Lindsay's novel of the same name.[16] This scene too – in both book and film – is enacted in a gymnasium. Irma is the only known survivor of a party of girls, and a teacher, who are lost (presumed dead?) on the eponymous Hanging Rock. She returns to Mrs Appleyard's ladies' college having been found in circumstances as mysterious as those in which she and the others disappeared. A period of exposure to the elements has apparently left her with retrograde amnesia and she can (or will) say nothing of what happened to her. In this scene she is ushered into the school's small gymnasium where the other girls are performing synchronised exercises to musical accompaniment. She is to leave the school shortly and this occasion is intended to be a bidding of fond farewells. In fact it very quickly degenerates into a terrifying orgy of recrimination as the other girls, led by one who, had she not fallen

15   The fact that the Girl, one of only three female characters in the film, is never named is subtly elided in Gavin Lambert's recent memoir of Anderson and their work together. In a description of the closing moments of *If...* Lambert refers to her as 'Christine', a blurring of the character with the actress by whom she is played – Christine Noonan. 'Mick Travis on a [...] rooftop [...] opens fire with a machine-gun [...] joined [...] by Christine, Wallace, Phillips and Johnny (Knightly).'

16   J. Lindsay, *Picnic at Hanging Rock* (London: Vintage, 1967/1998).

behind, might also have disappeared on the rock, crowd about her and demand that she tells what they are sure she knows of the others' fate. Such is the intensity of the pent-up emotions released that one timid schoolmistress cowers, mouse-like, behind her piano stool. Order is only restored when another, no less shocked and terrified by events perhaps but somehow still more self-possessed, administers to the riot's ringleader the universal cure for hysterics – a slap. Only then is Irma, 'fastidious Irma, who deplored all female odours', released from her temporary captivity, 'hemmed in by angry faces enlarged in hateful proximity to her own'.[17]

In common with *If...*, *PHR* could hardly be said to have a con-ventional narrative: 'there is an emphasis on character and sensibility, rather than strong story lines', but *PHR* is somewhat more easily summarized.[18] The location is a college or seminary for young ladies on the edge of the Australian outback in the year 1900. With the exception of the Cinderella-like character Sara, the girls set out on their annual Valentine's Day picnic. In the drowsy afternoon, four venture onto the rock. One of the girls turns back but three go on. It may be that these three are drawn to venture further but neither their whimpering friend who declares the rock to be 'horrid' and will go no further, nor we, can hear or see as they do – 'there is a thick cloud upon the mount' obscuring our vision of their vision(s).[19] Seen to leave by no one, a teacher later departs from the picnic ground, perhaps in search of the girls, and does not reappear. Irma is found on the rock, though almost at the cost of his own life, by a young man who is, in truth, driven to search not for her nor any of the others but for the character Miranda, by whom he has been preoccupied since having one fleeting glimpse. As her Shakespearean namesake before her, she tantalizes this knight-errant. The paper chase trail he lays allows his groom (squire?) to complete the rescue of the missing girl even when he himself has fallen down exhausted. The remainder of the film charts the dissolution of Appleyard College. 'It is Irma's

17   Lindsay, op. cit., pp. 136–7.
18   S. Dermody and E. Jacka, *The Screening of Australia: Anatomy of a National Cinema*, vol. 2 (Sydney: Currency Press, 1988), p. 106.
19   Exodus: 19: xvi.

presence rather than absence with Miranda, [and] Marion [the other lost girl] and [the teacher] Miss McCraw that destroys [it].'[20] Sara, is an orphan whose guardian has not paid her fees for some time, and on whom Mrs Appleyard 'has fixed [...] as symbolic [cause] of the breakdown of order and the familiar at the College',[21] – making her, to the cash-strapped headmistress the naughtiest girl in the school. She dies in mysterious circumstances, as does the school itself – pupils are withdrawn, staff resign. It only remains for Mrs Appleyard to lose her life on the rock that has apparently deprived her of everything else she once owned or valued.[22]

The films

If... is an absurdist masterpiece. I admire it greatly despite concurring with the contemporary reviewer for whom it had 'fascist implications'.[23] *PHR* is sometimes unfavourably compared to the book, though both are rich in melodrama.[24] The excessive plot devices of the book are preserved intact in the film. (Not least the subplot involving Sara, the College's resident orphan, a philanthropist's ward, and her brother Albert, the groom who finally brings Irma off the rock.) But to these the film adds its own touches. (I find the weepy pan pipe accompaniment both symbolically leaden and audibly irritating.) Like

20   J. A. Wainright, 'Desolation Angels – World and Earth in *Picnic at Hanging Rock*', *Antipodes* (December 1996), 121–3 (p. 123).
21   Wainright, op. cit., 123. Sara's death is generally understood as murder but has been taken to be a suicide. See J. Dawson 'Picnic under Capricorn', *Sight and Sound* 42.2 (1976) 96.
22   This event, described graphically in the book, is only alluded to in the film – variously in a voice-over or an on-screen text depending on the version one sees.
23   D. Speirs, review of *If...* in *Screen*, 10, 2 (1969), 85–9 (p. 89).
24   '[Joan] Lindsay never lets us forget how the threads of the [story's] tapestry are woven together, the warp and woof are woven together [but these] remain ultimately inscrutable to Peter Weir's *auteur* eye' (in Wainright (1996), op. cit., 123).

If..., I admire *PHR* despite my objections but unlike *If...* I can imagine *PHR* as a better film. Only bad art is ever definitive, but it is perhaps a mark of truly high art that, as in the case of *If...*, one cannot easily see how it could be improved. I base this judgement as to the value of *If...* as art primarily on two things. First amongst its achievements stands the ultimate sundering of authorial intent and audience perception in the accidentally achieved but consummately employed switching between colour and monochrome.[25] (Like a gambler, a genius may sometimes make his/her own luck and Anderson was nothing if he was not a lucky man.) Second in my list of causes for calling *If...* truly great comes its exploitation to the fullest extent of delicious ambiguity in its final moment.[26] (Those unfamiliar with the film are best advised to see it as no mere description can quite express what happens, or does not happen, at the end. Suffice to say the film simply ends, with no resolution of the plot.) It is however also this final moment that moved David Spiers to take Anderson to task as follows:

> Disquietingly, at the end, we find ourselves [...] fighting for pure instinct [...] in other words in a fascist position. The[se] fascist implications [...] are made even more disturbing [by] coming [...] from somebody who has always aligned himself with the left.[27]

If...'s final sequence has always struck me in similar terms: firing on unarmed civilians is hardly to be condoned, even if it seems as though

---

25   The circumstances behind this, the product of a shortfall in finance, are discussed in Lambert, op. cit., pp. 142–3. See also L. Anderson, 'Notes for a Preface' in his and D. Sherwin's *If...: A Film by Lindsay Anderson and David Sherwin* [published text of script] (NY: Simon and Schuster, 1969), pp. 9–13 (p. 10).

26   In the mid-1980s, when Anderson's career was stalled, there was a proposal for a sequel to be made but no satisfactory way could be found of resolving the ambiguity of the final moments of the original. Who is to say if the world was denied or spared *If... 2*? (Lambert (2000), op. cit., p. 233).

27   Speirs (1969), op. cit., p. 89. Intriguingly this, to my mind, most intelligent of reviews is omitted from those (I count fourteen in all) surveyed in Richards and Aldgate (1983), op. cit., p. 160. Of which only one (in the *Listener* – 'the most hating film I know', quoted in Richards and Aldgate, op. cit., p. 152) is judged unfavourable.

no blood is actually spilled until the headmaster's death and even if the civilians do arm themselves and fire back in the end.[28] Anderson defended himself against such charges by saying: 'I find the last sequence of the film exhilarating, funny [...] [and] plainly metaphorical.'[29] *If...*'s central conceit is its abusurdism: absurd devices are used to depict absurd realities – what other language could suffice? This being so, the final sequence can be seen as no less absurd than anything that has gone before – 'plainly metaphorical'. And yet...

Above all else *PHR* is a costume drama. This term is often synonymous with historical fiction but it has rarely been as apt as when applied to *PHR*. The film begins with the lacing of corsets and ends with the straight-laced Mrs Appleyard coming apart at the seams. When Miss McCraw is 'seen' (not seen by us but reported as having been seen by another character after she has left the picnic unnoticed) ascending the rock she has stripped to her undergarments – which are perhaps the blue stockings that her academic calling might seem to imply/require. Of the girls who disappear on the rock it has been said: 'The[y] [...] are swallowed up [...] because of what they are [...] Victorian girls were meant to be "delicate" [combining] refinement [and] sickliness. Corsets [were] the physical expression of [this]

---

28   Those reflecting on *If...* have sometimes been moved to remark on the resonance between this final scene and the public school rebellions of the eighteenth and nineteenth centuries. '[*If...*] could all be regarded as real, even the final rebellion...the Great Marlborough Rebellion in 1851, when the boys [...] arranged a great firework explosion [could be seen as] a pyrotechnical precursor of *If...*' (Richards and Aldgate, op. cit., p. 157). But if literal precedent is needed then something more appropriate may be the outbreak planned at Standon Farm Approved School in 1947 when 'a handful of boys [...] laid plans to burst in on the monthly staff meeting with Bren guns'. These were to be stolen from the armoury retained in the school for the use of its military cadet force, a common feature of elite British boarding schools, but perhaps more surprising in an approved school – a residential/custodial establishment housing young offenders (R. Adams, *Protests by Pupils: Empowerment, Schooling and the State* (Basingstoke: Flamer Press, 1991), p. 46). A literary antecedent for *If...* is suggested by Michael Bracewell in the shape of the 1947 novel *The Castle Children* by Nancy Hayes: see M. Bracewell, *England is Mine: Pop Life in Albion from Wilde to Goldie* (London: HarperCollins, 1997), p. 26.

29   Anderson (1969), op. cit., p. 12.

deformity.' 'Miranda's [...] is the beauty of pain – the corset.'[30] From the producer's memoirs[31] it is evident that as much care and attention went into the outfitting of the young actresses in the film as was the case in the late-nineteenth and early-twentieth-century ladies' seminaries and private schools on which Appleyard College is based.[32] Perhaps authenticity can be achieved by many means.

In the title I have described *PHR* as one of two films of *British* boarding school life and on the one hand, Australian commentators have not been reticent in disavowing it as an Australian film. '*Picnic at Hanging Rock* [...] has an air of perverse Britishness – or Europeanness.'[33] But on the other, it has been said that:

> *Picnic at Hanging Rock* signals an important turning point. It made no apology for being Australian. But that does not mean it insisted on its parochialism. On the contrary, it found the very means by which to transcend the limitations of the parochial. It was cleverly and deliberately painterly in its portraiture – apt as a period reference but also as a coded reclamation of the local, i.e. national.[34]

Certainly *PHR* has some degree of European precedent. Even if 'the subject [of the supposed disappearances on the rock] has rapidly worked its way into the national folklore [of Australia]', the study of the emotional culture of girls' boarding schools has distinctly European precedents.[35] Disregarding genre works of schoolgirl fiction, ex-

---

30   I. Hunter, 'Corsetway to heaven: looking back at *Hanging Rock*' (1976), re-printed in A. Moran and T. O'Regan (eds.), *An Australian Film Reader* (Sydney: Currency Press, 1985), pp. 190–3, pp. 191 and 192. 'In a sense, the corset [is] a machine for the erotic production of seductive femininity', V. Steele, 'The Corset: Fashion and Eroticism', *Fashion Theory*, 3.4 (1999), 449–74.

31   P. Lovell, *No Picnic: An Autobiography* (Sydney: Pan Macmillan, 1995), p. 158.

32   See, for example, G. Avery, *The Best Type of Girl: A History of Girls' Independent Schools* (London: Andre Deutsch, 1991), pp. 292–5.

33   Dermody and Jacka (1988), op. cit., p. 105.

34   A. Mitchell, 'Tripping the Light Fantastic: a bit of a look at Australian film', *Sydney Studies in English*, 23 (1997/8), 7–23 (p. 11).

35   Dawson (1976), op. cit., p. 96. Surprisingly, nothing to do with the story of a fateful picnic at hanging rock *does* appear in the principal reference work on

amples to be brought forward here might include *Olivia*, a thinly veiled autobiographical story published as though written by the eponymous heroine (hence sometimes known as *Olivia by Olivia*) by Dorothy Stratchey Bussey and Charlotte Bronte's novel, also largely autobiographical, *The Professor*.[36] It is in works such as these that the textual/textural conventions of the institution known variously as the ladies' college/seminary or *pension demoiselles* (= a punishment of girls?) have been established. But if *PHR* has any direct European precedent it is perhaps the fiction (in different versions and under different titles: a film, a play and a novel) which for convenience I shall call *The Child Manuela* (*TCM*). [37] *TCM* makes *PHR* possible by coining the emotional currency that is spent in *PHR* – mortification: punishment of girls. That, I charge, is the underlying theme of all fictions of this sort.

Australian folklore. G. Beed Davey ed., *The Oxford Companion to Australian Folklore* (Melbourne: Oxford University Press, 1993).

36   D. Strachey Bussey/'Olivia', *Olivia* (London: Hogarth Press, 1949); C. Bronte, *The Professor* (London: Dent, 1852/1910).

37   Christa Winsloe's story was first (1931) a film, directed by Leontine Sagan with the German title *Mädchen in Uniform* (Girls in Uniform); in 1932 it appeared in London as a play, which Sagan also directed, under the title *Children in Uniform* (though with a significantly revised, indeed reversed ending); in 1934 it became a novel – the English title of which is *The Child Manuela*. The novel extends the scope of the film and the play in that it details the 'back story' of the life of the eponymous heroine before her arrival at her school. The film and the novel share the same ending – Manuela is successful in the suicide attempt she aborts at the conclusion of the play. 'Readers [of the novel] already familiar with Leontine Sagan's film version [or the play] [...] may [...] find their sense of time disrupted. The film and play are set firmly in the years of their making [...] the novel is set much earlier [...] in about 1901', A. Hennegan, 'Introduction' in C. Winsloe, *The Child Manuela* trans. A. Neill Scott (London: Virago, 1934/1994) pp. vii–xviii (p. ix). See also the text of *Children in Uniform* in *Famous Plays of 1932–1933* (London: Victor Gollancz, 1933). Such is the understandable confusion caused by this proliferation of texts and formats that while the *front* cover of the Virago edition of *TCM* claims that it is 'The novel of the film', the *back* says it is the 'novel on which the famous film [...] was based'. Neither statement is strictly correct though the first is 'less wrong' than the second.

Response to the scenes in detail

At this point I turn to some explanation of my interest in the chosen scenes. To repeat: my concern is not so much with what I may have learned from these scenes but how I have been prompted to think since viewing them. 'We each possess inside us a sort of *imaginary museum* (original emphasis) of the cinema where we keep the various films and film fragments that have touched us deeply or made a profound impression on us.'[38] I consider below how and why I have been impressed by two such exhibits from my own imaginary museum. In the first place then, I turn to *If....* My theme here is simple. On viewing the scene involving Wallace and Philips in the gym, the scene which begins the affair that will end with the latter tucked like a teddy-bear in the bed of the former, I am inevitably reminded of the homosocial subculture so long associated with elite British boys' boarding schools.[39] This 'tradition' is deep-rooted and vexed. The 'unreformed' public schools that existed before the 1860s were often places of fearful repute.

> Late Victorian old gentlemen, looking back at their early Victorian, or pre-Victorian, schooldays, found it difficult to believe that those times of rabid licence had ever really happened.[40]

At Harrow in the 1850s John Addington Symonds, autobiographer and pioneer sexologist, was witness to what was effectively male rape.[41]

38   M. Lefebvre, 'On memory and umagination in the Cinema', *New Literary History*, 3.2 (1999), 479–98 (p. 480).
39   It is probably more correct to say elite *English* boys' boarding schools, because both culturally and historically such schools are more deeply rooted in England than anywhere else in Britain. See S. A. C. Gorard, 'Fee-paying schools in Britain: a peculiarly English phenomenon', *Educational Review*, 48.1 (1996), 89–93; and G. Walford, 'How important is the Independent sector in Scotland?' *Scottish Educational Review*, 19.2 (1987), 108–21.
40   J. Chandos, *Boys Together: English Public Schools 1800–1864* (Oxford: Oxford University Press, 1985), p. 153.
41   P. Grosskurth (ed.), *The Memoirs of John Addington Symonds* (London: Hutchinson, 1984): see especially pp. 94–5. See also Chandos (1985), op. cit., pp. 307–39.

But it was only from the late 1860s onwards that concern with sexual morality grew in the world of public schools.

> [F]or early Victorian headmasters such as [Thomas] Arnold, the words 'immorality', 'vice', 'sin' and so on, emphasised the wickedness of indiscipline [...] and drunkenness, rather than sexual impurity [...]. But [...] immorality with an increasingly explicit sexual connotation was already becoming a frequent theme of sermons by 1860, and by the 1880s [...] had become an obsession.[42]

In thinking about the Philips/Wallace scene in *If...* and the literature associated with the homosocial subculture of the public schools,[43] I came to realize that there is not as yet an accepted language for exploring the shift in attitudes associated with the period from the 1860s to the 1880s. Quite simply, it was then that I understood this shift represented a *moral panic*: 'an extremely heightened form of [social] awareness and concern'.[44] Here lies the scene's value as far as I am concerned. It has inspired me to find a way to speak about the past, where before I lacked the necessary language. Challenged to think by what I had seen and needing a language to render it I stumbled on an association I might otherwise never have made. Indeed, so far as I can tell, it is an association that has not hitherto been made. That is to say: the literature on the homo-social subculture of the public schools does not describe the attitudinal shift of the 1860s to the 1880s as a moral panic and the literature on moral panic does not refer to that attitudinal shift as an example of the

42   J. R. de Symons Honey, *Tom Brown's Universe: The Development of the Victorian Public School* (London: Millington Books, 1977), p. 167. In passing: amongst the most disturbing stories of Anaïs Nin is 'The Boarding School' in which an episode of terrifying sexual violence breaks out in an elite Brazilian boys' residential school. See her *Delta of Venus and the Little Birds* (London: BCA, 1996), pp. 41–4.

43   In addition to discussion in passing in such general historical works as those of Chandon, Honey and J. Gathorne-Hardy (*The Public School Phenomenon, 1597–1977* (London: Hodder and Stoughton, 1977)), see also the most specialized text: A. Hickson, *The Poisoned Bowl: Sex, Repression and the Public School System* (London: Constable, 1995).

44   E. Goode and N. Ben-Yehuda, *Moral Panics: The Social Constitution of Deviance* (Oxford: Basil Blackwell, 1994), p. 103.

phenomenon.[45] There is I think no feature of the archetypical moral panic that this shift does not satisfy.

> [R]eactions to unconventional behaviour do not arise solely as a consequence of a rational and realistic assessment of the concrete damage that the behaviour in question is likely to inflict on the society [involved] the reaction is out of proportion to the threat, [and] we are led to ask why it arises.[46]

The 'obsession' which emerged in the pivotal period of the 1860s to the 1880s was not the product of a 'rational and realistic assessment of the concrete damage [...] likely to [be] inflict[ed] on the society [of the public schools]' and it was 'out of all proportion to the threat [posed]'. Debate still exists amongst those who make most of moral panic as a category of analysis as to the circumstances in which panics come to occur – in a medical analogy we might say the vectors by which they spread – but this does nothing to interfere with my central claim.[47] Further:

> [Moral] panics are not like fads, trivial in nature and inconsequential in impact; they do not come and go [...] without trace [...]. Moral panics are a crucial element in the fabric of social change. They are no marginal, exotic, trivial phenomenon but one key by which we can unlock the mysteries of social life.[48]

As surely as it satisfies the test of irrationality and disproportionality, the shift I have already described satisfies this criterion of lasting importance.

In the example given above I have tried to show a benefit accruing to one who watches *If...* and ponders what it shows. I turn now to a final pair of 'lessons' to be learned from watching one scene in *PHR*. When Irma is mobbed in the gymnasium, I find two things borne in on me. First I am reminded that school life has often been a

---

45 Two recent and extensive surveys of the literature on this subject are Goode and Ben-Yehuda (1994), op. cit. and K. Thompson, *Moral Panics* (London: Routledge, 1998). Public school homosociality features in neither.
46 Goode and Ben-Yahuda (1994), op. cit., pp. 29–30.
47 The 'grassroots', 'elite-engineered' and 'moral entrepreneur' models of moral panic causation and spread are described in Goode and Ben-Yahuda (1994), op. cit.: see especially pp. 127, 135 and 138–9.
48 Goode and Ben-Yahuda (1994), op. cit., p. 229.

form of costume drama, and secondly I am moved to think about hysteria in schools. I explore these themes in turn below.

In her red outfit (as detailed in the book and faithfully depicted in the film), what are we to make of Irma?[49] The scene works for me as a vivid contrasting of ladies' seminaries and girls' schools. In 1900 elite educational culture in Britain and its empire stood poised on the cusp of change in at least one important respect. The ladies' college/ seminary, where 'one [would] never have smelt instruction'[50] in formal academic subjects, was not replaced *at once* by the girls' school with its 'pretensions [...] to prepare girls for [...] active and useful roles in the public and private spheres'[51] but this transition was well under way.[52] It has been argued that, in certain deep ways, the ladies' seminaries which endured largely intact[53] from perhaps the late 1700s to the middle of the twentieth century, with their curriculum of 'accomplishment[s]', their homely atmosphere of 'parlour boarders' and their emphasis on girls' deportment and gentility, resembled the

49   '[H]emmed in by the laughing, sobbing girls, a tuft of [her] scarlet feathers trembling, rising and falling [she was] like a wounded bird' (Lindsay (1988), p. 136). Before the scene degenerates in this way it does depict an activity typical of girls' schools in Australia in the period. See R. Burns, 'Dis/ease: discourse in Australian health and physical education' in A. Mackinnon, I. Elgqvist-Saltzman, A. Prentice (eds.), *Education in the 21st Century: Dangerous Terrain for Women?* (London: Falmer, 1998), pp. 67–80.

50   J. Austen, letter to her sister Cassandra on a visit to a ladies' seminary, 20 May 1813, in R. W. Chapman (ed.), *Jane Austen's Letters* (Oxford: Oxford University Press, 1969), pp. 305–9 (p. 308).

51   K. E. McCrone, '"Playing the Game" and "Playing the Piano": physical culture and culture at girls' public schools 1850–1914' in G. Walford ed., *The Private Schooling of Girls: Past and Present* (London: Lawrence and Wishart, 1993), pp. 33–55 (p. 35).

52   For a description of an extant seminary operating *c*.1901 see G. Raverat, *Period Piece: A Cambridge Childhood* (London: Faber & Faber, 1952), pp. 65–74.

53   It has been suggested that there was a transitional stage between the ladies' seminary and the girls' school in the shape of the ladies' college, emerging towards the end of the 1840s and 'closer in type to the new schools established for upper-middle-class boys in the previous decade' (E. Jordan, '"Making good wives and mothers"? The transformation of middle-class girls' education in nineteenth-century Britain', *History of Education Quarterly*, 31.4 (1991), 439–62 (p. 440)). I freely admit that I have largely elided this distinction but not, I hope, unreasonably so.

apparently progressive girls' schools that first emerged in the last quarter of the nineteenth century.[54] But I think that this debate can be put aside for the present. Suffice it to say that in style, if not necessarily in substance, the two types of institution were markedly different. In the gymnasium scene, we see these two – the seminarians and the schoolgirls – toeing the line like rival boxers. In her hat, gown and cape Irma is a lady. In their gym-slips the girls are – simply girls. She is sexualised by her dress. They are trivialized. This scene is truly costume drama. She is going out into the world ahead of them and already they and she are a generation apart.

The demise of the ladies' seminaries significantly contributed to the creation of the category '[school]girl'. This was both effected by and reflected in the emergence of uniform for girls attending elite schools. And this of course is something anyone might find out easily enough in much of the literature available.[55] But there is no device that I know of more graphic and more memorable than a viewing of this scene in *PHR* to make that point. Here I turn to the second thing I take to be memorably demonstrated here.

The study of outbreaks of school hysteria is a distinct field of enquiry – and one which boasts a surprisingly large body of literature.[56] Whatever other conclusion(s) may emerge from such study it seems possible to be unambiguous in asserting that hysterical outbreaks in schools are an enduring phenomenon.[57] How and why such

---

54   McCrone (1993). I have long tended to be persuaded by McCrone's point and found it all the more credible when I began work on this piece and stumbled across the photographic study of Cheltenham's most famous school made by Sue Packer where the sulky schoolgirl jostles for position alongside the sultry sophisticate. Here the culture of the ladies' seminary seems only overlaid on, not replaced by, that of the girls' school. See *Cheltenham Ladies: A Portrait of Cheltenham Ladies College, Photographs by Sue Packer* (Manchester: Cornerhouse Publications, 1989). For a more recent account of the depiction of girls resident in a boarding school see: S. de Bruxelles, 'School criticised for "provocative" calendar photos', *The Times* (15 December 2001), p. 15.

55   For example, Avery (1991), pp. 287–295.

56   R. E. Bartholomew and F. Sirois, 'Epidemic hysteria in school: an international and historical overview', *Educational Studies*, 2.3 (1996), 285–311.

57   'Two Kenyan boarding schools have been closed following invasions of ghosts, it was reported yesterday. Gigoto secondary school, in Kinangop, was closed after ghosts attacked boys on Thursday night and pupils stampeded, said the

things occur, whether the school context is necessarily or only contingently related, what cultural and other considerations may predispose certain groups to be more likely to be so affected and so on are not questions to be tackled here. My point is simply this: as before in *If...*, this scene in *PHR*, this depiction of epidemic – if short-lived – hysteria, drives home something I think worthy of note. Significant emphasis was placed in the construction of the new-pattern girls' schools on rationality. In doing this it seems to me that in effect their founders – the Busses, the Beales, the Doves and the rest – sought to use the academic as a cure for the epidemic.[58] The discourse of the girls' school from the late nineteenth-century onwards (perhaps even into the twenty-first) emphasises calm sobriety over febrile impetuosity. The gym-slipped girls in the gymnasium are *dressed* to be the next generation of their sort, but they are not *ready* to be that generation.

Conclusion(s)

In this piece I have striven to give a personal demonstration of the way(s) in which one interested in the history of education might employ films not so much as sources of facts but as sources of inspiration. Facts are plentiful; inspiration is rare. I for one do not reject any reasonable source of inspiration lightly and I believe that others might profitably adopt the same attitude.

Daily Nation. Kambaa girls' school, Kiambu, was allegedly invaded by spirits on Saturday', *Daily Telegraph* (19 July 2000), 20.

58   Mary Francis Buss, 1827–94, North London Collegiate Ladies' College; Dorothea Beale, 1831–1906, Cheltenham School; Francis Dove, 1847–1942, Wycombe Abbey.

KEN JONES

7 Rhetorics of Educational Reform: Britain 1945–1947

I

In a speech which heralded the policies his government adopted after its 2001 election victory, Tony Blair spoke in the autumn of 2000 of his vision of secondary education. It would be rigorously segregated, via setting; it would be 'personalized' – that is, responsive to the needs of individual learners; and it would via such means contribute to the rebuilding of a national community, in which everyone would feel that they had a stake.[1] Their frequent reiteration since Blair's speech does not make these various goals and techniques any more easily compatible.[2] Segregation does not sit well with personalization, since it imposes restrictions which may be incompatible with personal aspiration; neither fits comfortably into a project of national cohesion. Yet these are tensions which the policies and discourses of New Labour, like those of previous social-democratic governments, have in some way to handle. They are the necessary product of positions, shaped by conflicting social interests, that on the one hand emphasize differentiation, and on the other hand validate what are held to be the emancipatory powers of education, and the community of interests which it can create. In this chapter I want to explore the ways in which such tensions were worked out in the discourses of an earlier period, that of the immediate post-war years in which the British welfare state was constructed. In doing so I will suggest that the contemporary dis-

---

1   P. Wintour, 'Blair plans schools revolution', *The Guardian*, 9 September 2001, 1.
2   Department for Education and Employment, *Schools: Building on Success* (London: Stationery Office, 2001).

cursive contradictions of New Labour are not entirely novel. The chapter will have a double focus, on both the textual and the visual rhetorics of differentiation, emancipation and community.

By 'rhetorics', I do not mean a deployment of language to deceive. Rhetoric is not something intrinsically 'false', to be counter-posed to a 'reality' which it is assumed to misrepresent. In the classical Aristotelian theory which has in recent years provided a stimulus to the thinking of a new generation of social linguists, rhetoric is improvised or partly-improvised speech which draws from a pre-established repertoire of linguistic resources. It is designed not necessarily to mislead but to persuade – to move an audience and to effect particular actions. To do this, the rhetor – the speaker – has to discover available means of persuasion and to link them to strategies appropriate to situation and purpose. Rhetoric thus stems from the speakers' reading of his/her audience and the suasive challenge they present; and from his/her ability to utilize communicational resources appropriately.[3] Here, I extend rhetoric's original focus on the medium of speech and the context of face-to-face communication, to other media and other communicational situations. The texts I consider, both written and visual, can usefully be understood in terms of their suasive strategies, and of their attempt to combine particular intel-lectual and affective resources to achieve effects that are in a broad sense political and that in their more specific aspects have to do with the reconciling of social contradictions within a single discourse.

I will suggest that these rhetorics were mutually reinforcing. In writing and through visual representation, discourses of reform oper-ated to develop a critique of the present and a vision of the future that was both emotionally powerful and politically within reach. At the same time, in a crucial paradox, they acknowledged and sustained established social hierarchies, so as to create effects that were both utopian and deferential. Both written and visual rhetoric worked to construct ensembles of meaning in which themes of childhood, nature, authority and social reform were combined in ways which supported and at the same time transcended a particular political programme:

3   Aristotle (*c*.335 BC), *The Rhetoric of Aristotle*, trans. L. Cooper (New York: Appleton-Century, 1932).

contemporary issues of policy were connected, by word and image, to impressions that linked sentimentally the everyday and familiar to promises of collective improvement and personal development that inspired without threatening. The visual – and the representation of the visual in written form – was an important element in such discourses, all the more so because it could operate less at the level of formal argument than, as it were, paratactically, compressing complex clusters of social meaning into single frames or short sequences. In doing so, it presented what could be called an affective case for reform.

II

Between 1944 and 1947 the education systems of England, Wales, Scotland and Northern Ireland were substantially changed, via a series of Education Acts – in England and Wales in 1944, Scotland in 1945 and Northern Ireland in 1947. The central aspect of this legislation was the provision of 'secondary education for all'. The Act's initiators claimed to be shifting British schooling from a nineteenth-century system in which secondary education was available only to a minority, to one in which it would be the birthright of all children, the means of securing economic advance and of building an inclusive national community. This was its central promise, and the basis of its mass appeal. It was also the locus of its ambiguities and the source of the conflicts which later came to surround it.

'Secondary education for all' in practice meant a system divided into three parts, all of which were supposed to enjoy a parity of esteem while actually receiving different levels of funding and promoting different sorts of curriculum. The Spens Report of 1938 had sketched a system based on a tripartite division into Modern schools, Grammar Schools and Technical High Schools. The Norwood Committee in 1943 had decided that these distinctions corresponded to the facts of social existence. Individuals had 'enough in common as regards cap-

acities and interests' to justify the separation of individuals into
'certain rough groupings'.[4] In first place there was the type of student
'who can grasp an argument or follow a piece of connected reasoning'
who was 'interested in causes', 'sensitive to language as expression of
thought' and alert to 'the relatedness of related things, in development,
in structure, in a coherent body of knowledge'. This was the kind of
student suited to, and developed by, the academic grammar school.
Second came the pupil 'whose interests and abilities lie markedly in
the field of applied science or applied art', and destined therefore for
Technical School. Then came a third grouping, composed of students
who 'deal more easily with concrete things' rather than with ideas. Into
this group, allocated to secondary modern schools, fell the majority,
who were 'interested in things as they are'. For the first few years of
the new system they had no opportunity of taking public exams; there-
after a small minority stayed on at school to take GCE exams at 16.

The Norwood Report imagined an entire mental and emotional
universe for its groupings, each of which lived, to switch metaphors,
on different worlds, inhabiting different subjectivities. It made plain
that far more was involved in the reconstructions of 1944–47 than the
setting up of an institutional system: what was also at stake was the
role of education in cultivating particular types of individual, who
were imbued from birth with specific abilities and aptitudes – which
natural qualities the school would nurture. The civil servants who
shaped the thinking of the Ministry of Education had a similar tripartite view of the child population, but their vision, in which questions of rule and order were close to the surface, was a harsher one
than Norwood's. Deriving their authority from classical philosophy –
in particular, from Plato – they referred habitually to the divisions of
humanity established by Socrates in Plato's Republic. 'You are all of
you in this land brothers,' Socrates wants to tell the citizens of his
imagined society, using terms perfectly compatible with wartime rhetorics of community. 'But when God fashioned you, he added gold in

---

4   The Norwood Report, *Report of the Committee of the Secondary Schools
      Examination Council on Curriculum and Examinations in Secondary Schools*
      (London: HMSO, 1943), p. 1.

the composition of those who are qualified to be Rulers; he put silver in the Auxiliaries, and iron and bronze in the farmers and the rest.'[5]

Plato's myth, of course, involves not just the identification of particular almost-fixed types of human being. It also attempts, by naturalizing difference, and suggesting that it is an intrinsic feature of the social order, to strengthen social unity: 'You are all of you in this land brothers.' Taken as a whole, the educational discourses of the post-war years attempted to hold on to both aspects of the Platonic project – hierarchy and community, though these themes were variously inflected in different documents, and by different interest groups within the policy elite.[6]

III

'Community' was a byword of post-war discourses about the social, in which 'education' came to signify not so much the inculcation of established values, as the development of a new kind of human being, embedded in a national community organized around values of democracy and citizenship, and experiencing daily the effects of a school system that was attentive to the whole range of her needs. Ellen Wilkinson, Minister of Education, wrote of the new kind of schooling that was being created, with 'laughter in the classroom, self-confidence growing every day, eager interest instead of bored uniformity'.[7] The *Times Educational Supplement* imagined children as 'wards of the state' each of whom would be given by benign authority 'the fullest

5   Plato (*c*.380 BC), *The Republic*, trans. D. Lee, (Harmondsworth: Penguin, 1955), p. 160.
6   J. Ozga and S. Gewirtz, 'Interviewing the education policy elite', in G. Walford, *Researching the Powerful* (London: UCL Press, 1995), pp. 121–35.
7   E. Wilkinson, 'Foreword', in *The New Secondary Education* (London: HMSO, 1947), p. 5.

opportunity to develop every innate power'.[8] The London County
Council, probably the most innovative of local authorities, envisaged
education as 'a matter of all-round growth and development' and
thought it 'indefensible to categorize schools on the basis of intellect
only'.[9] A burgeoning individuality was in this way linked to a national
community in which social bonds were stronger and class divisions
weaker: R. A. Butler, prime implementer of the 1944 Education Act,
imagined that it had created one nation not two.[10] The LCC wanted
schools to promote 'a feeling of social unity among adolescents of all
kinds and degrees of ability'. Tom Johnston, Secretary of State for
Scotland, concerned for the 'future generation of the race', called into
being an Advisory Committee on Education, and gave it the 'most
urgent' remit of promoting in schools a sense of common citizenship.[11]

The appeal of 'community' rested in part on the inclusive identities of war-time. But it also had a wider frame of historical reference.
'The rapid industrialization of the last century', noted a Ministry of
Education pamphlet, 'has brought with it many material benefits.'[12]
But at the same time, it was a process that aroused trepidation. 'For
the town-dweller' it entailed a loss: of standards of craftsmanship, of
'directness and simplicity' in social relationships, and of a 'sense of
community'. The 'closeness of nature' enjoyed by those brought up in

8   D. Thom, 'The 1944 Education Act: the art of the possible?', in H. Smith (ed.)
     War and Social Change: British Society in the Second World War (Manchester:
     Manchester University Press, 1986), p. 102.
9   G. C. T. Giles, *The New School Tie* (London: Pilot Press, 1946), p. 77.
10   R. A. Butler, *The Art of the Possible: the Memoirs of Lord Butler* (London:
     Hamish Hamilton, 1971), p. 96.
11   J. M. Lloyd, 'Tom Johnston's Parliament on Education: the birth of the Sixth
     Advisory Council on Education in Scotland 1942–3', *Scottish Educational
     Review*, 16 (1983), 104–15. Then, as now, the Scottish education system
     remained legally and administratively distinct. To a greater extent than in
     England, there was an element of comprehensive secondary education – in
     some smaller towns and rural areas there were 'omnibus' schools. But in
     Scotland, as in England, policy-makers resisted calls, even from their own
     advisory committees, to generalize this limited experience.
12   Ministry of Education, *New Secondary Education* (London: HMSO, 1947), p.
     31.

traditional communities had been lost. It was education's job to 'give back' to the student some of these 'good things that had been lost'.[13] It could do this by concentrating its attention on a 'balanced and harmonious development' in children, in which intellectual growth was seen as just 'one facet' of the whole child. Thus education was assigned a role in relation to industrialization – to what another Ministry pamphlet called the 'deadening routine of much industrial work' – that was both critical and compensatory.[14] The modality of the compensations it offered was extra- or pre-industrial. Behind the new secondary school stood the lost village: the future would restore a forsaken past. Yet the hierarchies that underpinned this past silently remained, implicit only in the cultural evaluations embedded in the texts of reform.

The famous document of the Sixth Advisory Council on [Scottish] Education, just as much as that of its English counterparts, was preoccupied with the role of mass education in a society damaged by industrialization, by the 'vast incoherent complex' of urbanization and the new kinds of culture they promoted.[15] If the social preferences of English educationalists were for the country village, then those of the Committee were for the country town which preserved something of the 'simple and stable community life of earlier times'.[16] It celebrated the 'homely, natural and pithy speech of country and small town folk in Aberdeenshire and adjacent counties' and in other parts 'outside the great industrial areas'. It deplored the cultural life and linguistic habits of the conurbations, where language had 'degenerated' into a 'worthless jumble of slipshod ungrammatical and vulgar tones, still further debased by the less desirable Americanisms of Hollywood'.[17] And just as sternly as the reports of the early part of the century it demanded that schools 'war unceasingly against' the mass of 'debased and incorrect speech', in a 'campaign against the speech of the street,

13   Op. cit., p. 31.
14   Central Advisory Committee – England, *School and Life* (London: HMSO, 1947), p. 58.
15   Scottish Education Department, *Secondary Education: a report of the Advisory Committee on Education in Scotland* (Edinburgh: HMSO, 1947), p. 11.
16   Op. cit., p. 11.
17   Op. cit., p. 181.

the cinema and the illiterate home'.[18] This was a rhetoric that summoned an imagined past and a culturally secure community in an effort to rescue education from depravation and change. As McPherson and Raab suggest, what motivated Scottish reformers was not a socialist egalitarianism – their imagined community was located far from the Clyde or the coalfields – but a vision of cultural continuity.[19]

Approaches like these defined for education a role in relation to the building of community. They invoked organic unities more than they addressed the needs of occupationally divided societies, and to this extent their rhetoric circumvented questions of hierarchy. This was not the case with the main advocates of government policy, who in their defence of the tripartite system both confronted and revalued occupational divisions. Labour's first post-war education minister was Ellen Wilkinson, who had in her own words 'fought her way through to university from a working-class home' and in the process developed strong loyalties to the selective secondary education which had helped her to do so.[20] Wilkinson's political background was in the socialist education movements of the 1920s and the hunger marches of the 1930s, and she brought from this experience a passionate, if not always convincing belief that the road to educational improvement lay through a revaluing of the dignity of labour, via the work of the secondary modern. With her Parliamentary Secretary, David Hardman, she sought to convince public opinion, that all secondary schools, of whatever kind, now enjoyed parity of esteem. Parents must be convinced, she reminded her civil servants in 1946, 'that the grammar school is now a specialized type of secondary school and not the real thing, any others being substitutes'.[21] This was not a view that was universally shared. It was challenged in parliament by the Labour

18   Op. cit., p. 63.
19   A. McPherson and C. Raab, *Governing Education: a Sociology of Education since 1945* (Edinburgh: Edinburgh University Press, 1988).
20   R. Barker, *Education and Politics 1900–51: A Study of the Labour Party* (Oxford: Oxford University Press, 1972), p. 89.
21   G. McCulloch, *Failing the Ordinary Child: The Theory and Practice of Working Class Secondary Education* (Buckingham: Open University Press, 1998), p. 62.

Left, and by evidence to the government's Central Advisory Council on Education, which suggested that the new system was not based so much on parity as on 'three social grades, arranged in [...] order of prestige and preference'.[22] Against this strengthening current, one of the last things Wilkinson did before her death in 1947 was to compose an eloquent preface to the Ministry's pamphlet – *The New Secondary Education* – in which she attempted a socialist defence of the tripartite system. She linked the existence of different types of school to an argument about the uniqueness of the individual child, and the consequent necessity of developing forms of education that could relate to individual needs and interests. 'These plans', she wrote, 'put the child first [...]. Their variety is designed to suit different children, not different income groups.'[23] She contrasted this approach with the demand put forward by her critics in the National Association of Labour Teachers, who were demanding at the time a 'grammar school education for all'. 'No child', she argued, 'must be forced into an academic education which bores it to rebellion, merely because that type of grammar school education is considered more socially desirable by parents.'[24] In fact, Wilkinson went further, to call not just for an acceptance of educational divisions, but also for a revaluation of the hierarchies of the labour process – the hierarchies which underpinned differentiation in schooling. Manual work, in this perspective, took on a new dignity. The world war had brought about a 'revolutionary change' in public attitudes to the 'craftsman' and the 'prejudices of three hundred years' were being swept away; a 'civilized community', people now understood, is dependent on its 'farmers, transporters and miners, its manual and technical workers'. From this perspective, the secondary modern was not an expedient means of handling mass education, but a crucial element in a project of social and cultural recognition.

The pamphlet itself reiterates Wilkinson's concerns, basing itself on the one hand on a commitment to differentiation, and on the other

22   Op. cit., p. 70.
23   Ministry of Education, *The New Secondary Education* (London: HMSO, 1947), p. 3.
24   Op. cit., p. 4.

to positions long associated with the progressive movement in education. The former involves a Norwood-like belief that while 'some are attracted by the abstract approach to learning' others, the majority, 'learn most easily by dealing with concrete things'.[25] The latter seeks to dignify the lower levels of the hierarchy by linking it to child-centredness, freedom and experiment. 'Everyone knows', the pamphlet asserts, 'that no two children are alike', and it follows from this that 'the curriculum must be made to fit the child, not the child the curriculum'.[26] This principle entails a break with a past that is imagined as being one dominated by deskbound rote-learning. Secondary moderns must not be pale shadows of the grammar school, and must break from academic models of learning. From now on, experimentation will be the norm, guided by teachers enjoying an autonomy in curriculum development, and encouraged to focus on learning through activity, rather than through books. This was a norm supported not only by Labour, but even, temporarily, by the Conservative Party as well, in a 1945 Conference resolution. Accompanied by such claims, invested with hope, the mass school began its development as an institution both segregated and experimental, second-grade and 'free'.

IV

Children's Charter (1945) was a film directed by Gerry Bryant and produced by the Crown Film Unit – closely linked to the Ministry of Information. Its subject matter was the 1944 Education Act. It was intended for showing in 'public places' rather than in commercial cinemas. Its background in the institutions and traditions of British documentary film-making has been well treated by Peter Cunningham, who points to the ambivalent position of the Crown Film Unit. On the one hand it was heir to the radical documentary work of the

25   Ministry of Education, *The New Secondary Education*, p. 23.
26   Op. cit., p. 22.

1930s; on the other it was closely linked to government information strategies.[27] I will not retread ground ably covered by Cunningham in his treatment of the institutional context. Rather I want to explore ways in which the tensions embodied in education's differentiated expansion were elaborated in a documentary rhetoric which was itself subject to contending pressures.

British documentary of the 1930s and 1940s sought to discover and make beautiful the ordinary processes of work and community. In doing so, it aimed to contribute to the construction of a society that was both more egalitarian and more conscious of its own implicit aesthetics. This is the framework in which *Children's Charter* belongs, but not without tension. For, like other films such as Jennings's *Listen to Britain,* it depicts not only a society in which the mundane is given an aura of beauty, but also one in which at the same time existing hierarchies are dignified. The film thus contributes the tensions of its own systems of representation to the discursive field of education, or, as Cunningham puts it, to the 'public space in which educational policies and ideologies are promoted'.[28]

27   P. Cunningham, 'Moving images: propaganda film and British education 1940–45', in *Paedagogica Historica*, 36.1 (2000) 391–405.
28   Op, cit., p. 391.

Figure 17: The examination room.

The film lasts fifteen minutes. In its course, it moves from darkness to light. The darkness is that of the examination room, where a gowned figure, back to camera, presides. Children, sitting at their separate desks, are taking the '11+', the test whose results enable the separation of children into different sectors of secondary education (Figure 1). The light of the film's final sequences is that of education outdoors, amid lakes, hills, fields. The film's authoritative and univocal commentary moves in a similar way. It begins by describing and personifying the different categories of children brought into being by the 1944 Act. It goes on to show the tender ways in which the education system copes with their different aptitudes. It concludes much more generally by setting aside its concern with selection and specialization and evoking instead the future that the Act makes available to *all* children. But in doing so, it does not set its later images against those of its first few minutes. On the contrary, the earlier images – those of children destined for different educational futures – are re-offered to us as desocialized examples of the general category 'children', a category distinguished by vulnerability, curiosity, and the quality of inwardness that the cinematography of British documentary characteristically imparts to those who are its subjects. We're invited to respond to children, in their everyday, 'unstaged' behaviour, as dignified, natural, quietly sensuous – the arm round the waist – subjects. In this pastoral aesthetic, something is gained – a certain democratisation. But much, including the children's probable futures, is overlooked. The final sequence of the film depicts a journey of hope rather than an experience of frustration and opportunity denied:

> These are some the things the new Education Act is setting out to do. The best schools in the country have already shown what can be done.
>
> *Medium long shot. Teachers and younger students entering school from playground. One girl at the back of the line has her arm round another.*
>
> But alongside them are these...
> *Medium close-up of facade of urban elementary school – St Matthews. Railings are prominent. Camera moves down to boys.*
>
> and these...
>
> *Dissolve to uneven playground, children all over the place.*
>
> and they're still in the majority.
>
> *Another dissolve to long shot of a nineteenth-century three-decker school building – the classic urban elementary school.*
>
> We must have new buildings.
>
> *Dissolve to medium long shot of new school; the camera moves along it.*
>
> And most important of all, teachers of the right type, who will make the pursuit of knowledge an exciting adventure.
>
> *'Adventure' is the cue for a cut to an outdoor shot. Boys on a hill, against the sky. A male teacher is with them.*

Every child must be given the chance to develop his talent and abilities to the maximum.

Cut to younger children in medium close up, entering school gate.

This is the first condition of a happy and interested citizen.

Boy eating ice cream. Medium close-up. Working-class urban street.

A thriving democracy depends upon each one of us thinking for himself and accepting his responsibilities as a citizen.

Cut to classroom discussion with older children.

Good citizenship depends upon good education. There cannot be one without the other.

Cut to three young girls, behind a railing. Medium close up.

We shall need more than laws to make this scheme a reality throughout the land.

Cut to long shot of industrial town.

Don't say we can't afford it.

Cut to cooling towers of power station. High angle shot.

The cost of four days of war alone would keep that scheme going for a year.

Cut to high-angle shot of a piece of artillery, in manufacture.

We can afford anything when we are buying the future of our children. Let us make this new Education Act a real Children's Charter.

Dissolve to trees, children (boys) running down to a lake. Long shot across the lake, blurred images of boys in the foreground. Music.

Cut to children (boys) sitting on a bank. Camera moves right along the line of children, then down the bank. Sunlight. A skyline.

The end.

Figure 18: The future beyond social division.

The visual elements of this complex rhetoric work to elaborate some of the key motifs of post-war reform. Perhaps the most important of these is so central and obvious that it can be easily overlooked: the construction of the child. Much more is involved here than the mere presence of children, as recorded by an objective camera. The figure of the child serves as the focus of an unspecified hope, in a secularised narrative of redemption. The film takes us from particular urban locations, condensations of the ugliness and poverty of the industrial revolution, to a space which is both natural and symbolic of an expansive, uncosted 'future'. This is the space that children, finally, inhabit. The soundtrack at this final point speaks a language of citizenship and democracy. The images provide a richer rhetoric, for whose purposes children's bodies are recruited. The half-naked boys whose image (Figure 2) concludes the film are embodiments of free-dom, vulnerability, naturalness, collectivity. They work to support an image of the future that is positive, hopeful and vague; unregimented, natural and beyond social division. I think that, in the moment of the film, this 'works' – it moves the audience; at least, it moved me. For a moment, it magically resolves the problems of an education system pulled between a pledge to the needs of all and the everyday privileging of the interests of a much smaller section. It chooses a different route from Wilkinson's, but accomplishes, more successfully, a similar kind of reconciliation.

V

'All our children'. It is a familiar phrase in public discourses about education. 'All' and 'everyone' have been part of the vocabulary of reform since the 1920s, at least, and since 1997, with a New Labour government, they are used more frequently than ever. These occurrences are signs of difficulty: their very continuation as slogans of change over seventy years is a strong indication of enduring failure. Yet they have a potency which is not entirely exhausted. Addressing us as members of a community, *Children's Charter* encodes aspirations that relate not just to institutional reform but also to much deeper motivations about the care and nurture of children. It has powerful effects partly because of the resources of which it makes use, and the availability of these resources depends upon a new balance of social and political forces. The immediate post-war years, following the defeat of fascism and the emergence in many countries of strong movements for social change, provided conditions in which discourses such as child-focused romanticism, radical and socialist imaginings of the 'golden city', and democratic anti-fascism could flourish. They provided *Children's Charter*, and many other documentaries, with a repertoire and a set of associations which do much to explain its force.

The rhetorical complexity of the film lies in the way that it combines a deployment of this repertoire with a respect for established institutions and social processes, to create an ensemble which is ultimately, one feels, conservative, but that leaves open a space for more democratic and egalitarian imaginings. The film serves to assure audiences that tripartite segregation is not the essence of the new education; and that the new system works in universally beneficial ways. But because aspects of its aesthetic quietly celebrate the 'ordinary' rather than the high-cultural, it points also to other social possibilities, in which 'all our children' serves as a basis for a different educational politics.

By contrast, the deployment of the same phrase in the texts produced by the current British government seems less powerful. The discursive repertoire glimpsed from the vantage-point of New Labour is remote from the ideologies – romantic or in some way socialist – that sustained earlier projects of reform, and perhaps as a consequence has no very attractive affective component. International competitiveness, partial privatization, accelerating institutional differentiation, and performativity in relation to a set of narrowly defined tests and targets do not provide resources for a persuasive rhetoric of change, even though they may amount to a coherent justification for it. This deficiency may help explain the discursive repetitiveness of New Labour, as well as the strong element of centralist direction that it brings to education: both prolixity and centralisation might be read as substitutes for successful persuasion. But what does seem plain, across a gap of nearly sixty years, is the persistence of educational divisions which policy-orientated rhetoric must somehow still seek to address.[29]

---

29 Sections II and III of this chapter article draw upon K. Jones, *Education in Britain 1944 to the Present* (Cambridge: Polity Press, 2003).

NICK PEIM

8 Dangerous Minds? Representing the Teacher

In *The Savage Mind* Claude Levi-Strauss defines myth or mythological thought as a kind of intellectual bricolage.[1] Bricolage makes use of ready-to-hand materials and tools. These components of construction are not necessarily designed for the task in hand. The rule of bricolage is to make do with whatever is available, to use in a new structure the remains of previous constructions and destructions.

Levi-Strauss's account of bricolage comes out of a structuralist project concerned to define the so-called 'primitive mind'. Poststructuralism problematizes the positivist assumptions of this position and, in short, may be characterized as regarding all cultural production and knowledge systems as effects of bricolage.

For discourses in the history of education this problematizes certain key concepts, and in doing so also introduces a certain mobility of forms and procedures. The apparently stable continuities, procedures, objects and structures of history may be seen as the effects of different kinds of bricolage. Their definitive character is lost. On the other hand, the characteristic stuff of history – archaeology, genealogy, the archive – may be seen as being positively opened to the same *productive* logic of 'bricolage'.

Two texts came my way via quite different routes from different fields of representation, different ways of knowing, different 'archives'. I put these two texts together in a kind of semiotic bricolage. What educational discourse could conjoin these (apparently) radically different beings within the frame of a unitary account of 'the school' and one of its key symbolic figures, 'the teacher'?

---

1   C. Levi-Strauss, *The Savage Mind* (Chicago: The University of Chicago Press, 1966), p. 17.

Figure 19: Mr Shoveller, 1896.

Figure 20: Michelle Pfeiffer, 1996.

1.1 Interesting things can happen sometimes by placing two texts of radically different identity together. The texts can be 'read against' one another. This can be a technique for reading that highlights, and problematizes, perhaps, the relations between texts 'themselves', the textual orders they belong to and processes of sense-making.

1.2.1 The current paper is concerned specifically with two such texts of different status and identity. One is a photograph that has the status of a historical document, being kept in a civic photographic archive and being referred to in a respectable history of education. The other text is the popular film *Dangerous Minds* starring Michelle Pfeiffer. A hundred years separates the time of the production of these texts. What brings the texts together is the idea of the representation of the teacher.

1.2.2 The archival stability of the photograph is not what it might at first appear to be. The precise identity of the photograph is uncertain. There are two conflicting accounts of it. According to one version, it is a picture of a class and their teacher in a special school, perhaps a Barnado school. In the other version, the identity of the photograph is very specific: it is a Mr Shoveller, the headteacher of a board school in Bermondsey.[2] This difference may not actually affect the meaning of the photograph for current purposes, since either way, Barnardo or board school, the meaning of the teacher-figure remains consistent. But it does introduce a question over the stability of identity of this text, and perhaps of all such texts and how they 'come down' to us.

1.3.1 The technique for reading one text against another of different status identified above is complex and layered. In the first place, two texts of different orders can be linked 'thematically', in this case, the figure of the teacher is what brings them together. This ('violent') yoking makes visible the fact that the field of representation is differentiated, and that this has important implications for techniques of reading, for interpretation, and gives rise to questions about the nature and status of documents. 'In what sense is it possible to read the

2   P. Horn, *The Victorian and Edwardian Schoolchild* (Gloucester: Sutton, 1989).

photograph of Mr Shoveller and his class as a historical document?' is a question no less complex, I would suggest, than the same question applied to *Dangerous Minds*.

1.3.2 This technique can be deployed in different contexts. I have used it in the past to bring out questions of textual identity and authority in relation to the textual field in English teaching. Reading *Hamlet* against *Terminator 2*, for example, or *The Tempest* against *Twinkle* (the little girls' magazine) or *Romeo and Juliet* against *Home and Away* was a way of indicating the arbitrary nature of some powerful textual distinctions operating in the name of the subject. Doing this kind of reading from within the subject with year-ten students (fourteen to fifteen year olds) introduced a further layer into this act of problematization. A yet further layer involved presenting such work for assessment in formal and public examinations where the authority of the subject and of its assessment procedures are called into question.[3]

1.3.3 Within the context of the proposed double reading of Mr Shoveller with *Dangerous Minds*, the question of interpretation, of sense-making and meaning, is complicated by the different orders of representation that the texts (appear to) belong to. The photograph has historical resonance that comes from its belonging to the archive, from its location in historical researches and from the surface features that lend a historical flavour to its composition: its greyscale colouring, the marks it bears of an archaic photographic technology, its historical aura. *Dangerous Minds* lacks this historical dimension, given that it is marked by the signs of the more ephemeral order of popular culture and the genre from which it takes its form and style. It is in recent times that techniques for the reading of such textual material have come into being, through Media Studies and Cultural Studies, although these techniques have not seriously invaded historical discourses.

3   See N. Peim, *Critical Theory and the English Teacher* (London: Routledge, 1993), pp. 67–115.

1.3.4 But textual orders are not necessarily stable, although often deeply institutionalized.[4] This comparison or contrast raises an issue not just about a history of media texts but about the role of popular texts as historical documents that speak to (and against perhaps) other more familiar kinds of historical document. In this move there is likely to be some effect of problematization of the idea of 'the archive' – of what properly constitutes data in the field. The game is to introduce an unlikely element into a stable order. What happens is not just that the techniques for reading popular cultural texts are then added into the textual practices of history, but that the established techniques of reading historical documents are troubled by the intrusive element of the popular and the procedures it brings with it. One way of encapsulating this effect is to consider the question: In what ways does Michelle Pfeiffer constitute a historical figure? A host of related issues spring from this question.

2.1.1 Techniques for reading visual 'media' texts are *fundamentally* no different from techniques for reading any texts, though the techniques deployed in the newer, upstart disciplines of Cultural Studies and Media Studies do not necessarily have general currency across disciplines, in spite of their theoretical depth.

2.1.2 The available procedures for reading visual 'media' texts include approaches that can be characterized as: semiotic, narratological, generic, intertextual, discursive and deconstructive. Beyond this there are techniques or methods for reading that can be characterized by reference to the word 'audience'. These techniques or methods have been significantly adopted by Media Studies which has opened up the field of research known as 'audience studies', a generally anti-formalist approach to textual practices.

---

4   See M. Foucault, 'What is an author', in David Lodge (ed.), *Modern Criticism and Theory* (London: Longman, 1988), pp. 197–210.

2.1.2.1 *Semiotic*: derives from de Saussure's description of the sign and claim for a semiology, a 'science of signs in society'.[5] Semiotics is concerned with relations between the signifier, the material component of the sign, and the signified, the conceptual or ideational component that the signifier 'points to', as it were. Semiotics is also concerned with sign *systems* and with *texts* that are located within sign systems and that deploy signs – signifiers and signifieds – according to implicit rules in established patterns of combination to produce effects of meaning.[6]

2.1.2.2 *Narratological*: derives from the privileging of narrative as a fundamental textual form. Narratology is concerned to define the fundamental characteristics of narrative: the semiotic (symbolic) but also the hermeneutic and cultural properties of narratives.[7]

2.1.2.3 *Generic*: is concerned with both the taxonomy and structures of textual forms. What different types of text are there and what are their characteristic semiotic and narratologic modes? To what textual orders do they belong, how are they constituted and what are the characteristic ways that they get read and used in social contexts? Although perhaps structuralist in tendency, a genre approach may go beyond the limits of structuralism and explore characteristic textual 'habitats', modes of reading and using and responding to texts.[8]

2.1.2.4 *Intertextual*: is concerned with the referencing, borrowing and the common stock of signs deployed in texts. Signs are imbued with references from their previous uses. Meanings in texts are constantly

5   F. de Saussure, *Cours de linguistique generale* (Paris: Payot, 1922), p. 33: 'une science qui etudie la vie des signes au sein de la vie sociale'.

6   See for instance T. Hawkes, *Structuralism and Semiotics* (London: Routledge, 1991).

7   See R. Barthes, *S/Z* (New York: Hill and Wang, 1974) and G. Genette, *Narrative Discourse* (Oxford: Blackwell, 1980).

8   See D. Duff (ed.), *Modern Genre Theory* (Harlow: Longman, 2000); N. Lacey, *Narrative and Genre: Key Concepts in Media Studies* (Basingstoke: Macmillan, 2000); D. Longhurst (ed.), *Gender, Genre and Narrative Pleasure* (London: Unwin Hyman, 1989).

being borrowed from other texts and all texts have recourse to a common stock of signs in circulation. Texts are also clustered into textual fields that generate specific modes of cross-reference.[9]

2.1.2.5 *Discursive*: concerned with the larger textual arenas. Texts are not free floating but inhabit specific discourses, textual 'realms' that deploy particular modes of production, of reading, of sense making. Discourses belong to institutions and determine practices of production and reception.

2.1.2.6 *Deconstructive*: is concerned with identifying the 'aporias' and contradictions in texts, their unbounded nature and the productivity of reading and interpreting. Texts operate with oppositions that are locked in general patterns of thought, the great binaries that organize thought: nature/culture, civilization/barbarism, occidental/oriental, masculine/ feminine. These oppositions cannot sustain a strict separation between their opposing terms. A deconstructive reading is concerned to establish the oppositions and the precise ways that they appear in the text and to identify how they compromise their difference from one another.[10]

2.1.2.7 *Audience*: is concerned much less with the signifying elements in a text, how they are structured and what texts mean. The goal of audience-oriented theories of meaning is to identify the different kinds of sense and use that different audiences make of particular texts. This has been especially significant in media theory where ideas about cultural imperialism have been challenged by researches into specific reading practices and textual uses and the audience theory that has arisen from them.[11]

9   See G. Allen, *Intertextuality* (London: Routledge, 2000); M. Iampolski, *The Memory of Tiresias: Intertextuality and Film* (Berkeley: University of California Press, 1998).

10   See J. Derrida, *Disseminations* (Chicago: University of Chicago Press, 1981).

11   See, for example, I. Ang, *Living Room Wars: Rethinking Media Audiences for a Postmodern World* (London: Routledge, 1996).

2.2.1 Structuralist readings of text claim to be able to account for the signifying components of any text and its configuration within a recognizable form. Semiotic and narratological textual readings depend on this notion of the encoding of constituent elements within generic frameworks (see, for example, Barthes's famous codes).[12] These processes give access to the meaning of texts by identifying the cultural value of signs, the rules and regulations of sign systems and the positions of readers.

2.2.2 A poststructuralist position, exemplified most trenchantly and complexly in Derrida's deconstructive techniques, suggests that such structuralist accounts of texts, and of reading practices, fail to take into account some of the underlying conditions of signification: its dependence, for example, on the logic of the trace where meaning is always deferred along a bidirectional or multidirectional chaining, where spacing (the absence of a sign or the gap between signs) is a condition of the presence of any given sign, and where meaning is always dependent of the supplement of the non-present, giving rise to the remarkable phenomenon of the interdependence of presence and absence.[13] The position of the reading subject, in so far as it is a function of signification, is similarly fraught with difficulties of determination.

2.2.3 The upshot of Derrida's position, as Derrida has often been at pains to point out, is an insistence on the embedded nature of certain key meanings that work through the dominant oppositions of a system of thought that carries through certain cultural distinctions. The system of thought that is referred to as 'Western metaphysics'. These meanings are institutionalized in the everyday transactions of social life. Their habitual signifying practices and habits of thought are embedded in everyday discourses, as well as informing, for example, the more abstract discourses of knowledge. In other words, in various ways and at various levels, meanings are institutionalized and main-

---

12   R. Barthes, op. cit.
13   J. Derrida, 'Structure, sign and play in the discourse of the human sciences' in *Writing and Difference* (London: Routledge and Kegan Paul, 1978), p. 280.

tain what consistency and stability they do through the institutionalized practices that hold them in place and provide occasions for their
being.

2.2.4 According to this position, textual readings are, on the one
(signifying) hand, potentially endlessly mobile and open, but on the
other (institutional) hand are caught up in generic determinations.

2.2.5 The logic of the trace, the supplement, of spacing, features of the
principle of difference, all insist against the conventional metaphysical
wisdom of being-as-presence; differ*a*nce insists that the idea of a
consistent unity of meaning cannot be guaranteed by a stable presence
of 'text', textual elements, structure, author, reader or other 'subject'.[14] This has implications for the unity and stability of textual and
generic instances, forms and meanings: what's more, just as textual
boundaries cannot be fixed in time and place, so the limits of the
archive cannot be set. What, then, can prevent the coming together of
Mr Shoveller and Michelle Pfeiffer, both ghostly inhabitants of quite
different realms of representation and different orders of knowledge,
but both imbued with the halo of meanings that envelop the figure of
the teacher?

3.1.1 Mr Shoveller inhabits the realm of the 'authentic', established
archive of historical images. But there is an interesting 'twist' to the
status of the image that frames Mr Shoveller's 'presence'. It is important, perhaps, to begin a reading of Mr Shoveller with a reminder of
the status of the photographic (or any otherwise 'graphic') sign. The
image of Mr Shoveller in the photograph is a *trace*, and represents the
absence of Mr Shoveller at the same time and as much as it represents
'his' presence (or the presence of 'his' image). What we witness, in
other words, is a *trace* of Mr Shoveller (rather than Mr Shoveller
'himself') and what I offer in the following paragraphs is a *sup-*

---

14   J. Derrida, *Positions* (London: Athlone, 1987), pp. 19–26. The use of the word
'differ*a*nce' is fully introduced in J. Derrida, *Margins of Philosophy* (Brighton:
Harvester, 1982), pp. 1–27.

plementary reading that aims to propose additional substance to the orginary trace.

3.1.2 Mr Shoveller represents the figure of the teacher that belongs to the post-1870 period, the period of the coming of state education as a central social technology of the nation-state transformed through the movement from sovereign to governmental power. According to this position, the school system is less an instrument of a sovereign central state power, and is more the capillary extension of the state into the population.[15]

3.1.3 At the centre of this change is the new human technology of the elementary school. This is a mechanism for person transformation. The ideal end product of this social technology is the self-governing individual, imbued with the characteristics of care of the self that are necessary for civic life.[16] The dominant principles of this regime are the pastoral and the disciplinary. This description accounts for fundamental features of the modern school through to its present form where the logic of pastoral discipline prevails in the surveillance of the person. The form or modality may have changed since 1896 but the governmental function and its key strategies remain.

3.1.4 At the centre of this institution and this social technology is the indispensable figure of the teacher, defined and moulded through the practices of early training schemes and the frameworks developed for the persona and deportment of the teacher figure. The ideal condition for this key social figure includes a number of features: but above all

15   See M. Foucault, *Discipline and Punish* (London: Allen Lane, 1977) for an account of the transformation of government from sovereign to capillary power and N. Peim, 'The history of the present: towards a contemporary phenomenology of the school', in *History of Education*, 30.2 (2001), pp. 177–90 for a description of the school as an expression of governmentality.
16   J. Donald, *Sentimental Education* (London: Verso, 1992), pp. 17–48; I. Hunter, *Culture and Government* (London: Macmillan, 1988) and *Rethinking the School* (Sydney: Allen and Unwin, 1994).

'he' [*sic*] is to be close in class and cultural origins to the working-class populations he is to shepherd.

3.1.5 It is through this framing that I read the meaning of Mr Shoveller and make sense of the photograph in which he 'appears'. This seems to me to be a curiously double procedure. On the one hand it seems obvious and self-evident that the photograph doesn't provide this framework of interpretation for itself. But in bringing to consciousness and foregrounding the fact of framing my procedure for reading the photograph simply replicates whatever happens when a photograph or any other text is read. The text does not provide the conditions for its own reading. It will be read according to the frameworks for reading I have set up, established and elaborated here (or partly, anyhow).

3.1.6 The photograph has the generally recognizable form of the school photograph. There is a pose and an order. The pupils are organized into ranks: the teacher is set to one side. There is a general consistency with the generic pattern of the school photograph. Here the potentially wayward and disorganized collection of pupils is configured into a pattern of order. The potential for disorder and the organization of the group into order is visible in the arrangement of bodies – where both order and disorder appear in tension. Clearly, the management of bodies and the positionings and deportment of bodies is an enduring function of the school as a technology for control and for the training of self-control. This 'choreography' is evident in the photograph.

3.1.7 On the other hand the photograph doesn't quite fit entirely into this generic mould. There are a number of disruptive features that perturb the generic security and that also perturb the smooth governmental interpretation of the figure of the teacher within the school that I outlined above. The class has a certain kind of mobility that is semiotically visible in a number of features: hair that is in various states and degrees of unkemptness; the irregular presence and positioning of caps; the irregular folding of arms and in perhaps more than one case the overly tight folding of arms where the folding or arms indicates a posture of self-control imbued by the requirements of the school for regulation of the wayward body.

3.1.8 The photograph signifies this work: this struggle to bring the wayward body and bodies of pupils into order. The significance of this aspect of the photograph is heightened in terms of the interpretation I want to offer by the fact that the bodies in question are evidently 'working-class' urban bodies and this effort of regulation belongs to a particular, and particularly momentous, history of the school, of the state, that is continuous with the contemporary school and state.

3.1.9 It also represents in ideal form the figure of the teacher, the indispensable agent of this relatively new and vital governmental function. Mr Shoveller, if that's what we may call him, given the ambiguity of this 'information', represents and embodies semiotically this figure of the teacher. The posture he adopts signifies the modelling of the bodily self-management that is his calling to develop in his pupils. At the same time the photograph signifies his proximity to his charges. While set to one side he remains among and perhaps in some way also of them. He doesn't not baulk at touching them, either, as is evident in his beautifully ambiguous relation with the pupils he has laid hands on in a gesture that seems to hover between care and control. His demeanour is paternal and his gaze is interestingly distinguished from those of his pupils who mostly and more or less adopt the proper gaze required of the group photograph, a straight looking back into the eye of the camera. Mr Shoveller remains true to his calling: his gaze is the gaze of the teacher as pastoral disciplinarian.

3.1.10 Mr Shoveller embodies this new figure which is both an agent of the 'new' (roughly post-1870) governmental role of elementary education and which is also the teacher as embodiment of an ethic of disciplinary care, a regime of authority which is concerned with social transformation and the cultivation of the self. This is the point at which Mr Shoveller connects with Michelle Pfeiffer.

3.2.1 The film *Dangerous Minds* belongs to the order of popular culture. It does not have the automatic status of a historical document and doesn't stand inside an existing archive. Its textual status is more likely to prove problematic in the context of 'the academy', conventional academic reading practices tending to dismiss such artefacts as stereotypical, lacking complexity and depth. It will be important to suspend questions of cultural value, hopefully to return to lay them to rest later, in order to indicate how the film relates to the text characterized here as its other and to suggest why this text is interesting in terms of the representation of the teacher figure and what 'deep' genealogies it keys into.

3.2.2 The film *Dangerous Minds* adds in the complicating dimension of narrative. The narrative format of this film is deeply familiar in films of teachers and schools. A number of examples might be cited: *To Sir with Love, Dead Poets Society*, etc. Here the teacher is represented in dramatic form as the transformative figure, the outsider who is close in sympathy to her charges and who operates with a dedicated ethic of care. Interestingly, if predictably, this ethic is not rooted in sociological knowledge or socialist principles. It is represented more in the style of a personal attribute, rather like the familiar *noir* detective's inexplicable commitment to integrity of conduct and the pursuit of truth.

3.2.3 The narrative takes a characteristic and recognizable form with some interesting variations. The teacher-hero (LouAnne Johnson/ Michelle Pfeiffer) is represented as different from the body of teachers. She is distinguished from the somewhat jaded professional who in effect has given up on the 'academy' kids and distinguished from the administrative bureaucracy which is concerned to maintain procedural proprieties. This difference is in terms of commitment, care, 'charisma' and is expressed in a resourcefulness which goes beyond the limits of given practice. The difference is also signified in terms of dress. LouAnne Johnson begins to dress casually, reflecting her developing personal-professional style. Her deportment is more varied and informal; she has recourse to a wider range of speech repertoires than colleagues and, interestingly – in terms of a politics of (the representation of) teaching materials – she deploys more 'unconventional' material and terms of reference, bridging the popular culture/high culture divide. In all of this, LouAnne Johnson has some claims to proximity with the disempowered students who she teaches and may be defined at odds with current ethos of 'the school'.

3.2.4 There are interesting complications here in relation to the heroic status of this heroine. In spite of her marine toughness and karate expertise, LouAnne Johnson has been a battered wife. LouAnne Johnson appears as an unlikely, even reluctant entrant, uncertain, untrained but with a romantic view and a commitment 'to teach'. She combines a worldly knowledge with an ability to exert authority and to control by commanding attention. She emphasizes the capacity for individual choice: 'There are no victims in this class', but she also fails to save Emilio, for instance. In a neat self-referential irony Emilio reminds 'us', as he reminds his would be saviour-teacher, that he has 'seen the same movies as you have'.

3.2.5 The film depends on a number of features which we can characterize as generic to this particular popular cultural form. The central character, LouAnne Johnson, is played by the established 'star' Michelle Pfeiffer. The film depends for some of its effects on this double identity LouAnne Johnson/Michelle Pfeiffer and the star image carries with it an 'aura'. The Michelle Pfeiffer effect guarantees or at least offers a strong promise of certain characteristics: feminine insouciance, integrity – an array of heroine qualities. As LouAnne Johnson, there is also the difficult past with the brutal husband, the martial past with the experience of the marines. Star status overlaid with fictional qualities enable the LouAnne Johnson/ Michelle Pfeiffer figure to represent the teacher as saviour. Her fictional past guarantees her capacity to win through against the social odds.

3.2.6 When LouAnne Johnson expresses a feeling of uncertainty about her calling near the end of the film, it is the students who demand that she remain a teacher. She is identified as their 'light'. This reinforces the sense of her 'true' vocation calling back to her to confirm her rightful, ideal identity.

3.2.7 When Calley becomes pregnant she intends to change schools as is the custom. She decides to remain under the tutelage of Miss Johnson and gets LouAnne's support for this groundbreaking, code-breaking stance. Again, the proximity LouAnne enjoys with her charges is reflected in the tendency to break the inhibiting rules or codes of professional conduct.

3.2.8 LouAnne's dress styles reflect her particular attitude to professional identity. For classroom work she dresses down and enjoys a kind of sartorial relation of informality with her charges. For going out, as in her trip to the restaurant with Raul, and parents evenings, she dresses up.

3.2.9 Her speech codes vary too. To establish street credibility again a relation of cultural proximity is signified by code switching into a more vernacular speech style.

3.2.10 The film's references to music are interesting in this respect. The soundtrack is contemporary. Coolio's 'Dangerous Minds' with its rap-based style connects with black otherness and its music codes. In her teaching LouAnne mediates elements of the curriculum through popular culture; but uses Dylan, removed by a generation and closer to enjoying a kind of canonical status. The students' own, more rhythmic, more body-oriented music is represented as belonging unequivocally to the domain of popular culture. Dylan's 'Mr Tambourine Man' is the mediational text that enables the culture of the school (the curriculum, pedagogic styles) to speak to the radically other culture of the student. Another layer of mediation is evident in the figure of the sympathetic teacher who makes this alien music intelligible in terms of the street culture of the students. This replicates neatly David Stow's famous early-nineteenth-century vision of the cultural significance of the playground, the point of intersection of the 'street' culture of the urban child with the not-too-distant and morally infused culture of the teacher.[17]

---

17 Numerous accounts exist of Stow's Model Infant School and the Glasgow Normal Seminary of 1836, including Stow's own: D. Stow, *The Training*

3.2.11 LouAnne Johnson, then, appears in idealized form as the quintessential teacher figure. In her image is combined the early prototype of the schoolteacher envisaged in David Stow's conception of the primary cultural function of the culturally proximal teacher (shared by James Kay-Shuttleworth) with its contemporary form as the streetwise, culturally and linguistically flexible, informal, pastoral figure.[18] She is both tough and caring, embodying the twin poles of teacher identity: the pastoral and the disciplinary. The film both idealizes and glamourizes, through the narrative and the effect of star aura, this teacher figure. The film represents the teacher as being essentially above and beyond the (mere) curriculum, representing in herself a powerful cultural value and function. This figure also promotes the idea of social salvation mediated through education. Through this figure of the heroic teacher ideas about teaching and education as natural are also promoted. No amount of training or technique can produce this charismatic teacher figure. Heroes are both ordinary people and people of rare substance and commitment. Heroes stand out for integrity; hero teachers have epiphanies and have the courage to liberate through defiance of conventions. Teaching is a heroic and solitary business. No collectivity, no aspiration for reform, no politics is embraced by this model. Real learning is outside school for both teachers and pupils. The real teacher is *not* an academic. Practical professional studies, represented in the film by Lee Cantor's book, are thrown aside and personal resources called upon.[19]

3.2.12 The film also problematizes the 'proximal teacher' ethic and represents some of its gaps and contradictions. The narrative is not a smooth and unequivocal realization of the narrative of the hero-teacher. The cultural struggle for values is represented as unevenly balanced. The forces of darkness are set against the 'light' of the teacher. Social salvation is fragile. Survival is at stake. A crisis of

---

System, the Moral Training School, and the Normal Seminary (London: Longman Brown Green, 1850).
18   See I. Hunter (1994), op.cit., pp. 82–4.
19   L. Canter, *Assertive Discipline: Positive Behavior Management for Today's Classroom* (Los Angeles: Canter & Associates, 2001).

identity is induced as LouAnne Johnson loses the battle to save Raul. The film leaves this unresolved problem hanging and seeks no neat narrative resolution or transcendence. Rather it suggests that the victories of the hero-teacher are piecemeal, that the saving of an individual is a *kind* of saving of the whole world, but that the whole world in a worldly sense remains problematic.

3.2.13 LouAnne Johnson's professional qualities are specifically feminine. Her toughness is all the more admirable and effective for being feminine. Her gender identity might be characterized as a kind of worldly, tough femininity. Having been a marine she has good credentials of toughness, a woman surviving in a masculine world. She has the ultimate qualification of toughness, being a karate expert. The film also represents her as having been and having gone beyond being a victim of male domestic violence. She is thus able to stand up for herself, but also to stand up to and for her pastoral charges.

3.2.14 While this narrative form represents the institution, it does so in a highly sparse, metonymic manner to restrict vision to a limited perspective. The institution is represented by a limited number of metonymic signs: the urban landscape of the catchment area, the suburban context of the school, the principal (glimpsed as busy, struggling with public pressures, internal problems and looking for immediate short-term solutions to a welter of administrative difficulties, including staffing). The institution is represented minimally but is the absolutely necessary condition for the existence of the teacher-hero.

3.2.15 The film problematizes its own capacity to represent what it claims, nevertheless, to be representing. As LouAnne Johnson/ Michelle Pfeiffer attempts to convince the street wise Emilio Ramirez, he warns her: 'You trying to figure me out? Here let me help you […] I seen the same fucking movies you have, man.' We are clearly within the domain of the (postmodern) self-referential film; but there is a parallel with the self-conscious school photo, already an established form by 1896.[20]

3.2.16 What is the meaning, then, of the 'popular' and the 'historical' but locally institutional representation of the teacher? Why is the idea of the teacher here (in both cases) so represented: with its emphasis on the 'desire' of the teacher, the imaginary, idealized figure, the mission and the cultural positioning of the teacher figure with its questions about proximity on the one hand and aspirations for social distinction on the other? How might cultural distinction be involved in the figure of the teacher as here represented? And how might cultural distinction be involved in the uses, pleasures and purposes of audiences of these texts?

4.1 The relatively recent idea of the audience as an interpretative category, which provides a necessary check on the force of interpretation, cannot be authoritative; but can shift the dynamics in the production of meanings. Audience theory, born out of media and cultural studies, shifts the grounds of meaning from its enclosure in a textual or strictly institutional frame and makes a principle of the shifting and varied composition of a radically differential 'audience'. Only detailed empirical researches can represent, though never exhaustively, the possible strictures on the movement of interpretation.

4.2 The instability of meaning in audience theory is paralleled by the mobility of meaning in poststructuralism (Derrida's trace and supplement, for instance). Both cases in the end seek to define institutionalized meanings as necessarily partial and incomplete. Can there be a theory of the document after deconstruction? Historical evidence presents a particular case of textual data. A range of documents have entered the field of historical studies of education. Can there be limits set to this archive? Or does the poststructuralist, postmodern, postcolonial rethinking of textuality and language imply a rethinking of the field of historical data? Of the archive itself or of the very notion of 'an archive'?

20   See for instance N. Rosenblum, *A World History of Photography* (New York: Abbeville Press, 1997).

4.3 Can there be a stable and delimited archive which determines the nature of data, its status as data and the methods for its interpretation? This positivist, rationalist project seems to have been supplanted. What, then, are the implications of textual material to the function of a history that is always working with a shifting 'object' with subjects that are hybrid and with textual fields, fields of knowledge that are contained, or not contained, within shifting boundaries?

4.3.1 If the archive is not strictly delimitable nor self-defining: and the same necessary instability applies to the frameworks for the interpretation of documents, any phenomenology must equally be an open account. Structures must be structures for contestation – provisional frameworks to provide, as much as anything, forms of contention. This implies an always-agonistic view of knowledge...

4.4 To what extent does teacher education, for example, engage with the issues that might be raised by such an exploration of the representation of teacher identity? To what extent might such representations inform the conscious and unconscious thinking of teachers about the meaning of their work? To what extent is governmental policy influenced by ideas about teacher identity that might be read off from popular and historical forms and instances of representation? ('No one forgets a teacher' is the recent slogan for a teaching recruitment campaign in the UK.) And how much are teacher discourses – departmental discourses, staffroom culture, professional documents or casual conversations – influenced by different representations of teacher identity?

4.5 In other words, what is the relation between Mr Shoveller and Michelle Pfeiffer/LouAnne Johnson, this unlikely historical pairing? Clearly, the discourses that currently frame them and their identities would tend to keep them apart from one another. Bringing them together, within a certain determined framework, opens the possibility of engaging with a discourse (historical? contemporary? both?) of teacher identity, of the energies that inform professional desire and practice and their representation across apparently remote fields of representation.

KARL CATTEEUW, KRISTOF DAMS, MARC DEPAEPE
AND FRANK SIMON

9 Filming the Black Box: Primary Schools on Film in Belgium, 1880–1960: a First Assessment of Unused Sources

We perceive a growing tendency to devote increased attention to visual sources and to visual aspects of education in the history of education. Behind this trend lies a research programme, coming from outside educational history, that is, from the theory of 'cultural studies'. But this route runs the risk of sidetracking us.

We believe educational historians should primarily follow their own research line, and what concerns us is the 'realistic turn' towards social and cultural history or 'classroom history'. It seems a logical step from there to developing a new area of research. This will build on earlier research and we do not dispose of what brought us to where we are today as a body of modernist prejudices that should be studied to see how people used to live rather than for its content. The visual image can play a role here, but it remains to be seen how helpful this is. On the basis of a concrete example, we shall show that film clips and commentaries, which either directly or indirectly provide information about daily life in primary schools between 1880 and 1960, did not lead to any new conclusions. They failed to provide any insights that had not already been gleaned from our research using traditional source material. Indeed, we believe that if we are truly to understand the educational past, the study of films should be interpreted in the light of traditional source material.

The neglected visual

Some time ago we carried out a study of classroom history in Belgium. Our results are noted in a book called *Order in Progress*.[1] We based our research on traditional source material, mainly educational journals, but we also interviewed former teachers and used reports of teachers' conferences and monographs on schools. During our research we referred indirectly to visual sources. We gained access to photographs and some films, but quickly realized that this did not teach us much more than we already knew. We left those sources aside and finalized our research exclusively from written sources. Since then, we have been made aware of increasing calls to pay more attention to visual sources, and we are forced to step back and question whether we dismissed these visual sources too quickly. Should we have given them greater importance in our research? The answer to these questions depends on the answer to another: can one study these photographs and films from a different angle to that of the immediate and day-to-day realism as seen by the person in the street?

In our research into 'classroom behaviour' we looked at photographs and films from a 'realistic' point of view, that is, we concentrated on its content: what really happened in the classroom that was being filmed? Clearly, this perspective – which for us is the perspective of common sense – seems no longer to be acceptable in the dominant scientific circles. Interpreting an image, based on content rather than on form, betrays a positivist attitude to visual sources that, according to modern thinking, is hopelessly outdated.[2]

1   M. Depaepe *et al.*, *Order in Progress: Everyday Educational Practice in Primary Schools: Belgium, 1880–1970* (Leuven: Leuven University Press, 2000).

2   J. Ruby, 'Visual anthropology', in D. Levinson and M. Ember (eds.), *Encyclopedia of Cultural Anthropology* (New York: Henry Holt and Company, 1996), pp. 1345–51. In 'a post-positive and post-modern world', writes Ruby, we realise that films and photographs are always concerned with two different things: the culture of those who are filmed, and of those who film (p. 1345). Studies of photography and films in different spheres have concentrated for some time more on 'the social contexts of making and using images' (p. 1346).

Recent trends (and here we are referring to Cultural Studies) assert that when using visual sources in the study of the past, the content of images is less important than their form. If we seek to criticize films analytically and in a way which will enables us to advance in our research, the first step should be to study the technical and artistic aspects of photography and film: centring, lighting, choice of background and foreground and the behaviour of those being photographed.

This chapter will firstly discuss this trend and enumerate the reasons why, as educational historians, we are disappointed. We find no technical or heuristic problem in approaching visual sources from that angle, but it does pose a problem of content. Our belief is that such an approach departs from the proper field of educational history, and enters other branches of historical research such as the history of film and photography and the history of taste. We do not believe it is possible to use technical and symbolic interpretations of photographs as a basis for anything other than peripheral conclusions about educational history. For other reasons, the same holds for a realistic interpretation. We illustrate this failure of 'realistic' and 'symbolic' interpretations from images of classroom-history in Belgium taken from the 1930s and the 1980s. Finally, we identify a number of possibilities for a more positive and useful attitude towards the use of visual sources in the study of history of education.

So visual anthropologists are dedicated to the cultural study of photographic behaviour. The interpretation of the images should be understood as 'something negotiated rather than fixed' (p. 1346).

'Cultural studies', 'theory': what progress to be made?

While we were working on our study of classroom history in Belgium, attention was increasingly being directed within the field of educational history towards the use of visual source material. We did not observe this interest passively, but actively participated in it.[3] The idea of a 'pictorial turn' began to take hold, but the origins of this trend came from outside our field. It was imported from the field of studies known as 'cultural studies' or 'theory'. Today, there is talk of a new paradigm or a paradigm in the making. The term 'paradigm' implies more than a simple appeal to pay more attention to visual source material or visual aspects of the past. It implies a whole programme of research. In the past, other fields of research have been introduced into the history of education, and it has been fruitful even if the results were not always successful.[4] So we were wary and questioned whether this type of research and this paradigm would benefit educational history more than the current trend, and whether it answered an internal need. Based on the developments of the past decades, is it a logical step? Let us look at the programme in the context of its origins, that is 'cultural studies' or 'theory'.

What are 'cultural studies'? What is 'theory'? Both terms can give rise to confusion. Culture has been studied for a long time, certainly since Burckhardt, and also the term 'theory' was coined some time ago. There are different definitions of 'culture' and, equally, various definitions of 'theory', such that supporters of 'theory' or 'cultural studies' cannot establish an identity. Yet, in the Anglo-Saxon world, these vague definitions constitute a whole direction of thought, a field or a school of style. It is difficult to define this field with any precision. Some people talk of a 'cultural studies

---

3   M. Depaepe and B. Henkens, *et al.* (eds.), *The Challenge of the Visual in the History of Education* (Ghent: C.S.H.P., 2000). Also see the special issue 36 of *Paedagogica Historica* (2000).

4   H.-E. Tenorth, 'Lob des Handwerk, Kritik der Theorie – Zur Lage der pädagogischen Historiographie in Deutschland', *Paedagogica Historica*, 32 (1996), 341–61.

movement', but it can also be described by neologisms prefaced by 'post', for example in 'postmodernism', which is certainly the best-known expression, but 'poststructuralism' has also become an accepted term. Other variants of these expressions enter our language, coming from individual authors, and expressed in different kinds of variants that might be synonyms or may have specific meanings, although never formalized, such as 'postempiricism' or 'post-rationalism'. The prefix 'meta' has also become very popular, and books and articles increasingly contain the word 'context'. Even the term 'subtext' pops up now and again.

Although so widespread, this trend cannot be classified under one label. Academic supporters of 'cultural studies' and 'theory' are rooted in other fields of knowledge such as history, sociology, film science, anthropology and many others, but their like-minded 'meta' attitudes keep them distant from their own field; so they communicate with each other rather than with colleagues in their own field of research. They normally research less for empirical conclusions, instead seeking forms. They are concerned less with specific facts than with a 'critique' of 'dominant thinking, dominant ways of looking and feeling', about whole 'paradigms'. But do they have enough insight into their own specialisation to be able to incorporate new trends into the investigation? Are they not simply meddling in the international movement of abstractions, which are empty of any substance? By limiting the content to vague generalities they can communicate with others all over the world about multi-disciplines, but does that not depreciate the transfer of knowledge? For the practical craftsman, it appears that the supporters of 'theory' and 'cultural studies' in every separate field are just pushing empty boxes back and forth. But let us temporarily suspend negative judgement and look more closely at what they have to say about role and meaning, and all that is visual.

Image has taken the place of text

The visual aspect is a new turn in a school of thought, so to say, that has always strongly identified with text and all that is textual. Central to this was the analysis of text as 'discourse', to which an independent force was imputed, in the sense that it was creating reality because it fixed objects and decided what could or could not be talked about. Precisely what this 'fixation of objects through language' means in practice is far from clear. What is clear is that the general trend implies that everything is a 'construct'. Everything, social or not, is constructed, and nothing is *natural*. That something natural can exist with no cultural definition is considered to be 'naive'. For example, the human body is not simply a body, but 'an interwoven construct of flesh and speech'.[5] As far as we can judge, such terms were born out of a feeling of discontent with the more general common-sense concept that there is, on the one hand the body, and on the other a vision of that body which decides what is allowed or not and how a person has to behave. Setting 'nature' against 'culture' in this way is called a 'dichotomous ratio' or 'binary speech'. We do not understand what has been gained by lumping everything together, and explaining that the introduction of a clear distinction between phenomena testifies to a rigid way of thinking whereas in reality everything interlocks and overlaps. It is unnecessary to enter further into this argument: such concepts are adequately known. The last two decades have given this school of thought, under its various aliases, enough of a reputation and support, and everyone has formed their own opinion: some support it wholeheartedly, others believe it is hysterical nonsense.

However, this is not the place to go into the value of this academic cultural phenomenon, at least not in general terms. But we

---

5   For example, the American pedagogue McClaren wants to free the body from the hold of text, but recognizes that it is not possible to set the 'brute' body against text: bodies are already cultural artefacts, an interlacing of flesh and meaning. The so-called 'enfleshment' that McClaren aims for is no easy insertion of flesh into the order of representation. There is also an investment besides that of body/flesh in representation. For more information, refer to G. Biesta: 'The identity of the body', *Comenius*, 51 (1993), 274–90.

are concerned about its impact on educational history. The textual trend had a certain influence, although it was really more of a colouring, an ambiance, a *je-ne-sais-quoi*; one often talks about perspectives, 'speech' and 'social constructions', but this was more a question of being in with the crowd, submitting to the pressure to belong; wanting to show that you were not ignorant, that you kept up with the thinking of your time, that you were not fossilized in the past, limping along behind the rest, and that you did not, for example, still work pathetically as a Frankfurt Marxist! This colouring tended to appear in the introduction and conclusion of books and articles. In the body of the text, it was usually business as usual and was fine like that. All things considered, this textual school of thought can claim few methods or techniques from which we can benefit; its influence really was more of a colouring of the type that vanishes after several washes and it seems that we can now start rubbing away the last remains. It was good while it lasted, but now it is over.

There is also some activity in the field of cultural studies. They have created their 'new paradigm'; or rather, they say they are working on it and that they are slowly starting to define something; they are not totally sure what it is they are starting to define, but it could indeed be a new paradigm. It is not necessary to present the search for a new paradigm as having great overview or coherence. The procedure followed for this type of research is that everyone who can think of something that can be directly or indirectly connected with the visual in all its forms is requested to write an article for a new academic coffee-table book, in which are discussed such questions as the post-psycho-iconological subtext of *Basic Instinct* and how Cardinal John Henry Newman believed in an invisible world while others of his time believed only in what they saw, which indicates the surprising presence of divergent 'scopic regimes' at the same time and in the same place. This colourful concoction is used by way of a conclusion by the editor, with the remark that the physiological view that the eye not only receives light-rays but sends them, is today abandoned but can nevertheless express a symbolic truth. We just don't know which.[6]

If there is anything credible about this 'new paradigm', it is this: it translates into visual terminology the well-known and used views which have been used for some time regarding text. Tactically, this is a substitution: image has taken the place of text. For the rest, very little has changed. It seems to us that the sudden revival in a diminishing trend can best be described with the Scottish word 'fey'. The word means sudden feverish joy at the prospect of imminent death. To us this is like a desperate search for space in an area where everyone has for too long been packed in the same cycle, always hitting on the same critiques in an intellectual obsessional neurosis: the circle of stumbling figures of thought drag behind them lead balls and totally lack the will to escape, yet crave to know something, anything, as long as it is something real, something that exists. Eventually all this begins to hurt the reader not only psychologically but also physically. The mind is fought off and driven away. It becomes 'automatic writing', an accumulation of a priori and parti-pris, all presented in a tone that tolerates no objection. It is a practically worthless mechanical rose-wreath of 'perspectivism', 'power relations' and 'dichotomous ratios'. Compared to what has been produced in this field over the last several years, few texts have ever been so rigidly dogmatic and contorted with so little breathing space in such a narrow perspective, and therefore so painful to read. It is as if you had been picked up and swung against a wall.

What can the 'pictorial turn' do to this situation? The answer is nothing! The textual domain has been exhausted, but theoreticians continue, unperturbed, to plant their intellectual obsessional neurosis on new and fallow ground, where myopia and aporia will soon flourish as before. What was previously applied to text, is now applied to image. It is considered naive to take image as a representation of reality, because it is a 'construction' that has to be deconstructed. In the words of a 'believer', Martin Jay, who gives an insight into the enthusiasm of which a pictorially born-again man is capable, 'the new

6   T. Brennan and M. Jay (eds.), *Vision in Context: Historical and Contemporary Perspectives on Sight* (New York: Routledge, 1996).

fascination with modes of seeing and the enigmas of visual experience evident in a wide variety of fields may well betoken a paradigm shift in the cultural imaginary of our age'. And he goes on to talk about more than text: 'the figural is resisting subsumption under the rubric of discursivity: the image is demanding its own unique mode of analysis'.[7]

However, there is no trace here of this particular unique mode of analysis. A little later, Jay gives a more accurate characterization of the relationship between text and image in cultural studies, when he says: '"viewing texts" and "reading pictures" are now chiasmically intertwined'. But for us the important part of his thinking appears in the following passage: 'the optical unconscious now appears as a dark new continent ripe for exploration'. The expression 'a dark new continent' is what is important.[8] It seems to express a longing concealed behind the pictorial turn: it is a new way of looking, a new attitude that will renew everything and surprise us with Insight. The gap is as wide as it is deep: it is an initiative in which an undiscovered field of study is perceived; and in the rest of the article, as usual, it is the same old story as before. Like prisoners in their thoughts, keeping their gaze 'upon that little tent of blue which prisoners call the sky' they dream of totally new worlds, which are there for them alone.[9]

---

7   M. Jay, 'Vision in context: reflections and refractions', in Brennan and Jay, *Vision in Context*, pp. 3–11.

8   Op. cit., p. 3.

9   O. Wilde, 'The ballad of Reading Gaol', in *Complete Works* (London: Methuen, 1963), p. 725.

The unknown does not exist

The real substance of that kind of writing eventually proves especially futile, as illustrated in an article about our particular field, i.e. classroom history, by Eric Margolis, in which photographs are regarded as 'the hidden curriculum in black and white'.[10] Margolis's central question is: 'How can we understand the meaning of these photographs?' and in posing this question he approaches the same questions asked by Grosvenor regarding classroom history.[11] The fact that it is a depicted reality doesn't appear in Margolis. We concede that photographs are arranged, but it is reality that is arranged, so reality is also in the frame alongside the arrangement. We should not forget that the pictures were not taken in studios in staged classrooms, but in real classrooms. But Margolis's attention immediately heads off onto the arrangement, to the *mise en scène*. The photographs 'are frequently composed to symbolise social relations including: assimilation, order, discipline, purity, equality, patriotism, community pride and stability'. By printing such 'visual rhetoric hegemony' on postcards and sending them out, the public were convinced of the legitimacy of 'professional control of deviance'.[12] On photographs we can see that knowledge is not introduced as the 'open process of personal growth or something gained in family and community'; rather, knowledge is 'the property of the awe-inspiring institution behind the children through which they must pass. The children are ready for the challenge. They stand at attention, equidistant, not quite touching'.[13]

Margolis pays no attention to depicted objects. He concentrates on the symbolic. But then, we have to ask whether he really saw all that in the photographs? Of course he did not. This phenomenon goes under the name of *Hineininterpretierung*. Margolis can see in the

---

10   E. Margolis, 'Class pictures: representations of race, gender and ability in a century of school photography', *Visual Sociology*, 14 (1999), 7–38.

11   I. Grosvenor, 'On visualizing past classrooms', in I. Grosvenor, M. Lawn and K. Rousmaniere, (eds.) *Silences and Images: the Social History of the Classroom* (New York: Peter Lang, 1999), pp. 83–104.

12   Margolis, *Class Pictures*, p. 10.

13   Op. cit., p. 17.

photographs all kinds of things about which he has read something in a book. There is nothing to prove that the analysis of these photographs provides him with new insights. Of course it does, he argues: 'from a critical perspective, class pictures can be viewed as a historical record of certain elements of the hidden curriculum', he writes.[14] But is it a 'record' or an 'illustration'? You can see in those photographs that everything is neat and ordered and you conclude that the people liked order. They liked order in presentation, and in their pupils, they liked neat rows of desks, wall charts that were hanging straight, clean floors. They did not like pupils fighting, wall charts hanging upside down and stained books with loose and dog-eared pages, flung on the floor. All of this is true, and if such scenes occurred they were hard on the pupils, but this was not the way the school wished to present itself to the outside world. But we have known this for a long time. We do not need a pile of old photographs to tell us that. Margolis also says that we must not analyse photographs in isolation, but in conjunction with written sources and 'cross referenced', so to speak. That may be, but there is such a thing as cross-fertilization, and there is *Hineininterpretierung*.

In his enthusiasm for this source or reference, which can now be consulted over the Internet, Margolis begins to take some odd swerves of analysis and pictorial turns. For example, he regrets that there are no photographs of school-boards where decisions are made. He seems annoyed by this fact. If only we had pictures of board-meetings! There seems to be a distinct urge to throw everything overboard in order to renew everything. The suspicion expressed here is that all those old political histories of education, based on minutes of meetings, internal working documents, correspondence, newspaper articles, laws and the working documents of law-making; all these provide a one-sided and limited modernist view of history. They take no account of the human aspect and perception. But should we have had photographs of boards, then everything would become new. They are seeking a sudden flash of inspiration. Others refer more to private documents, but in general they are seeking a source within the deepest layers of the Hidden Meaning and from which rises pure Insight. The sad truth, however, is

14   Op. cit., p. 10.

that there is no Hidden Meaning. This is not some exciting adventure book for boys; it is historiography. There are no coded messages, written with invisible ink that needs candlelight to read it. There is nothing to decode. It is not a Swedish puzzle, it is quite simply historiography. There is no watchman guarding gates of history, refusing access to anyone who cannot decode the mystery. *There are many fewer things on this earth than our philosophy leads us to believe.*[15]

What we want to know as historians is quite simple, but so widespread that you have to bring it together. That means hard work and is not the same thing as imagining up one or two conclusions through looking at photographs. The toil of a previous generation of educational historians to meticulously bring together pieces of history into a meaningful whole is dismissed as archive fetishism. That was in any case one-sided and is now totally superseded given that it is possible to point to many modernist presuppositions: for example, that there was fact next to fiction whereas we now know that they are one and the same.

Eric Margolis seems to see some of these arguments. He puts forward many objections to the use of photographs as source material, with arguments such as that photographs only show one school scene, of teachers and pupils standing ready to be photographed. There are no photographs of school administration, and neither photographs of boredom, punishment or discipline and in general there are no photographs of 'conflicts and tensions in schools'.[16] In the final analysis, Margolis says, social relationships cannot be photographed. But what does this leave us with? It leaves one thing: the 'visual rhetoric of hegemony'. But this does not teach us anything we did not already know and if we are not careful, we can seize on innocent photographs as meaningful in situations where they are 'blameless'. Simply by interpreting the 'subtext' of this article, we can understand the 'hidden meaning' that says that there is nothing you can do with those photographs. But he does not admit this, preferring to comment that it is a pity we have no photographs of school administrations. Of course, if

---

15   F. Picabia, *Jésus-Christ Rastaquouère* (Paris: Allia, 1996, orig. 1920), p. 47.
16   Margolis, *Class Pictures*, p. 34.

we did have some, what would we do with them? Would we try and gain insights into school policy? We can check school policy in written documents. Or have they suddenly disappeared?

Subtext and visual unconscious

We have already come across this tendency in the analysis of photographs, in previous analyses of text as 'discourse'.[17] In discourse analysis, there is a tendency to think that relevant source information is coded and that we have to look for a switch on the desktop to open the bookcase. This tendency creates a belief that text creates reality, and subsequently that discourse analysis is the route to reality, not through a study of what the text represents but through a study of the linguistic markers in the text. The singular starting point used by these people is that we should not seek reality in the real educational rules, but that we have to read between the lines and study everything that cannot be said in words: for them that is reality. The clear, great humanist ideals that characterize educational texts have no meaning for them, but what they call the 'hidden text', the manipulation behind the rosy smoke screen, does.

Thomas Markus gives an example from school in his analysis, which is grafted onto Foucault's, of a pedagogical charter for the early nineteenth century in which he notes the illusory liberty given by the well-known educational figure: the pupils were apparently free. But in reality they were closely observed and manipulated. So, he came to certain conclusions about 'an education for the free market', in which there was the same illusory liberty. Markus's claim on 'reality' was in fact only based on the idea of a 'hidden curriculum' that will come into force and which is clever enough to find its own way.

We come across this approach more often in discourse analysis, but refer only to John Fowler who argued that the inferior position of

17   T. Markus, 'Early nineteenth century school space and ideology', *Paedagogica Historica*, 32 (1996), 9–50.

hospital patients was reinforced and legitimised through the discussion of their situation in newspaper articles using the passive sentence structure.[18] Fowler draws his idea from the science of literature (many passive sentence constructions in a novel express the feeling of fate-fulness of the writer) which he believes is important for the 'linguistic construction of reality'.

In our field, we have always regarded texts as representations of reality. We did no discourse analysis in our research. We thought that such associations (the passivity of sentences and people) bring us no closer to reality. Our first impression is that such far-fetched inter-pretations seem to be rather absurd, and we can see no well-founded reason to change our attitude. As indicated in the introduction to this chapter, our study of everyday educational practice was based on written sources. Our idea was that there is an observed reality. Those who believe that journals only spread 'ideals' or 'pure theory' should consider how difficult it is to fill a whole journal with pure ideals. To keep one's theory pure and clear from the intrusion of the 'everyday' is not a simple affair. Those theories must first be understood, incorporated and repeated. Everyday knowledge is always watching to get through. The starting point for a journal is always an educational ideal that seeks to be spread, but there is a desire to bring this ideal into line with daily reality: a school led by a curriculum, where one teacher is up against many pupils. They wanted to explain what these high ideals meant practically for the schools, ideals which, in general, were created for use outside school, often in a situation where there was one educator and one to be educated.

Educational journals are full of experience and the question is how to extract it from them. Which method did we apply? We did not have a specific method of extracting the information. Whether a particular mode of behaviour is purely an ideal, reality, or something between the two, it has to be analysed on a case-by-case basis. All we can say for certain is that it is a comparison between different educational circuits. Set against the systematic, well-reasoned and

18   J. Fowler, 'Power', in T. A. van Dijck, *Handbook of Discourse Analysis Volume 4: Discourse Analysis in Society* (London: Academic Press, 1985), pp. 61–82.

integrated educational science of academics or of philosophers such as Rousseau or Herbart, are the loose occasional articles in journals. Texts from different sectors and integrated to different degrees are carefully considered: academic texts will be better constructed and internal contradictions will be less evident. Firstly, the text is constructed according to a plan, whose foundations are theoretically well thought out. Then statements are read and reread, with the plan in mind. It is to be expected that an academic text is much 'cleaner' than a hastily-written journal article. With regard to educational advice for families, Jürgen Oelkers wrote: 'Medien ordnen Probleme einfach nebeneinander, während Moraltheorien den Nachteil haben sie zentrieren zu müssen' (The media simply place problems next to each other, while moral theories have the disadvantage of having to place them with respect to one another).[19] The hierarchy and the totality of moral theories is not the same as the juxtaposition of problems in the press. Furthermore, in 'day-to-day' life, problems are not placed in a hierarchical system, at least not in our lives; maybe in the *Alltag* of Immanuel Kant it was different. Whenever someone is considering a problem, for as long as this problem is a preoccupation, they will have particular views on particular matters. If the problem moves, so do other issues. Each particular problem and each topic imposes it is own way of thinking.

To clarify, an example of this concerns 'school discipline' in the sense of good behaviour. If 'discipline in school' is the subject of an article, the chances that we will learn something relevant to us is smaller than if the subject is only indirectly touched. If discipline is the central theme, an author will give the official version of the story. The official version may state that: (*a*) discipline was an emanation of the moral qualities of the teacher and (*b*) discipline takes place through a range of sanctions, going from a reprimand to expulsion. If this question is actually discussed as a side issue to the question of, for example, a model lesson, we learn totally other details, such as different kinds of microtechniques. So, during the 1880s, in the journal *Het Katholiek Onderwijs*, teachers discussed the question: during a

---

19   J. Oelkers, *Pädagogische Ratgeber: Erziehungswissen in populären Medien* (Frankfurt am Main: Moritz Diesterweg, 1995), p. 14

written exercise, should we impose a certain number of rules or is it preferable to allow a fixed amount of time for the exercise?[20]

Some thought that imposing fixed rules had the disadvantage that pupils finished the exercise at different times, and had time free time to cause trouble. In other words, in the discussion of a question of educational method, disciplinary questions were also taken into account, whereas in 'official discourse' these are two separate issues. On the one hand, there was an ideal didactical approach, and on the other, pupils had to be kept under control. But that was another item, namely 'the authority of the teacher', where one could read, for example, that authority was simply something a teacher did or didn't have. In the daily life of a school, these matters were of course indivisible, and if we look at the confusion of issues in the press, we can conclude that this is reality.

It is self-evident that the press is a prominent source of information, and there are historical reasons for this. The press, not photographs and films, was at the heart of the entire educational set-up. Photographs and films were marginal. Internal communication took place through journals, which were in fact creating reality, but only in part in the sense of discourse. You 'create' reality in a certain sense by talking about this and not that, or by connecting (*a*) with (*b*) and not with (*c*) except in the case of (*y*). It is always like this, but this ends in too far-reaching conclusions.

The texts were creating reality in particular by stating what precisely had to happen. In comparison to other educational advice books, school educational guidelines are now particularly suitable for a reality study. It could be said that it is impossible to study the history of daily life in school, because in school nothing was daily, at least not when the term 'daily' is understood as something of which we are actually unaware. A teacher had to be aware of everything he or she was doing. Complex reality was simplified in school by a standardization of behaviour. We can see this standardisation didactically (each lesson had to follow certain steps), but the rituals started outside as well. All of this can be read in the educational journals.

---

20   Depaepe *et al.*, *Order in Progress*, p. 172.

Social history of taste

Let us go back to some of the questions that certain people believe we should be asking on the subject of photographs. How are they arranged? What sort of symmetry do we find in these photographs? What can we learn from the lighting? How do the background and foreground relate to each other? How are volumes divided? This is the iconological alternative for text as a form of discourse, not the 'what', but the 'how' and the 'content of the form'.[21] The question as to what was *not* photographed is the next step. Firstly, this implies the question about which situations were not photographed, and secondly what was outside of the frame on the photographs that were taken. This type of research will no doubt lead us to marvellous discoveries, with 'hidden meanings'. This is the sphere of subliminal messages, images edited into films that the eye cannot see, but that we unconsciously observe, vinyl records played backwards, containing suicide assignments in the name of Satan.

We are willing to assume that the bulk analysis of piles of photographs can lead to the conclusion of specific dominant forms: set-up, type of pose, facial expressions. We can also observe changes and in this way could write a history of it. But what kind of information is this? Are we back in the collective 'optical unconscious' of school history? We do not believe that this is the case. We think that those who undertake this type of research will find themselves at the crossroads of the history of taste with the history of school photography. Here is a clear difference with texts, which were written by people involved in education. When we discover certain forms in texts and come across a layer of recurrent images such as 'outside life' or 'the beehive' in the case of reform education, you can assume that we can learn something about underlying motivations within the education system. If, on the other hand, you see this type of recurrence in visual compositions, you can assume that you find yourself in the

21 Quoted in V. Sobchack, 'History happens,' in V. Sobchack (ed.), *The Persistence of History: Cinema, Television and the Modern Event* (London: Routledge, 1996), p. 8.

sphere of the study of the attitudes of photographers, about their field of work and (possibly) their views on education.

To put it simply, are children laughing on school photographs or do they look serious? A whole history can be written about this. From the few photographs taken in the classroom, we can ask: are they assuming a pose or are they natural photographs? That is, are they assuming a non-posed pose, or are they in a relaxed pose – because all photographs are posed unless they are taken with a telephoto-lens. Again, we can write the story, which may be fascinating. Here, it is interesting to read the insights of Pierre Bourdieu on the social use of photography.[22] Bourdieu says that photography is not a natural language: it is a conventional system in which space is expressed according to the laws of a particular perspective. Or put another way: it makes people angry if you leave out the palm trees in the foreground of a holiday snap. There must be a foreground and a background. Everybody has become a photographer and everybody thinks about centring and wants to avoid clichés. On posing, Bourdieu says: assuming a pose is something only country people do. This is how they show their self-respect. Townspeople have a preference for the 'natural'. He adds that the contrast cannot be seen so clearly.

We could write an entire history of taste based on school photographs, and that could also be a social history, if one believes that the pursuit of distinction can also be expressed through photography. People fight for prestige and it is well known that in this fight, the most futile detail can be considered to be a stake. In any case, it appears to us that it is a better approach to the writing of a social history of centring, proportionality, behaviour within a photograph, than that taken by Martin Jay, who too easily saw entire visions of knowledge acquisition symbolized through the arrangement of groups of pupils in photographs.

In passing, we should comment that this kind of history of school photography cannot be written solely on the basis of photographs. We would need much more information about the circumstances of the scene, the extent to which the school (director, teacher) was involved

---

22   P. Bourdieu, 'The social definition of photography', in J. Evans and S. Hall (eds.), *Visual Culture: The Reader* (London: Sage, 1999), pp. 162–80.

in the setting. We would need to investigate how photographers may have been using the school to publicize their trade and to earn an income. Only when we knew all of that could we really interpret the photographs from a symbolic perspective; only then could we say if a specific placing of pupils symbolized the 'process of knowledge acquisition', or if placing was an expression of the skill of the photographer, or his aesthetic principles in the sphere of image composition. All this would be interesting to know, but the point is that it would be the role of the school photographer that would be discussed, his motives, his insights and his optical unconscious. But in the final analysis the school photographer played no significant role in education. To put it another way, we will certainly read a book about this, but we do not intend to go as far as writing it ourselves. It is a fine subject for a thesis, but it is not the Big Revolution of educational history.

In order for this to be an important field of study for us, much more would have to happen: inventories, identification of faces, seeking sources regarding the interaction between the school authorities and photographers (if they already existed), and even then, we wonder whether it is really worth the trouble? If we looked at photographs in the numerous tributes and memorial books that were published about educational history, we can see the answer: there is nothing to be gained from this field, neither on the image nor next to it; neither in the content nor in the form.

It might be argued, however, that this conclusion may not be relevant to film, where 'moving images' are in play. For reasons of space, a comprehensive review of the utility of all genres of Belgian film for educational analysis cannot be undertaken here.[23] Instead, we limit ourselves to two general comments before proceeding with a specific analysis of *De Witte* (a film based on the novel with the same title by Ernest Claes) designed to illustrate the general problems with using moving images as a source for educational history.

First, the potential for developing a significant analysis of educational history from Belgian film is severely limited by the fact

23   K. Dibbets, *Sprekende Films: De Komst van de Geluidsfilm in Nederland 1928 –1933* (Amsterdam: Otto Cromwinckel, 1993).

that Belgium is not really a country with a very high standing in native film-production.[24] Belgium did not have the necessary infrastructure to build a strong film industry and, in terms of quantitative data, this obviously limits what can be done. Second, and again for reasons of space, we limit ourselves to a detailed analysis of two different film versions of the novel *De Witte*. These are specific criticisms based on particular films but, with only minor amendments, the issues we raise could be easily applied to other film genres.[25] In all cases, we argue that visual images have little to teach us about the daily reality of education. Moreover, and a little ironically, what can be gleaned from popular, propaganda, didactic and amateur films depends on a prior knowledge of traditional textual sources.

School and Film

Not much of Belgium's limited film production has any relationship with education. However, in De Hert's *Blueberry Hill* (1989) and *Brylcreem Boulevard* (1995) and in *Les risques du métier* (1967) with Jacques Brel, school life in secondary education is a central theme.

There are no similar films with primary schools as the setting. Only a few films looked at children's life at primary school age where, more as a by-the-way than anything else, the little protagonists just stayed in a classroom. *De Witte,* the regional novel by Ernest Claes, in which a miscreant boy is punished mercilessly, is a prototype of this style. The book was filmed twice, by Jan John Vanderheyden in 1934 and by Robbe De Hert in 1980, and school discipline features prominently each time.[26]

---

24   R. De Hert, *Het Drinkend Hert Bij Zonsondergang: Het Jungle-Boek van de Vlaamse Film* (Leuven: Kritak, 1987); P. Duynslaegher, *Blik op Zeven: Flashback op 100 jaar Film* (Roeselare: Roularta Books, 1985).

25   An earlier version of this paper also analysed propaganda, didactic and amateur films.

26   See 'Wat staat er nu in "De Witte"' in E. Claes, *Ik en de Witte* (Antwerp: Standaard Boekhandel, 1960), pp. 204–12.

The first *De Witte* film has practically become a monument in the history of Belgian film. It is wrongly assumed that it was the first Flemish sound film, for the *Familie Klepkens* had been issued in 1930 with appropriate gramophone records.[27] The producer of that film, Jan John Vanderheyden (1890–1961), is one of the godfathers of the Flemish film industry. During the First World War Vanderheyden worked for the London division of Pathé and, at the end of the war, developed film distribution in his native city, Antwerp, first under the name Soleil Levant (Rising Sun), and then, after 1925, under the English name International Film Distributors. In particular, the company brought German films to the Flemish theatres, having first created subtitles. Vanderheyden met his future partner Edith Regelien-Kiel (1904–94) through business connections with the German Afaa-film. She suggested that he make his own Flemish full-length feature film, for which she wrote the scenario based on the Ernest Claes bestseller (that Claes had to translate partly into Dutch; Claes suspected her of having misunderstood some parts of the original). The duo used a German film crew, but recruited the cast from the Flemish theatre. The indoor scenes were filmed in Germany, with limited or movable scenery, while the outdoor scenes were filmed in the area where the story is set.[28]

Although Vanderheyden initially only acted as producer, Willem Benoy, the director, quickly failed to live up to his role through lack of film experience. Vanderheyden, who was a film seller rather than a film connoisseur, was a bundle of nerves and grumbled throughout the outdoor shoots that he was loosing 'his millions'.[29] Edith Kiel, the only one of the Belgian group with experience in film shooting (she had been an extra in *Der Blaue Engel*) took over his job.

27   F. Bolen, *Histoire authentique, anecdotique, anecdotique, folklorique et critique du cinéma belge depuis ses plus lointaines origines* (Brussels: Memo and Codec, 1978), pp. 117–25; J. Vincent (ed.), *Aslagwerk over de Vlaamse film ('Het Leentje')* (Brussels: CIAM, 1986), pp. 706–8.

28   E. Claes, *Toen De Witte werd verfilmd* (Zele: Reinaert, 1977), pp. 7–78.

29   '[He] always blamed his wife, Edith Kiel, who in fact knew more than the others what film production was all about' (L. Timmermans, 'I still was a child', in J. van Hemelryck (ed.), *Omkijken naar Ernest Claes (1885–1985)* (Tielt: Lannoo,1985), pp. 181–2).

So, *De Witte*, a film about a Flemish boy in a Belgian country classroom around the turn of the century, not only got a script from Germany and was filmed near Berlin after a German screenplay, but also was directed by a woman who grew up in Germany. Clearly, the film was not a close interpretation of the book. Firstly, the different chapters of the novel were stuck together with a love story that came straight out of the amateur theatre, complete with role exchange, anonymous letters and a festive denouement at a fair dance. The film has an opening sequence with images of the sea, of statues and historical façades of Bruges, Brussels, Antwerp and Ghent which have nothing to do with the story, but underline the slogan 'de eerste film van bij ons' (the first film from our country). According to Claes the film misrepresents the central role – the incomprehension the boy was fighting, the slaps he got after his practical jokes, the hatred of a punished child.[30] In his diary, Claes wrote about his disappointment, although publicly he defended the film for years by personally encouraging its production in Flanders and in the Netherlands.

> 13.09.1934. The first showing of the De Witte film took place today. The auditorium was crammed full. I am not happy with the film. It is a bland depiction of my delightfully wild little terror. And then, the story of the lovers is completely stupid. The film is full of improbabilities. I left it with pain in my heart, although I have to admit that the film was a great success with the audience.[31]

Former cameraman and actor Robbe De Hert produced the second screen version of *De Witte* – *De Witte van Sichem* (De Witte from Sichem) – in 1980. Unlike Vanderheyden's film, the funny and crude elements play only a background role, broad aspects are moved to the background. Although De Witte still kept getting into mischief, even using references to the first film version, he was mainly just a

---

30   See M. Depaepe, *De Pedagogisering Achterna: Initiative to a Genealogy of the Pedagogical Mentality in the last 250 years* (Leuven: Acco, 1998), pp. 158–9. See also in this connection, the interpretation by Claes's biographer, A. Boni, in *Ernest Claes: Een blik op zijn leven en levenswerk* (Leuven: Davidsfonds, 1948).

31   E. Claes, *Uit de dagboeken van Ernest Claes* (Leuven: Davidsfonds, 1981), p. 66.

deprived boy from a poor farming family, who got more beating than eating. De Hert strongly departed from the line followed by both Vanderheyden and Claes by portraying the little boy as he got to know striking workers, turning his world view upside down. The misery of the lead character who grew up too quickly was stressed by his failed suicide, with Vanderheyden's farmers only playing a background role. Although clearly, from a technical point of view, De Hert's production was of far superior quality than Vanderheyden's poor result, it was similarly spoiled by the 'comical' guest appearance of Flemish stars. The film was well received, but did not do as well in the box offices as its predecessor in 1934.[32]

Despite differences in film style and story line, both films contain three classrooms scenes, of which the first opens on romping children in a playground, who were then led in line into the classroom. In Vanderheyden's film, the playground is clearly recorded in a studio, and lighting and make-up are theatrical in their effect. The headmaster shouts, the children gather together, the headmaster inspects the rows while they are still pushing and pulling each other behind his back. And under close scrutiny the children march, singing lustily, into the classroom. All shots are long distance except for one close-up of De Witte. In the first scene, the class is being taught by the headmaster, while his assistant walks up and down the rows of children reading a love letter that appears later in the story. In a second classroom scene, the younger teacher is teaching in the same classroom. The classroom consists of a spacious room with windows on the left-hand side, a podium, a desk, a blackboard, and two rows of benches; the walls are bare. The classroom is remarkably clean and there are only some fifteen boys in the class which is remarkably homogeneous as far as age is concerned.

All the classroom scenes are inexplicably chaotic, with no introduction and structure, nor any educational moral lesson to be learnt: a catechism question-and-answer session is quickly followed by a geography lesson. The teacher asks questions to individual pupils, who automatically jump up beside their bench to reply, and the

---

32   M. Paquot, 'De Hert. Les années 80', in Jungblut *et al.*, *Une Encyclopédie des Cinémas*, p. 83; Duynslaegher, op. cit., p. 350.

more stupid the answer the better. Almost all the answers give rise to hilarity among the pupils and the teacher tries to regain peace and quiet by asking a new question, which has no relationship with the previous one. In both the second and third scenes, the teacher is called away to get an urgent message in the corridor, which is a signal for the classroom to erupt into chaos. On one occasion, all the pupils are gathered around one bench, shouting loudly. The teacher reacts by coming back into the classroom and waiting till silence falls and then saying furiously that everyone should go back to his bench.

If anything, the school scenes from Vanderheyden's film give an insight into the limited technical possibilities of 1930s cinema-tography, rather than Belgian school life at the end of the nineteenth century. The sparse decor is German. The lessons are used merely as a binding agent for the tricks pupils play with saliva, ink-pen nibs, marbles and shouting. When De Witte has to stay back after class, the teacher stays with him. In the same way as they would perform a dialogue on the theatre stage, both teachers wait until the pupils have finished making a noise to put an end to the racket.

Remarkably, there is a lack of violence in the film, in contrast to the original novel, where there was regular stamping and fighting, both by adults and children. This type of brute violence is taboo in the film. The teacher never lays a finger on his pupils.

In this sense De Hert's *De Witte Van Sichem* is slightly different. Firstly, the film is clearly placed in a specific time and place: in Sichem, the week after 15 July 1901. The playground is more spacious and extends into the street. The film is clearly filmed outside, in the courtyard of an old school building. Playtime is ended with a school bell. In this film only the headmaster, Bakelants, is in the classroom, and his colleague is obviously teaching another group, but this is not shown.

In this film, too, the lesson is very chaotic, but there is an explanation: as soon as the teacher starts his history lesson, the priest comes in to check the children's knowledge of the catechism. When the former is unable to keep them quiet through silent reading of a history text, he orders them to write down all the multiplication tables. While in the Vanderheyden film, the teacher's questions lead from one farce to the next, De Hert's teacher orders them to learn in silence, after which they get into mischief with marbles and apples. There is no hilarious laughter when the marbles fly around; quite the opposite: the class holds its breath, terrified, and all you can hear is the tap of marbles on the floor. The teacher shouts, questions, threatens those who were involved and hits the culprit while the class looks on in silence. It is only at the beginning of the third school scene that the class roars when the teacher humiliates De Witte at the blackboard by his poor knowledge of sums, which is connected with the loss of his clothes the previous day. In this film, the language is stronger and the story has more coherence. But does this make it a better source for study of educational history?

According to film dictionaries the use of long shots, such as those which prevail in Vanderheyden's films, elicit a more distant, analytical attitude on the part of the viewer. [33] We believe, however, that it shows rather the lack of film experience of the production crew. The film does not induce any feelings of sympathy with school children. De Hert's *De Witte* shows more technical sophistication, with a moving camera, medium-distance shots of pupils on the benches, close-ups of hands and the use of suggestive sound (for example, the tap-tap of marbles). Both directors film the classroom scenes among the pupils. De Hert places the camera on the podium when a pupil answers, but the camera angle still portrays that both directors want to show class life through the pupils' eyes, rather than those of the teacher. However, neither film gives a realistic image of primary schools in Belgium around the turn of the century. At no time, is it shown how a lesson is given. Vanderheyden's version is impregnated by (German?) military rituals, but paradoxically contains no corporal punishment and little psychological terror inflicted by teacher. De Hert's version shows more interaction between pupils and teacher, but the anachronisms of his version may lie in the ex-aggeratedly rich teaching material (even in the storeroom and punishment corner, where busts and models are still piled up), in the wall charts dating from the 1930s and in the school library. The language of the film, the pressure of the rhythm of the story and the

---

33   J.-M. Peters, *Pictorial Signs and the Language of Film* (Amsterdam: Rodopi, 1981).

obvious aim to communicate a certain perception of the situation prevail in both films.

In short, feature films made between the 1930s and 1980s are not entirely useful for the study of educational reality at the end of the last century. As far as using film as source material, we have to take the same position we took in regard to the novel, in that we have to assume that the experience of the writer as pupil or teacher is present in the production. Films say more about the personal experiences of the author from his or her school time than about educational history. If we watch this type of film in a naively realistic way, we come to the conclusion that we can gain nothing from the study of it. So we are obliged to see whether there may be another way of studying the film. The differences between book and film are interesting. In the films we have studied, punishments are presented more humanely than in books. Is this a historical development connected to the growth of taboo areas, including corporal punishment, or is it simply due to the different medium? It lies, of course, in both of these, but in order to gain any value from this knowledge, we have to consult written sources.

It is likely that violence decreased over time, although it was still present. But the classroom situation changed so that there were fewer children per classroom, better organized inspections, increased professionalism, more tradition and possibly less resistance on the part of the children. Generations of schooling had increased acceptance of the school's disciplinary regimes. We also have to recognise that film is another medium. If you write that a boy is kicked, it seems less violent than if you see it on screen. To render this scene harmless on screen it has to become slapstick. But how can this be reconciled with the fact that the 1980 film shows crude physical violence? Had the humanization of punishment reached a point where it actually came full circle and broke the taboos? Finding an answer to these questions would be purely speculative.

It seems futile to try and develop tricks to reach significant conclusions about classroom history, or educational history in general by using the inventive interpretation of technical-artistic aspect of film. What can we learn from slow montage and the widespread use of staging? Is it only that Vanderheyden was not influenced by the montage-experiments of Russian formalists, and was stuck in the tradition of filmed theatre? If this is all, we have embarked on a discussion of the history of film in Belgium, rather than educational history, a discussion of the influence of German *Heimat*-film, rather than German expressionism. An analysis of the quick montage and non-linear chronology of Oliver Stone's *JFK*, with its continual flashbacks and so on would tell us something about the American perception of politics in the 1990s. We could study *De Witte* for days, and still find no such insights!

Conclusion

Our standpoint in this article is that the 'pictorial turn', if we really need such a dramatic title for an appeal to gain more attention for the visual in the history of education, can only be useful in that it draws more attention to visual aspects of the reality of teaching and education, and so there is no need for infinite analyses about the 'representation of education and teaching in visual sources'.[34] We've already enumerated the reasons why we do not think this advisable, and they are all too obvious. The source material is too limited in its content and number to be a representation of reality and can only really be used as a complement to the textual sources with which it has to be interpreted.

We believe that the value of visual sources is as part of the historical education reality and not as a representation of it and this value should encourage interest in two particular spheres, the image as a medium of education and teaching, and the pedagogical gaze.[35] Over the course of time, images have been used in the same way as text as a teaching tool.

---

34   A. Nóvoa, 'Ways of saying, ways of seeing: public images of teachers (19th-20th century)', in Depaepe and Henkens, *The Challenge of the Visual*, pp. 21–52.

35   F. Pöggeler, *Bild und Bildung: Beiträge zur Grundlegung einer Pädagogischen Ikonologie und Ikonographie* (Frankfurt am Main: Peter Lang, 1992).

For years, pedagogues have been fighting over image and text. Ever since the time of Herbart, there has been an argument in the 'higher pedagogy' that, despite its derision in what we have called the 'lower pedagogy', image is more powerful than word and acts on a deeper level.[36] In New Education circles image was even more important and credence was given to the 'living image', over and above the 'real image'. We never see a drawing of the patterns of vein in a leaf, but we see the leaf itself. We do not see a stuffed owl, but are presented with a real one.

So already in 1880, there were doubts about the power of the word, and in 1930, it was given no credence at all, at least for the word as argument. Some space was allocated to emotional impressions. Arguments gave way to emotional impressions; that was New Education.[37] It was thought that those impressions had to be taken in directly through the senses, especially sight. The other senses, like touch, were neglected. But that was the opposition: word versus image.

Secondly, analysis of written sources indicated that the pedagogical gaze, the way of looking educationally (Foucault's or Bentham's approach is popular but probably much too general) played an essential role in the education process. Maybe the pedagogical gaze could well be analysed through all kinds of visual sources (a pedagogical-didactic study of wall charts, for example, can be relevant in this context). But in the final analysis we have to admit that yet again written text is the best source material, that it is necessary for the interpretation of visual sources and not the opposite. This is because communication in the course of the nineteenth and twentieth centuries happened more through text than image. This may well change over the course of the twenty-first century through internet culture. But this perspective is of no use to historical research. A

36   H.-U. Grunder, 'Die Verteufelung des Bildes in der Geschichte der Pädagogik', in Depaepe and Henkens, *The Challenge of the Visual*, pp. 53–71.
37   Compare the metaphors used by Peeters and Verheyen in Depaepe, *Order in Progress*, p. 87.

historical researcher must be careful not to use what is obvious and speculative in their time to interpret the past.

Catherine Burke

10 Personal Journeys: an Examination of the Use of the Concept of Time Travel in Constructing Knowledge of Past Educational Spaces

The consideration of space, place, site and imagery within an explorative and constructivist framework, characterizes new approaches to the history of education. This, together with a literature which speaks of the appreciation of cultural zones including the body as a kind of mapping has stimulated new considerations of pedagogical design in the subject.[1] 'Conjuring notions of place' is a theme explored by Jane McKie, who has taken the concept of the travel guide to illuminate tensions and dilemmas thrown up by the possibilities of online learning.[2] Allowing for autonomy whilst providing structure, support and guidance is a balance which should be achieved in any successful learning setting. And taking the travel metaphor further, on any journey to a territory which is strange and exotic – however defined – the traveller seeks for the possibilities of adventure and discovery: too much guidance can limit such an encounter.

> People who are constantly asking 'why' are like tourists, who stand in front of a building, reading Baedeker, and through reading about the history of the building's construction etc. are prevented from *seeing* it.[3]

1 See for example F. Biocca and M. R. Levy (eds.), *Communication in the Age of Virtual Reality* (Hillsdale, NJ: Lawrence Erlbaum Associates, 1995).

2 J. McKie, 'Conjuring notions of place', in N. Blake, and P. Standish (eds.), *Enquiries at the Interface: Philosophical Problems of Online Education* (Oxford: Blackwell, 2000), pp. 123–33.

3 L. Wittgenstein, *Culture and Value* (Oxford: Blackwell, 1980), p. 40e.

What does *seeing* in this context imply? And how does *seeing* in this sense allow for a freedom to learn through an envisaging of other landscapes rather than an acquisition of knowledge about them?

McKie cites the journalist Andrew O'Hagan who has suggested:

> Travelling with long out-of-date travel books is better fun than going with a contemporary guide: it helps you notice changes, to make contrasts, to conjure with previous notions of the place.[4]

Conjuring with previous notions of place is a concept which is characteristic of a pedagogical approach to the history of education which encourages the learner to actively engage with the layers of time and space which are captured in any one educational setting. Two distinct activities and their outcomes will be offered here as examples of contemporary practice within undergraduate programmes of study in the UK: the first, an example which exploits the possibilities of the Internet in a collaborative online learning framework; the second, which encourages the creation of new archives for the history of education.[5]

The first is an example of interactive computer-supported collaborative learning which uses a tailormade website to create the illusion of time travel through past sites of education and schooling in England.

Part of an undergraduate module entitled 'Children and Schools', the object was to allow for an examination and exploration of the origins of the present state educational system in England.[6] The approach encouraged the student not only to read and digest information found in the web pages and to follow links to appropriate other online sites, it required that a text based response should be made in role. For example, if by travelling from space to space through the web site the student found themselves with a schooling setting in a workhouse, the

---

4   A. O'Hagan, quoted in McKie, op. cit., p. 129.
5   For more on the importance of creating new archives, see I. Grosvenor, and M. Lawn, 'In search of the school', *Bildung und Erziehung: Virtuelle Bildungsgeschichte*, 1 (March 2001), 55–70.
6   C. Burke, 'Personal journeys: student evaluation of electronic role play in learning online', *Active Learning Journal*, 11 (December 1999), 3–8.

response might be made in role as a child, a workhouse keeper, a teacher, a parent or any other appropriate voice. The choice of role remained with the learner and the module leader or tutor also took on a role, sometimes initiating a discussion, sometimes responding. It was possible to slip with ease from one role to another but an important dimension to the exercise was that the imagined voice or view of the child could be considered. Since the child who is after all the subject of educational practice leaves little to the historian of primary evidence, it is just this perspective which fails to be incorporated into any analysis of past schooling systems.

A constructivist learning approach was adopted and the dilemmas thrown up with regard to authenticity, reliability and the creative response to sources provoked discussion and consideration. In so doing, it could be argued that a form of 'deep learning' had resulted.[7]

To successfully report, in this case to each other as part of a small group within an online discussion space, the student had to gain some insight into their new circumstances as an inhabitant of a past world. They were required to report their feelings, their observations and their knowledge with the voice of an other. Messages were archived and it was possible for a considered and reflective comment to be made at any time.[8]

Here is an example of a learner adopting the voice of a girl from the past.

> Papa doesn't think that sending me away to boarding school is worth spending money on. He thinks the money should be saved for my dowry. Besides I can learn all I need to at home. Mother is interviewing a Governess tomorrow so I will soon learn to read and write like my brothers.[9]

---

7   'Deep learning' as opposed to 'surface learning' is associated with the learning process being subject to discussion. See P. Ramsden, *Learning to Teach in Higher Education* (London: Routledge, 1992).

8   This is known as asynchronous online discussion, where the learner has flexible and continuous access to discussion threads.

9   Student, Bretton Hall College, 2000.

Social class, gender and location were hinted at markedly in the adoption of certain voices with distinct dialects and nuances peculiar to time and place. This was constructed entirely by the students involved and took on a dimension which in effect created an exclusive dramatic world. The particular use of regional dialect is illustrated here.

> I wish mamma would hurry up and cook the tea. I'm really hungry. The bairns are getting fractious. Of course as I'm eldest I've got to look after them. It wouldn't be so bad if it were just our Mabel, Jane, Seth, Freddie and Albert – I've always got to look after them while mamma's preparing for tea and we are waiting for father to come home. [10]

It was the intention of the approach to allow a critical stance to develop in the learner by means of entering an entirely 'other' world and by means of exploring the familiar amongst the exotic. In so doing the learner can become aware of and is able to articulate continuities and change in the experience of schooling over time.

The decision to stay and explore or to travel to other points on any journey represents a kind of freedom and autonomy. The ideal travel experience provides comfort, ease of travel, clear direction, discovery and chance. In the pedagogical sense, constructing learning as a journey is not a difficult concept to grasp. But until the advent of educational technologies such as web-based learning and hypermedia or hypertext[11] the control of flow of information and the route taken via a syllabus was very much in the control of the teacher. Internet-based learning appears to encourage the learner to enter a maze of uncharted territory, to become lost in the enormous range of available material which is often not clearly marked. But an element of structure and guidance can, it is argued here, stimulate a sense of freedom and exploration which works for some learners and which creates new perspectives on past educational spaces.

The second example of pedagogy which will be presented and discussed here does not utilise the possibilities of the Internet in teaching and learning but does require that the learner leave the

10   Student, Bretton Hall College, 2000.
11   Referring to information which is structured in a non-linear way, allowing for autonomy of choice in the learner's path through the experience.

classroom and engage in travel, exploration and *seeing* the familiar as exotic and 'other'. Using the metaphor of an archaeological dig, the notion which generates this approach is the recognition that within any one site of learning – for example, school, workplace, or college – there are to be discovered layers of evidence laid down over time which chart and record the impact on that space of human activity in the pursuit of education. With an understanding that 'proof and evidence might co-exist with ambiguity, contrast and layering' so the learning emerges from the setting up of a creative and useful tension between 'descriptions of a fixed space and a struggle over its meaning'.[12]

Figure 21: School classroom, date unknown, Featherstone, Yorkshire.

In this instance then, the student is required to explore a contemporary school site and to construct a journey through educational

---

12   I. Grosvenor, M. Lawn and K. Rousmaniere (eds.), *Silences and Images: The Social History of the Classroom* (New York: Peter Lang, 1999), p. 9.

time drawing on the primary evidence in both the built environment, the walls, the windows, corridors, floors and doors and on the memories of those who worked there as teachers or pupils. What can be revealed through such an exploration are materials which are imbued with educational policy and practice but also with memory and emotion.

> Memories of schooling offer a primary source of experiential insights into layers of social and educational history. Ideologies are seen translated into the physical environment and individual experience [...] it can be seen how although aspects of state educational policy have changed, elements of schooling ideology persisted from one generation to the next.[13]

Through a microstudy which attends to detail and specificity, the general or macro history in terms of ideology, policy and practice is starkly revealed.

> Featherstone [near Barnsley, Yorkshire] with its varied history of schooling has epitomised almost every aspect of education in working class England, from the charity schools through elementary and up to the present secondary and primary schools, all have been represented at some time in the area. The impact of government policy has been reflected in the many styles of school building present in the town. Government policy has also affected the curricula taught in these schools over the years and the built environment has often affected how the curriculum is delivered.[14]

In employing an 'active learning' approach, this form of pedagogy is enabling and affirming of the learner who can recognize that they themselves are in the process of revealing and recovering past educational histories and that indeed new archives need to be created.

13   Undergraduate assignment, Arts and Education BA (Hons.), Bretton Hall College, 2001.
14   Undergraduate assignment, Arts and Education BA (Hons.), Bretton Hall College, 2001.

We need to take photographs of children not only when they are smiling but when they are sad or maybe crying as this helps us to build up a complete picture of who they are.[15]

What these two pedagogical approaches have in common is the attention to the specificity of time and space in distinct educational settings. They both allow for the construction of knowledge within a framework which is structured but allows for autonomy. They allow for and encourage discovery, adventure and a reconsideration of the familiar as uncharted territory. They appear to generate a transformation in ways of seeing and a prolonged interest and engagement in the subject.[16]

Figure 22: School grounds, Yorkshire, 1950s.

15   S. Shuff, unpublished undergraduate assignment cited in C. Burke, 'Hands-on history: towards a critique of the "everyday"', *History of Education*, 30.2, (2001), 191–201 (p. 200).

16   One undergraduate student has recently located the whereabouts of one of the teachers, long retired, who taught at the time of the making of the photographic collection.

Supporting learning as a creative process necessarily involves the emotions and engagement with self as well as subject. It is difficult to be creative dispassionately! In both of the pedagogical approaches to a history of education discussed here, the learner is encouraged to reflect upon their own decision-making, their own impulse towards certain spaces and sites of interest, their own senses and emotions as they are caught up in an exploration of a system which has at one time impacted upon their own identity.[17]

Freedom in determining the route one takes through a learning experience is challenging to many students who wish to be directed and carried systematically through a syllabus or programme, but it is a feature which is integral to a pedagogical experience designed to encourage student autonomy and reflexivity.

The theoretical grounding of this form of pedagogy might be described as learning as a creative process whereby a form of world-making occurs within which the ambiguous flow of experience is punctuated and ordered in a creative act of sense making.[18]

'Flow Theory' attempts to explore the psychological state of learning when the learner is taken along by the experience almost in spite of self, the state in which people are so involved in an activity that motivation occurs seemingly naturally.[19] Flow occurs, it is suggested, when an activity 'frees the individual, at least temporarily, from other worries and frustrations and [...] all feelings of self-consciousness disappear'.[20] Rieber relates this to his own focus which is the role of play in learning. However, the evidence presented here argues that 'flow' can be achieved through a pedagogy which engages the learner actively in a critical approach to a real or constructed environment. The following remark made by an undergraduate student

---

17   See Burke, 'Hands-on history', where I have commented further on the emotional response to exploring the history of schooling.
18   N. Goodman, *Ways of Worldmaking* (Indianapolis: Hackett, 1978).
19   Usually associated with M. and I. S. Csikszentmihalyi, *Optimal Experience: Psychological Studies of Flow in Consciousness* (New York: Cambridge University Press, 1988).
20   L. P. Rieber, 'Seriously considering play: designing interactive learning environments based on the blending of microworlds, simulations, and games', *Educational Technology Research and Development*, 44.2, (1996), 43–58.

in reflecting upon her experience of taking the computer-supported 'journey' to other educational spaces suggests this form of engagement:

> When I first started, I felt I was in front of this machine, struggling with this computer. Then, when I entered the web site, I forgot all about the computer altogether – I was in there – in the 'journey' [...] it was as if Robert Owen and the others were still alive! I had fears that I would not be able to gather information through computers, but once I entered into the computer into my journey of education there was no ending to the information I gained. I forgot about computers and my identity – instead I became a character in the past.[21]

Experiential learning is recognised as an essential element of any learning situation at all levels. However, in the humanities, it is perhaps true to say that the higher the level of education, the less frequently experiential or even active learning is employed as a technique. Engagement in learning is likely to return pleasure as well as achievement. But scholars are divided as to its meaning. Clark Quinn explores the meaning of engagement in the context of computer simulation but his remarks could equally carry weight in a non-electronic environment. In attempting to define engagement, Quinn talks of a required combination of 'embeddedness' and 'interactivity':

> Embeddedness includes thematic coherence, meaningfulness of action to the domain of representation, and meaningfulness of the problem in the domain to the learner [...] embeddedness differs from immersion, which to me is the physical presentation directly and exclusively to sensory inputs, such as seen in virtual reality environments. People can get just as engaged in a non-immersive environment as they can in an immersive one.[22]

Embeddedness and immersion both imply that the learner is wrapped both cognitively and physically in the learning activity. Embodiment as a notion could be added here to draw attention to the reflexive stance taken in the learning process. Reflection and reflexivity has become recognized as a learning strategy which produces a form of

---

21   Undergraduate student, Child and Family Studies, BA (Hons.), Bretton Hall College, 1999.

22   C. Quinn, 'Engaged Learning' in http://it.coe.uga.edu/itforum/paper18/paper 18.html (accessed 20.06.01).

knowledge which essentially acknowledges the role of self and auto-biography in its production.[23] In any teaching and learning situation structure is imposed by teachers and learners, usually in unequal measures. A central feature of this structure is the hierarchy of power and control embedded in the 'classroom' environment. New approaches to pedagogy which draw on the interactive possibilities of the Internet as well as the long tradition of critical pedagogy which has influenced adult and community educational practice over many years, are becoming revealed as possibilities in higher education as everything becomes questioned within postmodern economies of knowledge.

Such a pedagogy offers the potential to challenge orthodoxies and to encourage a move towards autonomy in the learning process. The online environment can be designed as a virtual world but more importantly its obviously constructed character provides the opportunity for teachers or facilitators to reveal to the learner the essentially provisional basis of knowledge and their part in its emergence.

23   See J. Smyth and G. Shacklock (eds.), *Being Reflexive in Critical Educational and Social Research* (London: Falmer, 1998); M. Alvesson and K. Skoldberg, *Reflexive Methodology: New Vistas for Qualitative Research* (London: Sage, 2000); F. Steier (ed.), *Research and Reflexivity* (London: Sage, 1991).

DEREK BUNYARD

11 Montage on Autobiography

Introduction

The argument developed here is that an encounter with archival material is fundamental to historical experience, and that pseudonymous writing about personal experience through the medium of montage provides an effective propaedeutic for work on archival material, particularly when this is of a photographic nature.[1]

History's inflections

Socrates, in the *Phaedrus*, rejects the idea that epistemological categories are conventional. Our task is to observe 'the natural articulation, not mangling any of the parts, like an unskilful butcher'.[2] Today, of course, we have profound reservations about the notion that the world might be so naturally divided. Instead, in accommodating the possibility of diverse accounts, we tend to fall back on other foundations, such as sociology. From a sociological perspective there are some fairly obvious remarks that one can make about historiography.

There are at least three general statements that follow from accepting as valid multiple sources of 'truth'. In the first place, linguistic

---

1 The notion of pseudonymous writing is derived from Kierkegaard, who employed this strategy to evoke reflection upon 'subjective truth' in most of his writings.

2 Plato, *The Phaedrus* (Harmondsworth: Penguin, 1973), p. 82.

representations of historical events are creations, rather than linguistic 'mirrors' offering isomorphic images of an objective reality. This stance towards the writing of history entails abandoning viewpoints predicated on claims for external sources of truth outside of discourse. Secondly, the analysis of eyewitness accounts makes it abundantly clear that most are constructed in reverse: their structural form – particularly when seeking to offer explanations – depends on the identification of causal linkages that were not experienced as 'inevitable' at the time. Finally – and again a sociological common-place – most accounts are constructed on the basis of the interests and assumptions of the narrator.

To each of these sources of acknowledged error there are some equally familiar methodological responses: multiple perspectives are offered, divergent accounts are judged on the basis of 'reliable' evidence, and multiple stops along the supposed line of causation are made so as to estimate the extent to which any one line is the principal source of change, etc. In total, these refinements to historical method are all intended to avoid collapsing back to a position in which history itself is seen as artificial and lacking in substance.[3] Researchers within the discipline do not have licence to construct whatever narratives they choose. The 'real' of the past, even when conceived as irredeemably recondite and ultimately elusive, continues to trouble the present. In response to this cultural stance, an audience of readers and fellow researchers collectively maintain (and modify) well-recognized obligations towards the forms of representation deemed acceptable within historical work at any one time.[4] A consideration of the nature of historical archives, and our relationship to these, throws some light on the factors influencing these sophisticated 'rules of the game'.

In the first place, what, in a formal sense, is the nature of the threshold that defines everything on one side as within and belonging

3   That is to say modernist, and not simulacral. See J. Baudrillard, *Simulacra and Simulation* (Ann Arbor: University of Michigan Press, 1994), pp. 43–8 for an extreme statement of the view that 'history' simply names a set of cultural arguments – a discourse.

4   The David Irving trial being a case in point. More generally, the difficulties which many have with Holocaust fiction are illustrative; see S. Vice, *Holocaust Fiction* (London: Routledge, 2000).

to the archive, and everything on the other side as extraneous to it? One answer is to see the threshold as a non-neutral frame – as a necessary pretext of assumptions and rules without which the contents could not be constituted qua content.[5] But in trying to further characterize the nature of this act of confinement, a number of writers have been drawn to Foucault's analysis of the oculocentric discourses of the sciences.[6] However, locating the formal properties of the historical archive within this same discourse runs the risk of aping assumptions of distance and objectivity necessarily entailed in an account that was attempting to track *and interpret* the growth of scientifically inspired technologies of control. Locating the archive within this framework turns it into a body of material structured so as to present the observer with a perfect visibility of the observed, along with an effacement of the archive constructor.[7]

In following this panoptic ideal a misinterpretation of the nature of historical understanding itself is generated. What is at stake within the historical archive is not so much the visibility of mechanism as the

5   See, for example, J. Tagg, *The Burden of Representation: Essays on Photographies and Histories* (Basingstoke: Macmillan, 1988), particularly chapters 2 and 6; M. Rosler, 'In, around, and afterthoughts (on documentary photography)' in R. Bolton (ed.), *The Contest of Meaning: Critical Histories of Photography* (Cambridge, MA: MIT Press, 1992); J. Roberts, *The Art of Interruption: Realism, Photography, and the Everyday* (Manchester: Manchester University Press, 1998), pp. 72–97. More generally, the point is forcefully developed in Derrida's *The Truth in Painting* through his notion of the *parergon*.

6   For instance, G. Batchen, *Burning with Desire: the Conception of Photography* (Cambridge, MA: MIT Press, 1997); J. Crary, *Techniques of the Observer* (Cambridge, MA: MIT Press, 1990). As Nicholas Royle points out, this reading of Foucault should be contrasted with a more Nietzschean line of thought as exemplified in his *Archaeology of Knowledge*; see N. Royle, *After Derrida* (Manchester: Manchester University Press, 1995), pp. 24–7. A more philosophical analysis is offered in R. D'Amico, *Historicism and Knowledge* (London: Routledge, 1989), chs. 5 and 6.

7   This is a very contentious area. R. D'Amico (1989), op. cit., provides a useful review of the contesting views; the distinction made here derives from Dilthey: i.e., crudely stated, that science deals with causes and history with reasons. Foucault attempts a refutation of this through his idea of *la fonction enonciative*; see M. Foucault, *The Archaeology of Knowledge* (London: Routledge, 1992), pp. 79–105.

construal of intention.[8] To be more precise, the historical aspect of the archive is essentially an act of naming which signifies that the contents are relevant to a particular contemporary and culturally determined set of arguments about the past. The mistaken misreading of Foucault turns the archive into an atemporal record of 'symptoms' denoting past forms of perception, intention, and belief.[9] But taken at face value, one might still assume that the two stances were united in their assumption that the task of the archive constructor was to avoid muddled collecting and confused analysis – in other words, to get the facts straight and penetrate beyond the merely gratuitous. But the prefatory remarks to this section suggest rather more: whereas the scientist may continue to assume that s/he is not dealing with an evil God, determined to sow doubt and error in the path of scientific endeavour, the historian must assume not only that deception is an inherent part of the process of discovery but that her own credibility in carrying out the research is also open to question.[10]

This is, of course, a modernist interpretation of the historian's dilemma: s/he must be continually alert to the possibility of subversion from the 'edges' of the frame of representation – must attend to that which is rendered marginal by the dominant discourse.[11] The consequences of this extend further than might at first be thought. Unless the archive is very small, there are practical difficulties to any immediate presentation matching the ocular ideals of Enlightenment

8   Royle is again helpful: N. Royle (1995), op. cit., pp. 30–2.
9   In other words, the construction of a surface upon which history conceived as a record of causes can be inscribed upon the substance of the archive.
10   For example, R. Descartes, *Discourse on Method and the Meditations*, (London: Penguin, 1968), pp. 58–9. Not only is there the task of establishing relevance in ways that seem both more personal and more 'interpretative' than is the case for the scientist, with respect to the archive contents themselves there must come the recognition that what is misleading may be intended, and the very perfection of any 'set' represented may depend on deliberate distortion, e.g. J. Roberts (1998), op. cit., pp. 72–97.
11   Apart from Derrida, this point is extensively developed by Jean-François Lyotard: a postmodern account would assume 'an incredulity' towards the construction of any absolute claims for the metanarrative involved in 'framing' an archive. See J.-F. Lyotard, *The Postmodern Condition: A Report on Knowledge* (Manchester: Manchester University Press, 1999), p. xxiv.

science. One is, instead, far more likely to be confronted with an index providing access to the multiplicity that it is understood to stand for. The syntactical/rhetorical structuring of the index itself has then to correspond to the logical structure of the archive contents, and this, if all is 'well ordered', will correspond to the reality depicted.[12] What follows for the nature of this archive type is that the discursive position is inevitably 'centralized' in a way that is formally equivalent to the single viewing point of perspective representation. Similarly, for the investigator as for the viewer, this systematic representation has a reciprocal outcome: the 'visibility' of the archive is enhanced when the contents are 'viewed' from this central position, and is rendered difficult when any alternative investigation is attempted.

Obviously not all archives are constructed according to these principles, but it is often the case that in an informal way they present the same difficulty. In these instances the constructive assumptions arise from pragmatic estimates about likely patterns of use, rather than a more abstract conception of an underlying formal unity and its 'visibility'. The central Foucaultian proposition remains: an objective and scientific representational structure will 'incarnate' the viewer, and it is difficult to avoid the conclusion that these more utilitarian approaches will similarly work to locate the user through their 'helpful' adoption of a 'typical' point of view. But what follows for the historian interested in the vagaries of meaning and its generation – one who wishes to adopt the role of detective, rather than scientist or amateur psychologist, while building or using an archive? Any number of detective stories suggest the correct response: the 'detective' must attend to anomalies within the apparently unified surfaces of meaning that are being developed/offered, since such details have the potential to reveal the disguised heterogeneity of the archive itself.[13]

12 The quoted phrase is Locke's. See A. Pringle-Patterson, *Locke's Human Understanding* (Oxford: Oxford University Press, 1969), p. 91. It points to-wards the aspirations (and problems) of 'logical positivism' developed within the Vienna School.

13 Slavoj Žižek has used this metaphor for other purposes. See S. Žižek , *Looking Awry: An Introduction to Jacques Lacan through Popular Culture* (Cambridge, MA: MIT Press, 1997), pp. 48–66. Christopher McQuarrie's film *The Usual Suspects* makes this same (postmodern) point explicitly: the detective looks up

This assumption of inherent deception entails that each anomaly (including gaps, silences, and unexpected short cuts) becomes the pretext for enquiring what was intended to be achieved by the supposed unity of the dominant field of meaning, and by whom? The false move is to accept the given meaning within the field as the necessary delimitation of the range of enquiry – to work only within its 'common sense'.[14] Instead, it becomes essential for both the archive constructor, and its user, to achieve some distance from the assumption of immediate intelligibility – to engender a sense of estrangement so that an act of deception may be recognized for what it is. However, 'distance' in itself is not enough – what is required is a means by which the nature of the 'frame' constituting the contents can be better understood; this is an intrinsic and formal – perhaps even atemporal – stance towards the archive and its contents.[15] Assuming a practice of this kind is possible, there remains no absolute guarantee of perfection outside the detective novel. What, after all, prevents this second, 'distanced' perspective from containing new anomalies as products of its own self-generation? For the classical detective story the answer is straightforward: the detective's solution retroactively provides a final narrative that links all events, individuals, and anomalies in a satisfyingly complete sequence of cause and effect. In so doing, contemporary normality is restored and reconfirmed in its authority.

For the historian such 'victories' are hard won and temporary. Typically a degree of conditionality attaches to both the constructive

at the bulletin board alongside which all interrogations have taken place and 'sees' the heterogeneous items of information 'Verbal' has used to construct his apparently consistent narrative.

14   This emphasises the extent to which work with the archive falls within the domain of meaning generation. See Poirot's comments about the unusual position of a chair at the scene of a murder: 'It is completely unimportant. That is why it is so interesting,' in A. Christie, *The Murder of Roger Ackroyd* (London: Flamingo, 2001), p. 74.

15   Agatha Christie offers the following example. Poirot speaking to Dr Sheppard: 'You are like the little child who wants to know the way the engine works. You wish to see the affair, not as the family doctor sees it, but with the eye of the detective who knows and cares for no one – to whom they are all strangers and equally liable to suspicion' (ibid., p. 126).

and presentational decisions reached in building the archive and the interpretative decisions made while using it.[16] As indicated above, what is at issue here is not so much the final eradication of all anomaly as the degree to which such conditionality is recognized and located within historical discourse. Such explicit recognition is often exorbitant in the demands it makes. Sticking with the analogy of the detective, it as though the historian has to choose between adopting the roles developed by Agatha Christie with her Poirot, and that of Raymond Chandler and his Philip Marlowe. The first offers an extreme of closure and distancing, the second its opposite: self-involvement and continuing uncertainty. The first promises a heightened ability to spot anomaly, but at the risk of a too radical simplification of the initial field of meaning; the second so complicates this as to run the risk of never emerging from under its shadow.[17] These two poles introduce an explicitly subjective element to our consideration of the archive, and point towards issues more obviously involved with writing the self.

Autobiography (by way of anamorphism)

By foregrounding the work of signification it became possible to shift student attention towards the pedagogic potential to others of their own autobiographical analyses. The 'distancing' effect of montage production was found to be particularly useful in encouraging students to view their own representations as manipulable and renegotiable.

To talk of manipulating representations inserts possibility between the word and its object, and by this act of insertion both word

16   This is the political/cultural edge to Derrida's play of *différance*.

17   These two forms of the detective novel can also be read as modernist and (almost) postmodernist, in that Poirot will use his 'little grey cells' to find that component which will disrupt the prevailing assumption (an *avant-gardiste* strategy), while Chandler's Marlowe will end by being further confirmed in his melancholic sense of all-pervading corruption. See S. Žižek (1997), op. cit., pp. 60–3.

and object loose their stability. However, what makes possible this
same possibility? So far in writing about the archive the term anomaly
has been used to denote some aspect within a system of meaning that
seems 'out of joint', that perhaps fits, but only just. Another way of
interpreting this state of affairs is to return to the oculocentric presuppositions referenced earlier and suggest that one is here encoun-
tering a form of anamorphism – an inclusion that is at first seen as
senseless or distorted relative to the rest of the field of representation.[18] In terms of possibility, we again face a split between the
modernist and postmodernist stance. A modernist critical analysis will
involve detecting anomaly from the margin, so to speak, so that it can
subsequently become one amongst a number of possible systems of
representation, that is, can be seen as obeying a different but equally
consistent ordering. The alternative move – the postmodern – may
seem much harder. It requires us to recognize what is retained within
the primary field of meaning but which is apparently senseless within
it.[19] In other words, there is recognition that the anomaly is the
'nightmare' that one hoped could be avoided, i.e. that which renders
the primary field of meaning insubstantial – corrupt, but unavoidably
so because only with this 'thing' at the centre is the field of meaning
held together.

At this point an analogy from the visual arts may help to make
clear what is at stake. Most art practices incorporating anamorphism
make great investment in the notion of disguise: clouds conceal the
bodies of animals, shadows form the hollows of a skull, and landscapes reveal the disguised bodies of young women, soldiers, and
gods. The link here with deception is significant. When the anamorphic element is placed alongside or within a consistent scopic
system, such as is the case with the peculiar yellowish stain on the
carpet in Holbein's *The Ambassadors* – a picture in all other respects

---

18   In the following account, the visual arguments reproduce aspects of the
      undergraduate programme, i.e., we do not use a Derrida-inspired equivalent.
19   This 'blot' is the essential element of non-meaning (the supplement) which
      makes possible the 'sense' of the primary field's ordering. See J. Derrida,
      Dissemination (London: Athlone Press, 1981), pp. 156–71; C. Norris, *Derrida*
      (London: Fontana Press, 1987), pp. 28–62; N. Royle (1995), op. cit., pp. 13–38.

suggesting an uncompromising visibility – it becomes possible for the artist to convey meaning by evoking a special kind of performative response from the viewer. Viewed straight on, Holbein's use of central perspective shows us the two ambassadors standing alongside a collection of objects symbolizing their wordly power.[20] But if we stand on the extreme right of the canvas the carpet stain resolves into a skull – a familiar momento mori reminding us of the inevitability of death, rather that the magnificence of wordly achievement – indeed, viewed from this position it is wordly achievement itself that is now rendered obscure.[21]

In total, therefore Holbein's picture presents a meditation on the transitory nature of wordly achievement, and it does so by providing a hierarchy of subject positions (incarnations) instead of making a related point by presenting an explicit and unified hierarchy of objects, such as exists, for instance, in Raphael's painting *The School of Athens*. The additional viewing position developed by the anamorphic skull is also constructed according to a system of central perspective, that is, in viewing the anamorphic image we do not move into a scopic regime that is utterly different in kind, only encounter the 'master' system written upon a new surface configuration which allows the surreptitious insertion of discordant content.[22] In part,

---

20   This collection of symbols introduces a complement to the idea of anamorphism: anaphorism, or the expression of connection and resemblance between things. Using these two terms the archive becomes a system articulated by two organizational imperatives: on the one hand that of anaphora – the establishment of contiguities and resemblances; and on the other that of anamorphism – seen now as a system by which partial yet self-consistent views upon the totality are developed and presented. The terms also relate to the two poles of semiotic analysis: the syntagmatic and the paradigmatic. What should be added is that the anaphoric is also equivalent to the syntagmatic with respect to meaning: the archival contents under this form of articulation gain their signification through difference.

21   Lacan referred to this idea on a number of occasions. See, for example, J. Lacan, *The Four Fundamental Concepts of Psychoanalysis* (London: Vintage, 1998), pp. 85–90. See Žižek 's account of this painting in S. Žižek , *Enjoy Your Symptom* (London: Routledge, 1992), p. 137.

22   Compare this with the playful acts of subversion employed by Picasso in developing his collages. See C. Poggi, *In Defiance of Painting: Cubism,*

perhaps, we come to penetrate the meaning of the disguised skull through a literal re-enactment of the dominant configuration of secular and religious views common in Holbein's time; it is as though we mirror the principal roles within a tableau vivant. In so doing, we are reminded of the dominant field's bland omissions – and the corresponding object set needed to correct the totality of the field of representation, that is, that which provides a 'deeper' yet still intrinsic appreciation of its system of order. On this reading, what is not apparently available, therefore, is that postmodern recognition of ultimate senselessness – the object which would make it possible to 'see' the final contingency of the dominant system of representation.

What kind of embodied operation matches this other reading? While the modernist may seek, ultimately, a reconciliation between the anomalous order and the surrounding dominant – perhaps after experimenting with overt forms of subversion – the postmodern strategy offers no prospect of this final consolation. No balance point can be reached, and one is left with a restless shifting of the gaze in which signifiers are filled and then evacuated of meaning.[23] Reading Holbein's picture within a postmodern paradigm, it now acts as the true 'central prospect' that resists symbolisation – a perspective upon that which both horrifies and fascinates. Varying attempts at symbolization made from within the dominant field of representation will repeatedly fail at this juncture, and yet – returning to the supposed stance of the historian – the necessity of so doing becomes the leitmotif of postmodern research.[24]

It seems essential to make these fundamentally different formal stances towards historical substance available to dialectical analysis

Futurism, and the Invention of Collage (New Haven: Yale University Press, 1992), pp. 59–89.

23   For example, D. Crimp, *On the Museum's Ruins* (Cambridge, MA: MIT Press, 1995), pp. 282–325.

24   For example, S. Friedlander, *Probing the Limits of Representation* (Cambridge, MA: Harvard University Press, 1992). Although some authors in this volume locate the representational difficulty as 'beyond' the horizon of normal discourse, i.e., at the margin – others seek to locate it at the heart of the representational system, as that which resists and returns the subject's gaze (Lacan).

within any pedagogy involving historical study. What is required, if the foregoing is accepted, is a strategy directing attention away from content and towards form itself.[25] Yet if this is granted, the turn to autobiography adopted in our own undergraduate programme must seem perverse. It must be stressed, however, that in promoting this informal 'archive' to work on initially, we focus on understanding the 'how' of archival representation, rather than the 'what'. Such a pedagogic strategy attempts, therefore, to establish an initial position *before* asking students to respond to the expectation that they (and we) become more than the incarnated subjects of ideology – that we retain a capacity to stand apart.[26] In our view, this pedagogic ideal of critical distance before the facts all too readily pushes students towards picking up the burden of representation prematurely, rather than pausing to think about that which is senseless or contradictory.[27] What, then, is a more appropriate response? Hegel's *Phenomenology of Spirit*, in analysing the nature of 'idea', provides a focus:

> But that accident as such, detached from what circumscribes it, what is bound and is actual only in its context with others, should attain an existence of its own and a separate freedom – this is the tremendous power of the negative; it is the energy of thought, of the pure 'I'. Death, if that is what we want to call this

25 However, see the introduction to R. D'Amico (1989), op. cit., in which an analysis on purely formal grounds is rejected. Yet it can be argued that formality does not prevent the eventual reintroduction of the historian's interpretative responsibility and burden, and an 'ethics' of historical enquiry; for example, see the second and third chapters of S. Bann, *The Inventions of History: Essays on the Representation of the Past* (Manchester: Manchester University Press, 1990).

26 This also holds true for the archive constructor. One supposedly dominated by a particular ideology would be expected to produce an archive congruent with the scopic assumptions of the ideology with respect to both content and structure: for example, Nazi archives of Jewish degeneracy, Starkhonovite propaganda records of 'shock' workers, etc.

27 Žižek produces a fascinating analysis of Roberto Rossellini's films *Germany, Year Zero, Open City*, and *Paisan* as instances where the focus of the narrative is to stop at the point of non-meaning. See S. Žižek , *Enjoy Your Symptom: Jacques Lacan in Hollywood and Out* (London: Routledge, 1992), pp. 31–67.

non-actuality, is of all things the most dreadful, and to hold fast to what is dead requires the greatest strength.[28]

As Žižek explains in writing about this section of the *Phenomenology*, the problem expressed in this formulation is not so much the dissection of the real by the word – even less the recognition of the abyss separating word from act – but rather the means by which the act of disjunction itself can be thematised.

Obviously part of an overall pedagogic response to this state of affairs is to ask undergraduate students to work on both the construction and interpretation of archival material, and such experiences are offered in all three years of our own undergraduate programme.[29] However, as has been indicated, in the first year we preface this work with an initial analysis of autobiographical representation. During the first semester, we assume most students will mistake the 'fullness' of their own experience for truth, while in the second year, the disjunction between 'lived' experience and its theoretical representation will force an encounter with the loss of 'organic unity' through symbolic self-relocation (see below). The inclusion of these autobiographical components is, therefore, intended to realize a general intention that the undergraduate programme should be as much about educating to live as about the academic study of education itself. This must sound altogether too pious, but in wanting to invoke the ethical and interpretative dimensions of historical enquiry, we have allowed ourselves to be led by Kierkegaard. His arguments for employing pseudonymity as a means to begin articulating thoughts on the relationship between writers, writing, and autobiographical truth have been seminal to all refinements in practice.[30] For example, in the final

---

28   G. Hegel, *Phenomenology of Spirit*, trans. A. V. Miller, (Oxford: Oxford University Press, 1977), p. 19. See also S. Žižek (1992) op. cit., pp. 50–5.

29   During the second semester of the first year, students work on a comparison of the 1944 and 1988 Education Acts – apart from interview material developed through research they are also introduced to the analysis of selected sound and visual archives of the two periods. However, the main significance of this selection is that these are archives that relate directly to their own educational histories; the archives used in subsequent years are more 'distanced'.

30   For illustration, Kierkegaard's *Fear and Trembling* is currently used because of the multiple interpretations it offers of the triad God, Abraham and Isaac. In

year of the programme reflections on pseudonymity are supplemented by the addition of Kierkegaard's conception of the subjective thinker, resulting in an experience of dialectic as the loss of content but not, thereby, leading inevitably to 'abstract thinking'.

Instead of having the task of understanding the concrete abstractly, as abstract thinking has, the subjective thinker has the opposite task of understanding the abstract concretely. Abstract thinking turns from concrete human beings to humankind in general; the subjective thinker understands the abstract concept to be the concrete human being, to be this individual existing human being.[31]

To return to the first year, perhaps the greatest difficulty faced by all involved has been arriving at an appropriate recognition of what is to be understood by 'studentship'. The subtleties involved in this approach become clearer when one reviews what the first year programme deliberately eschews by asking students to work initially with the 'archive' of their past experience. Both the modernist and postmodernist approaches outlined above provide plenty of scope for false moves on the part of tutors. For example, cynically – but fully in the modernist tradition – one could adopt an approach in which accounts of student experience were resited within a pedagogic symptomatics that would triumph over their common-sense views. Equally, one could play at amateur psychoanalyst and invite students to dwell upon that which was most troubling or fascinating to them – using this as the pretext for suggesting that all of their supposed certainties should be considered as phantasmagoria built around whatever resisted 'pacification'.

Referring back to the metaphor of the detective, the problem with both of these approaches is that while they employ the notion of deception, they do so in totalizing ways that effectively render students dupes of a prevailing symbolic order. They omit any notion of deception as being conceivable by students themselves, not only within forms of self-representation made to a 'public', but also in

---

terms of Kierkegaard's own explanation, this is most explicitly developed in his *Two Ages*.

31   S. Kierkegaard, *Concluding Unscientific Postscript to Philosophical Fragments* (Princeton, NJ: Princeton University Press, 1992), p. 352.

terms of self-recognition before such deliberate acts take place. In other words, in order to develop a capacity for detecting anomaly, we reject early pedagogic operations intended to move students away from what is personal and familiar towards an abstract typology of relations applied to selected contents deemed to be 'educational'. Instead, we employ the principle of pseudonymity to allow students to continue working with what they consider to be their own experience, but to do so through the prism of 'writing' for a public: in practice, by constructing pseudonymous montages. The hope is, therefore, that students will be able to capture insightful reflections for a public, rather than having to deal directly with their own 'historical-actual' in any confessional or simple psychoanalytic sense.[32]

Montage and Pseudonymity

As has been indicated, an appropriate pedagogic response to the problems identified above has required the identification of a form of archival work that will best draw students' attention towards what is included within representation, which encourages the identification of false totality and perplexing inclusions, and which also makes explicit the responsibility of acting towards one's peers. There have been, and continue to be, many difficulties in achieving this. At a pragmatic level, perhaps the principal stumbling block has been the fact that many students arrive at the course with limited familiarity with narrative forms and poor self-images of themselves as 'writers'. This has tended to compound a sense of unease generated by recognition that the complexity of causation associated with autobiography can

---

32   Kierkegaard saw his own responsibility as one in which private and public experience was to be shaped into that which would evoke reflection (subjective knowledge). By grasping an underlying coherence he hoped to identify possibilities – he referred to these as 'ideal actualities' – imaginative constructions that hypothesized *in concreto*, rather than through scientific or philosophic abstraction.

become a major source of falsification. But such difficulties have been a continual spur to finding ways in which students might more easily achieve self-representations that locate and cite themselves within particular educational processes, and also act as a pretext to the formal dilemmas of archival representation outlined above.

At a theoretical level, it is the response of Kierkegaard to the Hegelian negative referenced above that has been of greatest help. His stress on the need to embrace the violence of the act of becoming, before a new symbolic order is instituted, has suggested both a means by which the act of disjunction can be thematized, and has also introduced a further justification for work that might continue to seem questionable in its focus on the self.

> The ethical is then present at every moment with its infinite individual's finding himself in a state exactly opposite to what the ethical requires. their peers and to their tutors, as they work to identify possibilities in their actuality. Within such a setting, students requirement, but the individual is not capable of fulfilling it [...]. The suspension consists in the themselves have been able to mount a direct interrogation of the processes involved in creating the frames/limits that their autobiographical representations rely upon. The claim is, therefore, Therefore, far from being able to begin, every moment he continues in this state he is more and more prevented from being able to begin: he relates himself to actuality not as possibility but as impossibility. Thus the individual is suspended from the ethical in the most terrifying way, is in the suspension heterogeneous with the ethical [...]. [33]

This disunity with ethical imperatives is used as the setting within which students are invited to become tutors of and about the self to that rather than seeing representations as existing prior to – or apart from – the direct experience of education, students become familiar with the cultural/educational work involved in any signifying process. Also essential, as indicated above, is the fact that this takes place within an ethical framework that the students themselves en-counter directly and largely determine. Ideally, then, their own ma-

---

33   S. Kierkegaard (1992), op. cit., pp. 266–7. In practice, Kierkegaard's book *Fear and Trembling*, is one of the key texts referred to in the final year of the course, but it is referenced at various points before then, including the work with montage described in the next section.

terial practices in relation to pseudonymous autobiographies support and move forward a burden of representation that belongs to them alone in the first instance.

What form does this take? Various trials and tribulations were encountered before our present practice was identified. Linear narratives, 'branching' stories, and photo-narratives were all attempted before montage was adopted.[34] None of the preceding practices gave grounds for pedagogic confidence in relation to the anomalous: the linear narratives all too easily collapsed into the expression of predictable sentiments; the branching stories drew too much attention to predictable decision points, rather than the intrinsic possibilities; and the production skills required for the photo-narratives proved to be more than most students could muster. However, experiments with photographic representation continued, since they promised links with a feature of photographic archives that had repeatedly drawn student comment: the peculiar anonymity and undecidability of even the most illustrative pictures.[35] Therefore the next pedagogic trial experimented with photographic tableaux. Few of the results avoided the stereotypical, but a significant number – often when deliberately cultivating the amusing – became also inclusive of disruptive elements.[36] The further modification of this practice in the direction of comedic montages became a relatively small step in imagination.[37]

---

34   For reasons of space, montage remains an untheorized concept here, but see, for example, J. Roberts (1998), op. cit., particularly pp. 40–57.

35   This is a much-ploughed field of analysis. See R. Barthes, *Camera Lucida* (London: Vintage, 1993); J. Berger, J. and J. Mohr, *Another Way of Telling* (London: Writers and Readers, 1982); J. Spence and P. Holland (eds.), *Family Snaps: the Meaning of Domestic Photography* (London: Virago, 1991); L. Rugg, *Picturing Ourselves: Photography and Autobiography* (Chicago: Chicago University Press, 1997).

36   The work of Duane Michals, with its combination of text and posed imagery, was first referenced when introducing photo-narratives – attention now shifted to his single images. See M. Livingstone, *The Essential Duane Michals* (London: Thames & Hudson, 1997).

37   Montage is used here to cover a range of techniques involving the construction of new meanings from disparate components. Photomontage is a term generally restricted to the production of unified photographic negatives derived either from direct manipulation of the negative itself or else from the practice of re-

The hope was that montage composition would give students access to a means of representing dilemmas and possibilities lying beyond their command of linear narrative. However, prior familiarity with the medium proved to be a stumbling block. Most students were already familiar with the use of photomontage from newspapers and magazines, and the related practices employed within political cartoons. But although political montage seemed very close to a visual equivalent of dialectical thinking, the form led to dilemmas being stated in a way that was typically biased towards a single conclusion – once again, the anomalous slipped away from an appropriate level of analysis.[38]

On balance, this risk has been accepted. If the public practice of pseudonymity were to be respected, the students themselves had to become the principal actors in the development of an ethics of presentation. Current practice, therefore, employs photographic components culled from magazines and newspapers, and these are used to explore the borders and limits of pseudonymous self-representation; pedagogic intervention is normally restricted todeveloping formal awareness within each group.[39] Following Kierkegaard, it is not the case that pseudonymity is used as a means to hide authorship. Instead, it is employed so as to allow students to explore the 'logic' of particular forms of self-representation – including any intrinsic contradictions. The pedagogic intention is, therefore, to direct students towards the production of photocollage 'masks' that will serve as objects for reflection upon the self and its condition. However, in order to offer students a means to move beyond simply illustrating selected beliefs

photographing composite constructions made from photographic and other material – as a consequence multiple copies can be produced. Photocollage is restricted to the practice of constructing single images composed of disparate photographic (and other) elements for the purposes of making a single artefact.

38 An enthusiasm for a particular political or ideological reading of experience often resulted in montages in which the horns of a policy dilemma were presented in an 'abstract' way, rather than through the conception of Kierkegaardian 'actual possibility'.

39 This is not to imply that responsibility for allowing troubling representations to be discussed is totally abrogated by the tutor. Instead the focus of critical pedagogic intervention is shifted towards supporting audience-led analysis.

and experiences – towards the production of what can evoke reflection in others – selected artistic practices are presented to student groups; principal amongst these is the work of Hannah Hoch.[40]

Results over the last three years have covered a wide range of responses. Some students have only ever offered simple 'accretions' of images around a theme, such as sport or religion, but most have been surprisingly good in their use of composition to present ideas to others. A few of these retain a capacity to astonish and intrigue beyond any individual group of students. The first illustration belongs to this last group (Figure 23). The montage featured the work of a student who chose to develop an image that featured what for her was the principal contradiction that she had experienced throughout her secondary schooling. Being blond, attractive, and academically able, she felt continually unsettled by the stereotypical expectations of her male peers and her own interest in academic study; her sexuality had seemed to be both a promise and a threat. The automatic assumption of sexual capability and involvement in a predetermined reproductive future was not only depressing, but also seemed linked to the sexual infantilism she associated with academic work.

40   For a discussion of Hoch's work see M. Lavin, *Cut with the Kitchen Knife: the Weimar Photomontages of Hannah Hoch* (New Haven: Yale University Press, 1993). Examples from the work of Herbert Bayer, Claude Cahun, Raoul Haussman, John Heartfield, Gustav Klutcis, Barbara Kruger, Aleksandr Rodchenko and Martha Rosler were also used.

Figure 23: Montage of the self, I.

Two further pedagogic interventions have been attempted, with varying outcomes: students have been asked to start the process of identifying subject matter by explicitly identifying contradictions that they recognized; and they have also been asked to prepare a short piece of writing to accompany the discussion of their collages.[41] The principal analytic themes to emerge through contradiction have been gendered life experiences, socioeconomic difficulties in relation to educational aspiration; and self-modelling as a learner. (All but the last of these being directly relevant to the archival work followed in the next semester.) However, when coupled with the request for some writing it has been generally misunderstood as a request for a preferred reading, resulting in a considerable degree of closure. Such representations encouraged recognition rather than reflection, and many of the students interpreted the request for a preferred meaning as an invitation to drop psuedonymity:

> the body in the picture is mine and as can be seen I do not have a real head, instead I have two different ones. One of these is a lion's and the other is that of a mouse. These two heads represent two strong and controversial sides of my personality that I recognise and that my friends, family and new people see. In contrast to the lion I have used the head of a mouse to represent the characteristics of the other side of my personality. This part is very quiet and timid [...]. The other words that describe this side are frightened, under-confident, shy [...] happy to be in the background unrecognised.[42]

It is easy to dismiss the expression of such stereotypes and ignore the fact that even at this level two essential components of archival work have already come into play: self-commitment in the presentation of an interpretation, and the development of interpretative criteria in

---

41   The use of contradiction stemmed from a combined Lacanian and Kierkegaardian perspective. Within each contradiction there would probably be a marked term (Lacan). If this was the case, the unmarked term had the potential to act as an anamorphic projection within the dominant scopic regime – offering a spectatorship for the subject that undermined the authority of the marked term and its imaginary. This last point can be linked to Kierkegaard's distinction between subjective and objective truth.

42   Permission to use the illustrative material given here has been granted by the students concerned so long as their anonymity is preserved.

relation to selection. The next two examples remain more 'open', and illustrate the quality of thinking that is generated. The first montage consisted of a reproduction of three Muybridge strips with the additional text 'Are batteries included?'. A particular feature of the example is the way in which the physical production itself became a focus for further reflection and the consideration of possibilities.

> It (the image) is not only a representation of a naked woman climbing over a trestle, but this action is also shown from three different angles, so we have a truthful knowledge of how her body performs this task. We are in no doubt of what is in the picture: naked woman, trestle, marked backdrop. The tension between science and nature is returned to by our seeing each photograph or 'still' numbered. This implies sequence, which could be parallel to the sequence of experience. The series is also in black and white – could this be seen as 'stark reality' or 'truth'? It could also denote a detachment from the occurrences in which the scientific reading would be suitable.
>
> It is through this ambiguity that I find it most interesting. It can be contrasted with the specific scientific nature, setting up a kind of tension as well as posing many questions. Hopefully the images I have chosen will direct the viewer in the direction of questions involving science over nature, the idea of trial and error, effort and reward. The nakedness of the woman could be seen as dealing with emotional/raw issues or indeed that some types of experience can only be had by our 'true' selves with nothing to hide behind [...].

The writer of this more distanced account was mainly interested in exploring the interplay of a number of 'essentialist' interpretations that she felt her particular form of self-representation embodied. In terms of the programme's aspirations, the main reservation would be that Kierkegaardian 'subjective thinking' is largely suppressed until the last line. The next extract suggests not only the 'shaping' of experience in order to invoke a public form of possibility, but also a move towards a modified form of autobiographical writing that dwells on the loss of self.

> I'm not sure that my montage is very honest; I tried to manipulate it so that it would only reveal what I wanted it to. I thought I had achieved this by keeping the picture simple and minimal. What I actually think I've done by doing this is revealed more than I had intended to.
>
> Everything involved in the montage is of some relevance, from the main image to the white background. The books that I chose, or, as I should say, the book titles, represent important and continuing chapters in my life [...]. The

books also represent in a slightly ironical way the well known phrase, 'It's what's on the inside that counts'. The revealed eye shows the person beneath peeking through, which shows that I cannot simply be measured by surface labels.

The naked body is also of importance. It not only shows how I feel exposed by the revealing nature of the montage, but it also represents exactly how much of a blank canvas my life and body are at this present moment.

Kierkegaard undoubtedly regarded pseudonymous authorship as central to his project. It was this element that was to provoke subjective thinking in others – a form of philosophico-poetic insight. In our view, not only is there an ethics to historical representation, there is also a poetry (in the Kristevan sense of a compacted symbolism), and it is the aspiration of the work featured here to initiate an equivalent level of engagement with the archive via montage. The student's work featured in the last example (Figure 24) described the production of her montage as an 'exercise which pulled together pieces of confusion without actually constructing an answer'. The montage illustrates the level of visual 'poetry' often attained through these simple means; extracts from her written commentary may help to locate the work.

At the time of constructing the montage I had conflicting ideas about my position in life. I was not sure if I had made the correct decision to begin a degree course and was feeling trapped both by my own expectations and the expectations of others. I had an overwhelming desire to 'break free' of my various roles in life and to use my travelling feet to change the situation [a direct reference to the walking boot, as opposed to the fashion shoe].

I have found that I can convey my feelings much more easily through this pictorial representation and have provided an insight for others in a more succinct way than through writing. In fact, it has been comparatively more difficult to express my thoughts in writing this piece.

Figure 24: Montage of the self, II.

Notes on Contributors

DEREK BUNYARD has a long-standing interest in with visual education, having previously worked on the development of computer-based graphics environments, photography education programmes, and aesthetic theory. He has held senior posts in teacher-education programmes, and is currently Field Leader in Education Studies (Early Childhood), University College Winchester.

CATHERINE BURKE is lecturer in education and coordinates the undergraduate programme, Childhood, Education and Culture at the School of Education, University of Leeds, UK.

KARL CATTEEUW is a doctoral student at the Centre for History of Education of the Katholieke Universiteit Leuven (Belgium). He is currently researching wall charts employed in Belgian primary education 1860–1960.

KRISTOF DAMS worked at the Catholic University of Leuven (Belgium) and the University of Groningen (The Netherlands). He is now finishing his PHD on family education advice in Belgium 1870–1930.

IAN GROSVENOR is Professor of Urban Educational History at the School of Education, University of Birmingham.

SIRKE HAPPONEN is lecturer in the Department of Applied Sciences of Education at the University of Helsinki, Finland. Her research field covers children's literature and illustration, especially the relationship between word and image.

KEN JONES is a Professor in the Department of Education at Keele University.

MARTIN LAWN is a Visiting Professor of Education at the University of Edinburgh and a Professorial Research Fellow in the School of Social Sciences, University of Cardiff. He has published widely on the sociology and history of teachers and increasingly on the cultural history of schooling (with Ian Grosvenor). He is the Editor of the *European Educational Research Journal*.

DAVID LIMOND lectures in the Education Department at Trinity College, Dublin.

ULRIKE MIETZNER teaches history of education at the Humboldt-University Berlin. She is particularly interested in images and photography as sources in qualitative research, in pedagogical anthropology, youth movements and Jewish history of the 20th century.

KEVIN MYERS teaches social history and education in The School of Education at the University of Birmingham.

NICK PEIM teaches in the School of Education at the University of Birmingham and has long been interested in theoretical issues concerning representation.

ULRIKE PILARCZYK lectures in the Department of Education at the University of Potsdam, Germany. She has research interests in the history of education, Jewish youth movements and new media.

FRANK SIMON is Professor in History of Education at the University of Ghent. He is editor-in-chief of *Paedagogica Historica: International Journal of the History of Education* and has longstanding research interests in the socio-historical aspects of education.

MINNA VUORIO-LEHTI is a research fellow in the Department of Education at the University of Turku, in Finland. She is preparing her doctoral thesis on the Finnish Matriculation system.